THE ANTI-SLAVERY MOVEMENT AND RECONSTRUCTION

A Study in Anglo-American Co-operation, 1833–77

THE ANTI-SLAVERY MOVEMENT
AND RECONSTRUCTION
A Study in Anglo-American Co-operation
1833–77

—————◆┼┼◆—————

CHRISTINE BOLT

Published for the
Institute of Race Relations, London
by
OXFORD UNIVERSITY PRESS
LONDON   NEW YORK   TORONTO
1969

Oxford University Press, Ely House, London W. 1

GLASGOW NEW YORK TORONTO MELBOURNE WELLINGTON
CAPE TOWN SALISBURY IBADAN NAIROBI LUSAKA ADDIS ABABA
BOMBAY CALCUTTA MADRAS KARACHI LAHORE DACCA
KUALA LUMPUR SINGAPORE HONG KONG TOKYO

Printed in Great Britain by
Richard Clay (The Chaucer Press) Ltd,
Bungay, Suffolk

TO IAN

AUTHOR'S PREFACE
AND ACKNOWLEDGEMENTS

The main part of this study concerns how the venerable but declining British anti-slavery movement of the 1860s found a new cause and a new lease of life in the needs of the four million Negroes freed by the American Civil War. For five years—from 1863 to 1868—through the medium of freedmen's aid societies, the leisured, philanthropic, and religious elements in Britain which had long protested against slavery in the States were able to exchange exhortation and pious hopes for action. Working in co-operation with the voluntary agencies for the freedmen in America, these associations raised an annual average of £24,000 towards the physical relief and education of the Southern Negroes.

Nowhere else outside the United States did freedmen's societies exist on such a scale, and they are interesting phenomena in Britain, since no comparable bodies had been established to care for her own West Indian freedmen earlier in the century.

However, in order to set these activities in perspective, the early history of the British anti-slavery movement and the attitudes of Britons in general to the racial aspects of the Jamaica Revolt (of 1865) and Reconstruction are separately examined.

Interest is not centred at governmental level, where the diplomatic disputes arising from the Civil War were all important, but other sources of opinion—diaries, letters, and the periodical and newspaper press—have revealed a surprisingly well-informed interest in America's post-war crisis, a strong desire to foster Anglo-American (or, as the Victorians put it, Anglo-Saxon) unity, an aim which the freedmen's aid movement fully approved, and, perhaps most interesting, an increasingly hostile preoccupation with questions of race.

I should like to acknowledge with sincere thanks the invaluable help, encouragement, and advice over this work of Professor Harry Allen of University College, London. I am also indebted to Professor Sam Shepperson of Edinburgh University, to Dr. Michael Thompson of University College, and Dr. Lucy Brown of the London School of Economics for their most helpful comments on the first version of the manuscript. Any errors of interpretation or fact which may unintentionally remain are, of course, my own.

Canterbury, October 1968

ABBREVIATIONS

Add. Ms.	Additional manuscript of a collection in the British Museum.
A.P. C. . ./. . .	Indicates manuscript from the Anti-Slavery Papers, Rhodes House, Oxford.
Ms.	Manuscript.

NOTES

Square brackets indicate a word or punctuation added to a quoted passage.

The Victorian press habit of completely capitalizing proper names and words at the beginning of a paragraph has not been followed.

The abbreviation '&' in quotations from manuscripts has been rendered in full.

Words underlined in such quotations have been italicized in this book.

CONTENTS

CHAPTER I

The British Anti-Slavery Movement
1833–60

'The effect of . . . [the Emancipation Act of 1833] throughout the American continent will no doubt be great; but whether it effects the general emancipation of the slaves there peaceably, or through a dreadful servile war, will, under Providence, . . . greatly depend upon the proper discharge of the duty which the religious public in this country owes to those who are rightly concerned on the other side of the Atlantic, . . . as leaders in the cause. . . . Let us, therefore, form a general crusade against this accursed [slave] system throughout the civilised world.'

JOSEPH STURGE, 1833[1]

On 29 August 1833 a bill for the abolition of slavery in the British colonies became law. This legislation marked the triumph of an emancipation campaign launched in the 1770s, which had already secured notable victories in 1772 and 1807, with the prohibition of slavery in England and the termination of the British slave trade. The year 1833 heralded changes in the leadership of the anti-slavery movement as well as in its objectives, but there was no thought of winding up operations in Britain: much still remained to be achieved.

In fact, the 1830s saw the appearance of several new emancipation societies, among them the British and Foreign Society for the Universal Abolition of Negro Slavery and the Slave Trade (1834); the Central Negro Emancipation Committee (1837–9), concerned with Negroes in British possessions, and giving place in 1839 to the British and Foreign Anti-Slavery Society; the Society for the Extinction of the Slave Trade and the Civilization of Africa (1839–43); and the Aborigines Protection Society, formed in 1839 and operating independently until 1909, when it merged with the British and Foreign Anti-Slavery Society. Only one major emancipation organization disappeared in the course of the decade—the Society for the Mitigation and Gradual Abolition of

---

[1] H. Richard, *Memoirs of Joseph Sturge*, London, 1864, p. 205.

Slavery Throughout the British Dominions, in 1839—its dissolution becoming inevitable with the abolition of apprenticeship schemes in the British West Indies, and with them, it was felt, the last remnants of the slave system in the colonies.

As the names of some of the new societies indicate, and as one would expect after 1833, abolitionists in Britain now felt free to take a wider view of slavery and obliged to devise and promote policies to advance emancipation throughout the rest of the world. They were encouraged to do so by the two successful world anti-slavery conventions held in London in the early 1840s, and the magnitude of the slave problem amply justified their concern.

In 1842 it has been estimated that the slave population of the United States was approximately two and a half millions; that of Texas, soon to be annexed, was a further 75,000; Brazil possessed around two and a half million slaves and Peru, 284,000; the West Indian colonies of Spain, 600,000; of France, 170,000; those of the Dutch, 17,000; and of the Danes and Swedes, over 43,000. These figures do not take account of the many millions more held in bondage in the British East Indies and by independent native powers in the East and Africa.[1] Moreover, according to Foreign Office estimates, the slave trade was on the increase, and between 1835 and 1839 no less than 135,000 Negroes were annually exported westward from Africa.[2]

But if the challenge was great, so too were the problems which harassed British abolitionists. Until 1838 success had been achieved through Parliament, and from the first, members of all parties had been drawn to the anti-slavery cause—men like William Wilberforce, M.P. for Hull, Henry Thornton, representing Southwark, Charles Grant of Inverness-shire, James Stephen of Tralee and East Grinstead, and Thomas Fowell Buxton, who sat for Weymouth. Their support brought the British movement prestige and helped to steer it away from extremism (though it should of course be remembered that many members of the Commons were equally interested in the maintenance of slavery, in the years before 1833).[3]

After the passage of the Emancipation Act, in political terms abolition became a distinctly marginal issue, because over most of

---

[1] *An Epitome of Anti-Slavery Information, or a Condensed View of Slavery and the Slave Trade, etc.*, London, 1842, p. 5.

[2] H. Temperley, *The British and Foreign Anti-Slavery Society, 1839–1868*, Ph.D. thesis Yale, 1960, p. 3.

[3] W. L. Mathieson, *British Slavery and Its Abolition, 1823–1838*, London, Longmans, 1926, p. 118.

the problems debated by the British societies Parliament was powerless to act. The former thus found themselves denied direct action; anxious spectators of the struggles of other nations; petitioning, corresponding, exhorting, quarrelling. Furthermore public opposition to their activities grew; as the Secretary of the Cirencester Anti-Slavery Society pointed out in 1839, 'When abolitionists directed the attention of the benevolent public even to our own colonies, we were constantly met with "Charity begins at home ... there is no occasion to go three thousand miles from home to relive misery." If such was the public feeling when the slavery to be abolished was the crime of our own country, what great efforts can we expect when the evil to be abolished is the slavery of foreign and distant nations?' The argument used by William Cobbett in the 1820s, that the abolitionists overlooked the factory slaves of Lancashire in favour of a 'a fat and lazy negro that laughs from morning to night', became more common as the problems produced by industrialization and urbanization increased.[1]

These difficulties were not apparent to all, however, even after 1838, and ambitious plans were laid for the future. Since the freedmen's aid societies, whose operations occupy the main part of this study, modelled themselves upon the British and Foreign Anti-Slavery Society, it is with this body that we shall now be chiefly concerned. But in 1840–1, directly under the influence of American abolitionists, the British anti-slavery societies split up, and the B.F.A.S.S. and its journal, the *Anti-Slavery Reporter*, represented only those groups which followed the American and Foreign Anti-Slavery Society in its opposition to William Lloyd Garrison, inspiration of the original American Anti-Slavery Society. (The schism in the American movement was caused primarily by Garrison's espousal of other good causes, such as women's rights, thus confusing the anti-slavery issue; his insistence on the need for immediate emancipation; and by the increasingly bitter attack Garrisonians mounted against the churches for their failure to support the cause of the Negro.)[2]

In the provinces the anti-slavery societies of Glasgow, Edinburgh, Dublin, Manchester, and Bristol, glad of an opportunity

---

[1] Brewin to Tredgold, 27 July 1839, Anti-Slavery papers, Rhodes House, Oxford, C14/29; Mathieson, op. cit., p. 137; and see charges in E. Williams, *Capitalism and Slavery*, University of North Caroline Press, Chapel Hill, North Carolina, 1947, pp. 193–5.

[2] Temperley, op. cit., pp. 337–40. I do, however, consider the views of Bristol and Glasgow Garrisonians, and some others.

to free themselves from metropolitan domination, remained steadfast in their admiration of Garrison, deploring the existence of the
'New Administration' group in London, attacking the motives of
its founders, and blaming it for misrepresenting conditions in
America, for excessive caution, and for reliance on pacifist
methods.[1] The B.F.A.S.S. was no less strident in its criticism of all
that the Garrisonians represented, especially during the period of
office (1839–52) of its conservative and unpopular secretary, John
Scoble. Relations seem to have improved once Scoble was succeeded by Louis Alexis Chamerovzow, if the testimony of American Garrisonian Sarah Pugh may be believed; for though she had
referred to Scoble as 'dishonorable and dishonest', his successor
was regarded as 'certainly . . . a true man'; and it is noticeable that
in the 1860s the provincial societies which had long opposed the
B.F.A.S.S. joined with its members in the work of freedmen's aid,
a gratifying as well as surprising tribute to the greatness of that
cause.[2]

Altogether between 1839 and 1869 there were approximately
100 auxiliaries of the London group in being, though not all were
active at the same time. Of these, about a third were female societies. Local associations were fairly evenly distributed in relation to
general population, though on the whole Ireland, Scotland, and
Wales were less well represented, while the societies of London,
Birmingham, Liverpool, and Bristol were always especially active
and prosperous.

The reasons for this are not hard to find. The anti-slavery movement began in London and the South, through the efforts of
prominent Quakers (working closely with the London Meeting
for Sufferings) and public men, the 'Clapham Sect' (so called from
the area in which they met), who looked to see slavery ended
through the action of Parliament, assembled in the capital. Its
tremendous resources of man-power, wealth, and influence made
the city the obvious starting point for any philanthropic crusade.

[1] See Glasgow Emancipation Society Minute Books III and IV, Smeal Collection,
Glasgow Public Library; R. D. Webb, *The National Anti-Slavery Societies in England
and the United States, or Strictures on 'A Reply to Certain Charges Brought Against the American
and Foreign Anti-Slavery Society, etc., etc.';* by *Lewis Tappan of New York, United States:
With an Introduction by John Scoble,* Dublin, 1852; Temperley, op. cit., p. 303 f.; and
letters in Estlin Papers, Dr. Williams's Library, London, 24.121 (19), (58), (101),
24.125 (53), 24.122 (51).

[2] Sarah Pugh to Mary Estlin of Bristol, 26 January 1853, 24.121 (25) and 15 March
1853, 24.121 (34), Estlin Papers.

Outside London, as indeed within it as the years passed, the anti-slavery cause depended largely on the efforts of interested individuals. Thus from the thirties great progress was made throughout the Midlands, where the influence of Quaker corn merchant Joseph Sturge radiated from his home in Birmingham.[1] Similarly, sterling work was undertaken in Liverpool by another Quaker merchant, James Cropper, while in Bristol the key figures were Dr. James Estlin, a well-known ophthalmic surgeon and Unitarian reformer, author of a study of American slavery, and Edwin Chapman, a fellow Unitarian. (In both Bristol and Liverpool interest in the slave issue was already strong, as a result of the commercial ties, mainly through cotton, which both ports enjoyed with the United States.)

Religion, commerce, and politics also played their part in determining the success of abolitionists in particular areas, and these factors, in addition to the most important personalities involved in the work in Britain, may now claim our attention.

The influence of religion upon nineteenth-century humanitarianism can scarcely be over-emphasized. As far as the anti-slavery movement is concerned, the three most important groups which lent their support were the Quakers, the Evangelical section of the Church of England, and the Nonconformists. The B.F.A.S.S., with a view to the practical advantages which would accrue from such an approach, as well as from conviction, consistently stressed the sinfulness of slavery. In this way the institution might be attacked wherever it occurred—the work of God could not be confined within national boundaries.

Although the early success of the abolitionists in Britain had been achieved through Parliament, they had been susceptible to charges of entering into a questionable political alliance with certain groups—the Whigs, for instance, and the East India interest—with the result that expediency had triumphed over principle. Reacting against the conservatives a group led by three Quakers, Emmanuel and Joseph Cropper, and Joseph Sturge, had broken away from the main Anti-Slavery Society to form the Agency Committee in 1831.[2] The new approach would, it was hoped, avert such incidents in the future. 'It was self-evident', recalled Sir George Stephen in his memoirs, 'that if the religious world could

---

[1] Sir R. Coupland, *The British Anti-Slavery Movement*, London, Oxford University Press, 1964, p. 137.
[2] Coupland, op. cit., pp. 137–8.

be induced to enter upon the subject, severing from it all its political relations, and viewing it simply as a question between God and man, the battle was won.'[1]

By making slaveholding a sin, abolitionists were distinguishing it from most other forms of social evil to appeal directly to the Christian members of the community, and a stern and uncomfortable awareness of their religious duty to the oppressed distinguishes almost all those active in the work. As Sir Edward Arnold expressed it in his popular epic the *Light of Asia*:[2]

> The woeful cry
> Of life and all flesh living cometh up
> Into my ears, and all my soul is full
> Of pity for the sickness of this world.

Most of the abolitionists had never experienced the sufferings which they deplored or looked on a black face; they were moved, not so much by the heart, but, in the words of Quakeress Catherine Gurney, by 'the only source of true strength, a principle of religion in the conscience'.[3]

Since Quakers had launched the first organized attack on the British slave system in 1783, and were again active in the Anti-Slavery Society of 1823, it comes as no surprise to find that of the sixty-seven individuals who held seats on the committee of the B.F.A.S.S. between 1839 and 1868, thirty-two, or just under half, belonged to the Society of Friends.[4] The Quakers also operated independently in work for coloured peoples, co-operating with their brethren in America, and after 1833 particular importance was attached to the religious and secular education of freedmen in the British colonies.

In 1845, following the visit to the West Indies of two English Friends, Edwin Tregelles and James Jesup, a Negro and Aborigine Education Fund was established. By the middle of the century, drawing upon subscriptions from meetings throughout Britain, the Fund Committee was spending hundreds of pounds annually on the upkeep of over 100 schools in Jamaica, Antigua, Berbice, India, Canada, Liberia, and Sierra Leone. Although the Aborigine

---

[1] *Anti-Slavery Recollections: in a Series of Letters Addressed to Mrs. Beecher Stowe, etc.*, London, 1854, p. 161.
[2] Quoted in H. Wigham, *A Christian Philanthropist of Dublin. A Memoir of Richard Allen*, London, 1886, p. 17.
[3] Quoted in R. H. Mottram, *Buxton the Liberator*, Hutchinson, London, 1946, p. 22.
[4] Temperley, op. cit., p. 50.

Fund wound up in 1877, the Anti-Slavery Committee of the Meeting for Sufferings was still active at the end of the century.[1]

The interest of other religious groups and individuals in anti-slavery work was similarly intense, so that the title of 'the Saints', which had been given to the earliest abolitionists in Parliament, might aptly have been conferred upon their successors.

It was thanks largely to the efforts of missionaries sent out by the various Nonconformist sects that during the first four years of the life of the B.F.A.S.S. fifteen auxiliaries were formed in the West Indies—eleven in Jamaica, one each in Trinidad, Demerara, Barbados, and Berbice—to help the Negroes adjust to their new found freedom. At the first world anti-slavery convention in London in 1840 some thirty church groups attended, including the Congregational Union of England and Wales, the Congregational Union of Scotland, the United Associate Synod of Scotland, the Midland Association of Baptist Churches, and various other local Baptist groups.[2] The same year, following the promptings of the convention, saw protests against slavery by the Wesleyan Methodists, and the Congregational and Baptist Unions.[3]

Prominent individuals may be found representing the approach of their respective religious sects to the anti-slavery issue in abolitionist organizations throughout Britain. In London the Evangelicals found spokesmen of substance in Captain Charles Stuart and Thomas Fowell Buxton (the latter being also linked by birth and marriage to the Society of Friends); the Rev. William Arthur of the Wesleyan Methodist church was a tireless champion of the Negro freedman and opponent of slavery both in America and the British colonies, while fellow Wesleyan George Thompson was a widely known reformer and orator of great power; in Bristol two of the leading families in the work, the Chapmans and the Estlins, were Unitarians by conviction; and during the thirties the Baptists possessed in Dr. Cox of Hackney a spokesman for the anti-slavery cause familiar with conditions in the United States, his

---

[1] See report *At a Yearly Meeting Held in London, Beginning the 21st Day of the 5th Month, and ending the 31st of the Same Inclusive*, London, 1845, p. 545 (in future simply *At a Yearly Meeting Held in London . . . 18 . .*); *Extracts From the Minutes and Proceedings of the Yearly Meeting Held in London (Printed by Direction of the Yearly Meeting)*, *1862*, London, 1862, pp. 36–7 (in future simply *Minutes and Proceedings . . . 18 . .*), for 1863, p. 72, 1864, pp. 44–5, 1866, p. 45, pp. 51–2, 1868, p. 61, 1869, pp. 48–9, 1870, pp. 48–9, 1873, pp. 49–52, 1877, p. 57, 1896, p. 109.

[2] Temperley, op. cit., pp. 87, 132.

[3] F.Thistlethwaite, *The Anglo-American Connection in the Early Nineteenth Century*, University of Pennsylvania Press, Philadelphia, 1959, p. 114.

B

mantle later falling on the Rev. J. Hinton, for many years secretary of the Baptist Union, and for a time editor of the *Anti-Slavery Reporter* and member of the B.F.A.S.S. committee.

But we should not deduce from individual interest that church groups in Britain presented a united front against slavery; all too often the approach to the problem was jealously sectarian. Enjoying close and cordial relations with their fellow-believers in the United States, the British Dissenting sects tended to reflect the divisions which beset the American reformers; to follow a cautious line when this was advocated abroad and to quarrel among themselves at home.[1]

In 1844, for instance, the Free Church of Scotland (which a year earlier had broken away from the established church) sent a successful fund-raising deputation to its Presbyterian brethren in the Southern States of America, and thus, while supposedly committed to the anti-slavery movement, became guilty of taking money from slaveholders. Other sects in Britain objected, as did the B.F.A.S.S., and a controversy was provoked which raged for several years.[2] Bitter feelings were again aroused by the attempt of British abolitionists to secure the support of the Evangelical Alliance, an international Protestant association formed in 1846, an attempt which failed because of the objections of some of the British clergy to the membership of slaveholders; upon American members of the Alliance threatening to resign unless neutrality on the slavery issue was preserved, stalemate was reached. The close connexions between English and American reformers, which have been so carefully documented by historians, brought difficulties as well as inspiration and strength.[3]

By the late forties and throughout the fifties we still find complaints from the anti-slavery wing of the Unitarians that churches on both sides of the Atlantic were sustaining the 'peculiar institu-

---

[1] Maria Weston Chapman to Mary Estlin, 24 November, 1867, 24.122 (51), Estlin Papers; D. P. Crook, *American Democracy in English Politics, 1815–1850*, Oxford, Clarendon Press, 1965, pp. 156–9; Thistlethwaite, op. cit., Chapter III.

[2] See G. A. Shepperson, 'Thomas Chalmers, the Free Church of Scotland and the South', *Journal of Southern History*, Vol. 33, 1957, and 'The Free Church and American Slavery', *Scottish Historical Review*, Vol. 27, 1958.

[3] See Richard, op.cit., pp. 373–83; also Thistlethwaite, op. cit.; G. C. Taylor, *Some American Reformers and Their Influence on Reform Movements in Great Britain, 1830–60*, Ph.D. thesis, Edinburgh, 1960; H. Koht, *The American Spirit in Europe*, Philadelphia, University of Pennsylvania Press, 1949; Crook, op. cit.; F. J. Klingberg, 'Harriet Beecher Stowe and Social Reform in England', *American Historical Review*, Vol. 43, 1938; G. D. Lillibridge, *Beacon of Freedom, The Impact of American Democracy Upon Great Britain, 1830–1870*, Philadelphia, University of Pennsylvania Press, 1955.

tion'; American abolitionist Dr. S. G. Howe appealing to 'the churches of England [to] . . . take high and stern ground, and declare they would not hold communion with churches composed of slaveholding congregations'; and the Rev. Samuel J. May of Syracuse, New York, declaring that 'there needs to be a revival of anti-slavery faith and . . . zeal in England' especially among the religious community.[1] Wilson Armistead of the Leeds emancipation society put the position most bitterly of all when he wrote to the Secretary of the B.F.A.S.S., in 1854, that 'There cannot be a doubt that professors of religion, and ministers of the Gospel, and Christian churches constitute the stronghold of Slavery. If, instead of conniving at its existence, they would throw their influence into the efforts of Anti-Slavery Societies, the evil would soon be abolished throughout the . . . earth.'[2]

As regards the economic strength of the British anti-slavery movement, it is necessary to consider both the abolitionists themselves and those interested individuals who lent support to the cause for other than philanthropic reasons. Most important in this latter category was the East India interest, who from the 1820s looked to emancipation of the slaves in the West Indies and the ending of protection for sugar from those islands to weaken its most powerful economic rival. East Indian sugar, though inferior in quality to the West Indian variety, was far cheaper, and only the imposition of a special duty to protect the latter prevented it from capturing a large share of the British market. And while slavery in British India was not legally abolished until 1843, Englishmen, living there were forbidden to own slaves, and in the Indian controlled islands of St. Helena, Ceylon, and Bencoolen after 1818 all slave-born children were set free, so that with some justification the East Indians could raise the cry of free-grown versus slave-grown sugar.[3]

Furthermore, as Eric Williams has pointed out, after 1783 'every important vested interest in England . . . came out against

[1] *Report of a Meeting of Members of the Unitarian Body Held at the Freemason's Tavern, June 13th, 1851, to Deliberate on the Duty of English Unitarians in Reference to Slavery in the United States*, London, 1851; Dr. Howe to Dr. Estlin, Boston, 29 March 1849, 24.125 (22), Estlin Papers; *The Duty of the United Kingdom Towards the Slaves of the United States. A Letter, by the Rev. Samuel J. May, of Syracuse, State of New York*, Bristol, 1860, p. 7.
[2] Armistead to L. A. Chamerovzow, 27 November 1854, Anti-Slavery Papers, Rhodes House, C27/62.
[3] Mathieson, op. cit., pp. 118–9; Coupland, op. cit., pp. 123–4.

monopoly and the West Indian slave system', as a relic of outmoded protectionism hampering Britain's capacity to absorb raw produce and thus export manufactured goods.[1] In time not only the East Indian merchants but also the sugar refiners looking to trade with Cuba and Brazil, the cotton manufacturers trading with India, North America, and Brazil, and the ship-owners who stood to benefit from any increase in business, interests represented in every important industrial and commercial town, joined in the attack.

Once emancipation was secured in 1833, these critics sustained their animosity to the West India planters by pressing for the termination of apprenticeship, under which, until 1838, white domination of the Negroes was perpetuated. The forties saw attention shift to the preferential sugar duties. Success was achieved partly because the abolitionists proper, for various reasons, supported the capitalist forces, and partly because of the growing belief, especially among Benthamite liberals, that colonial possessions were expensive, outmoded, often turbulent, and the cause of much unnecessary suffering and rivalry between the nations of the world.[2]

But though self-interest undoubtedly drove British capitalists to support abolition in the West Indies (and to condone slavery in Cuba, Brazil, and the United States), we should not conclude that all abolitionists were thus motivated, as Dr. Williams seems to imply.[3] Just as in America, many men of very different degrees of conviction adopted that title, so that the 'typical' abolitionist has become almost impossible to define.[4] Not all capitalists were drawn into the anti-slavery movement by pecuniary considerations, or showed themselves indifferent to suffering at home. Thus we find that Richard Allen of Dublin, who ran a prosperous drapery and tailoring business in the city, laboured against capital punishment and the corn laws as well as slavery; Stafford Allen, Robert Alsop, James Cadbury, and Joseph Thorp worked for abolition and the extension of popular education; and Samuel Gurney held seats on the executive committees of eleven philanthropic organizations, and was closely associated with several others.

From 1839 onwards the B.F.A.S.S. relied financially upon the

---

[1] Williams, op. cit., pp. 144, 154, 157–8.
[2] D. C. Somervell, *English Thought in the Nineteenth Century*, London, Methuen, 1929, pp. 176–82.
[3] Ibid., pp. 169–71.
[4] See 'Who was an Abolitionist?' in *The Anti-Slavery Vanguard: New Essays on the Abolitionists*, M. Duberman (ed.), Princeton, Princeton U.P., 1965, pp. 32–51.

regular, voluntary donations of certain rich Quaker families—in fact between a half and two-thirds of the Society's total income was derived from Friends. As Paul Emden has observed, 'By no means did they consider money to be objectionable; . . . made rightly and spent rightly money was, from every point of view, of the greatest value and usefulness.' The anti-slavery cause provided many Quakers with an opportunity for spending rightly the fortunes they amassed in brewing and banking, as merchants, manufacturers, and railroad pioneers.[1]

The most flourishing emancipation societies after—as before—1833 were in the great industrial cities of Britain, where such men were to be found; the abolitionists deliberately concentrated their attack on areas like London, Manchester, Liverpool, Birmingham, Sheffield, the West Riding of Yorkshire, and Glasgow, although over the years contributions came in regularly from smaller centres where interest was high.[2]

If the anti-slavery movement had simply been a convenient, capitalist crusade, one might have expected its resources to be more ample than they in fact were. In the 1840s the income of the B.F.A.S.S. ranged from £4,000 in 1841-2, to £800 in 1847-8, the average figure being around £2,000; while in the fifties and sixties, with declining interest in the country at large, and the number of local auxiliaries sharply reduced, the average income was only approximately £1,000. The largest number of donations received from an auxiliary in any one year was three, in 1843-4, even though there were at least seventy in existence at that time. Out of this income had to be found the rent of offices in London and meeting halls, printing and publishing costs, the price of stationery, books, and newspapers, travelling expenses, and the salary of the society's secretary and his assistants—Louis Chamerovzow, who held the former office from 1852 to 1870, drew £300 annually (though many part-time officials worked for nothing).[3]

Although the B.F.A.S.S. enjoyed its share of aristocratic patrons —notably the eighth Duke of Argyll, Lord Brougham, Lord Shaftesbury, and the Duchess of Sutherland—it was dominated by middle-class individuals and values. Wilberforce had commented in 1825 that 'It is by the union of people of the middle class of

[1] P. Emden, *The Quakers in Commerce: a Record of Business Achievement*, London, Sampson Low & Co., 1939, p. 13; and Temperley, op. cit., pp. 74-5.
[2] See Richard, op. cit., p. 84.   [3] Temperley, op. cit., pp. 73, 76.

society, amongst whom are comprised the greatest portion of virtue and understanding in any community, that we hope to render
our cause successful'; and middle-class opinion was indeed mobi-
lized through public meetings, pamphlet literature and maga-
zines, and the skilful use of paid agitators appealing to conscience,
commercial instincts, religious and missionary fervour, and the
Romantic tradition.[1]

All the leading Romantic writers, recent studies have revealed—
Shelley, Wordsworth, Coleridge, Southey, Byron, Hazlitt, Leigh
Hunt, Landor, De Quincy, and Lamb—were sympathetic on
theoretical and idealistic grounds towards the Negro, and a similar
sentiment may be traced throughout the lesser known works of
Thomas Hood, Samuel Rogers, Thomas Campbell, Thomas
Moore, James Montgomery, and John Galt.[2]

Given the fact that philanthropy was expensive and time con-
suming, the largest part in anti-slavery work was inevitably played
by those in the middle range of income, but poorer men also took
an interest. The most famous demonstration of working-class
sympathy for abolition was during the American Civil War, but
then, as in the earlier part of the century, this partisanship with
sides in the United States has been seen 'as a "veil" for social and
political antagonism in Britain' (just as the crusade of aristocratic
philanthropists against American slavery was often 'a backhanded
way of hitting at America', of proving 'the inherent falsity of
American democracy').[3] Also, among labour leaders like Bronterre
O'Brien there prevailed a conviction that the anti-slavery movement was a luxury which imperfect nineteenth-century society
could not afford, and one which served to conceal the hypocritical
attitudes of British philanthropists; 'How is it,' asked O'Brien,
'that we never hear the Buxtons or the Wilberforces complain
about slavery here at home? . . . it is because [they] . . . know . . .
that English slavery is indispensable for our highly civilized state.'

Nevertheless, old Owenists and Chartists in Britain had behind
them a strong tradition of opposition to slavery, and workers were

---

[1] Thistlethwaite, op.cit., pp. 105–7.

[2] See for instance H. D. Fairchild, *The Noble Savage: a Study in Romantic Naturalism*, New
York, 1961.

[3] See R. Harrison, *Before the Socialists. Studies in Labour and Politics, 1861–1881*, London,
Routledge & Kegan Paul, 1965, pp. 57–60; G. C. Taylor, 'Notes on American Negro
Reformers in Victorian Britain', *Bulletin of the British Association for American Studies*,
New Series, No. 2, March 1961, pp. 45–6; and *American and English Oppression, and
British and American Abolitionists: a Letter Addressed to R. D. Webb, Esq., by an American,
in his Fatherland*, London, 1853, pp. 13, 53.

prominent in the Anti-Slavery League founded in 1846 under the presidency of Chartist George Thompson.[1] The Manchester Anti-Slavery League, which seceded from the Manchester Union in 1854, and the London Emancipation Committee of 1859 were also founded partly at Thompson's instigation and looked up to him as their major British leader, in spite of his comparatively humble north-country background, limited formal education, and disadvantage of being poor, which, according to Maria Weston Chapman, was 'to be under a suspicion of being wicked, with the great majority' in England.[2]

In 1853 G. J. Holyoake sent an anti-slavery address to America signed by 1,800 working men, and attempts were continually made by emancipation societies to enlist the support of the humble through devices like the 'Uncle Tom Penny Offering', a proposal made in Edinburgh to collect at least a penny from every Scottish reader of Harriet Beecher Stowe's *Uncle Tom's Cabin*; in all approximately £1,930 was raised and sent out to America.[3] And during the Civil War, in spite of the Confederate sympathies of a large fraction of the labour press (including *Tait's Magazine*, the *Beehive* under Troup, the *Weekly Budget*, *The British Miner*, and *Reynold's News*), once the Northern government was steadfastly committed to Negro emancipation, working-class support was assured, on the grounds that liberty and 'the cause of labour . . . [are] one all over the world'.[4] Writing in 1863, F. W. Chesson, Secretary of the Aborigines Protection Society, assured American friends that 'The working classes . . . have proved to be sound to the core whenever their opinion has been tested', and George Thompson during the same year reported even more enthusiastically on the reception given to him by working-class audiences at anti-slavery meetings in Lancashire, Cheshire, London, Scotland, and the West.[5]

The political affiliation and debt to politicians of the British anti-slavery movement are harder to determine after 1833 than before it. As we have seen, before the Emancipation Act success

---

[1] Harrison, op. cit., p. 59.

[2] C. D. Rice, 'The Anti-Slavery Mission of George Thompson to the United States, 1834–1835', *Journal of American Studies*, Vol. 2, no. 1, April 1968, pp. 18, 30; M. W. Chapman to Mary Estlin, 29 October 1855, Ambleside, 24.122 (18), Estlin Papers.

[3] Harrison, op. cit., p. 59; *Uncle Tom Penny Offering. Statement of Committee*, in papers of the Glasgow Emancipation Society, Smeal Collection.

[4] Harrison, op. cit., pp. 64, 72.

[5] W. P. and F. J. Garrison, *The Life and Times of William Lloyd Garrison, 1805–1879, as Told by his Children*, New York, 1889, 4 vols., Vol. IV, pp. 66–7, 72, 75.

was achieved through Parliament, even though this aroused controversy; but the early 'Saints' were not a strict party group—William Smith usually voted Whig, James Stephen Tory, Wilberforce and Henry Thornton changed their allegiance as it suited them, and Buxton saw Parliament simply as the 'sphere in which I could do most for my Master's service'; 'I care but little about Party politics', he said, 'I vote as I like.' However, emancipation was carried by a Whig government, and by 1833 most of the leading members of the Anti-Slavery Society were Whigs (the Nonconformist element, it will be remembered, was very strong in this party), while the West Indian magnates were generally allied with the Tories.[1]

From this point abolitionists in Britain increasingly relied, where political action was possible, on the goodwill of all parties, while some M.P.s who had once given their support felt, like Thomas Babington Macaulay, that their obligations 'ceased when slavery itself ceased in that part of the world for the welfare of which . . . [they] were accountable'.[2]

The Whigs continued to be the party of reform, the Melbourne ministry, especially Russell and Glenelg, giving every support to the ill-fated Society for the Extinction of the Slave Trade and for the Civilization of Africa, and its major venture, the Niger Expedition of 1841. Palmerston, as Foreign Secretary from 1830–41 and 1846–50, and later as Prime Minister, was the inspiration and main support of Britain's coercive policy towards the foreign slave trade. But although Lord John Russell vigorously upheld Palmerston's policy, other Liberals like Cobden and Bright were opposed on economic grounds, and Gladstone, not entirely free from the influence of his slave-owning family background, held similar views, denying that Providence had ordained that 'the Government of one nation shall correct the morals of another'.[3] Nevertheless, in spite of the continuing reputation of the Tory party for opposition to emancipation, every successive British government after 1807 sustained the fight against the foreign slave trade, responding to the ceaseless petitions of British abolitionists, while the B.F.A.S.S. enjoyed the patronage of M.P.s from opposing parties, on humanitarian rather than political grounds. The appeal was

---

[1] Mathieson, op. cit., pp. 198, 220; Coupland, op. cit., pp. 81, 119, 188; Mottram, op. cit., pp. 36–7; J. Harris, *A Century of Emancipation*, London, 1933, pp. 20–1.
[2] Quoted in Williams, op. cit., p. 193.
[3] Ibid., p. 191; and Coupland, op. cit., pp. 174–5, 177–9, 182.

embodied in a resolution passed at a public meeting in Glasgow in 1841:[1]

> That Slavery being upheld by every class of Society independent of sect or party, it is equally important, successfully to oppose it, that the friends of the Slave should, irrespective of country, creed, party or sex, harmoniously co-operate for its overthrow.

From the late thirties to the late fifties the B.F.A.S.S. was dominated by the Quaker, Joseph Sturge. Born near Bristol of a modestly prosperous family, he quickly rose as a corn merchant in Bewdley (later moving to Birmingham), and as soon as the business was securely established, by about 1822, Sturge began to devote himself to non-commercial pursuits. By 1816 he had become a supporter of the London Peace Society, of which he became President in 1858, and during the fifties was to go on peace missions for the Quakers to Denmark, Schleswig Holstein, and Russia. Once established in Birmingham, Sturge became an active member of Thomas Attwood's political union, and some ten years later a Chartist, heavily involved in the Complete Suffrage Movement; his attempts to enter Parliament, however, were rebuffed on three occasions, in 1842, 1844, and 1847.

Never a man who shrank from commitments, Joseph Sturge described himself as one of those 'who have never been able to see that a Christian was not equally bound to discharge his political with his religious duties'.[2] Acting upon this premiss he laboured in many political causes, and was the chief founder of the Radical newspaper, the *Morning Star*.

In 1826, Sturge first became interested in the anti-slavery movement; he began as secretary of the Birmingham society, and went on to lead the movement's extreme wing in forming the Agency Committee; he campaigned effectively against Negro apprenticeship schemes in the British West Indies, and was instrumental in founding the B.F.A.S.S. and organizing the world anti-slavery conventions of 1840 and 1843. He remained a force to be reckoned with in the national society, even after Scoble became secretary, and was a corresponding member of the B.F.A.S.S. until his death in 1859, when tributes to him poured in from all over Britain and from America.

[1] W. P. and F. J. Garrison, op. cit., Vol. IV, p. 67; Coupland, op. cit., p. 188; and *Glasgow Emancipation Society Minute Book III*, Smeal Collection.
[2] Harris, op. cit., p. 57.

Sturge's career cannot be criticized on the familiar grounds that charity should begin at home. In his immediate neighbourhood he devoted time and money to the establishment of parks and open spaces for the use of working men, a reformatory for young criminals, and to day and Sunday schools. The stern conscience which seems so characteristic of many abolitionists, the earnest piety and inflexible singlemindedness which may repel as well as impress, these were his to a high degree. As a close friend observed after Sturge's death, 'His benevolence was the *philanthropy of principle*, as well as of feeling. . . . He felt it at once his duty and his privilege to do good: a sense of duty gave sanctity to the privilege, and a feeling of privilege imparted pleasure to the duty.'[1]

To an even greater degree, the B.F.A.S.S. relied upon the generosity of another prominent Quaker, Samuel Gurney, although the huge variety of this wealthy banker's charitable commitments meant that anti-slavery functions often benefited from his patronage rather than his presence. But such a man was as vital to the movement as Sturge, and the latter paid tribute to the financial debt of the London society to the Gurneys; Samuel Gurney Junior was a member of the B.F.A.S.S. for thirty-six years, and its President from 1864 to his death in 1882.[2]

The lives of several other important members of the society took the same course: hard work rewarded by early retirement, and the means and leisure to devote to philanthropy. Thus Robert Alsop, a prosperous Quaker chemist, retired in 1855 at the age of 52, to plunge into missions for the temperance and peace movements, educational reform, religious freedom, and the anti-slavery cause: he was a committee member and honorary secretary of the B.F.A.S.S. for many years, interests which were matched exactly by those of another London Friend, Stafford Allen, who laboured for abolition from 1837 (when he was 31) to his death in 1889, by which time he had become a Vice-President of the London society. Similarly, schoolmaster Josiah Forster, after retiring quite young, gave much of his time to Quaker business—he was an elder and clerk of the London Yearly Meeting for eleven years, visiting all parts of Britain as well as Europe and America; in addition Forster was a keen supporter of the British and Foreign Bible Society and for many years a committee member of the B.F.A.S.S.

---

[1] Richard, op. cit., quotation, p. 591; and F. J. Klingberg and A. H. Abel, *A Side-Light on Anglo-American Relations, 1839–58*, Lancaster, Pennsylvania, 1927, pp. 48–9, 56.
[2] Ibid., p. 48.

The major issue facing British abolitionists in 1833 was the apprenticeship system imposed on the West Indian Negro after emancipation. If the experiment of freedom failed to bring benefit to the islands, its failure might be used to argue the case against emancipation elsewhere in the world, and especially in the United States. The missionaries renewed their efforts with a will, and Buxton and Lushington after considerable effort obtained for the purpose of educating the freedmen the sum of over £110,000, left in 1710 by a Lady Mico for the redemption of Christian slaves in the Barbary states (to which the government added a temporary grant of £20,000 and individual abolitionists contributed generously).[1]

In Antigua and the Bermudas, however, emancipation seemed to have worked well without the transitional period of enforced labour imposed elsewhere, and a group in Britain led by Sturge, which had never been reconciled to the compromise act of 1833, felt that apprenticeship schemes should be discarded throughout the islands. A trip to the West Indies during 1836–7 by Sturge and three others (financed largely by the Birmingham Quaker) dramatized the issue as the 1836 Select Parliamentary Committee on Jamaica had failed to do, though the conclusions drawn from the visit were often biased, and generalizations were made on the strength of an acquaintance with only a small part of one island.[2]

But genuine grievances were also aired—the laws passed by colonial assemblies confining the freed Negroes to their former masters' estates or to specific localities; legislation sanctioning the apprenticeship of children; corporal punishment which might be excessive (as in Mauritius and Jamaica) and permitted the flogging of women; the appalling condition of the Houses of Correction to which offenders were committed; liability to arrest for vagrancy—for the Negroes (for instance in St. Christopher and parts of Jamaica) were sometimes unable to reconcile the idea of freedom with that of compulsory labour, and the availability of areas of wasteland upon which they might obtain plots made freedmen reluctant to continue in the hard toil of the sugar plantations. Many planters were forced, for want of labour, to give up growing provisions, and as the Negroes often grew only subsistence crops

---

[1] Harris, op. cit., p. 60; Coupland, op. cit., p. 144.

[2] Mathieson, op. cit., pp. 283–6; and by the same author, *British Slave Emancipation, 1838–1849*, London, Longmans, 1932, p. 15; Richard, op. cit., pp. 110–202; some local societies also opposed apprenticeship—see, for instance, *Glasgow Emancipation Society Minute Book II*, Smeal Collection.

on their new land, the colonies became increasingly dependent for food on the United States. Controversies arose over the freedmen's hours of work, and allowances for food, clothing, lodgings, and medicine were often skimped as the planters endeavoured to adjust to the new conditions. Special magistrates appointed to safeguard the interests of the Negroes were immensely hindered by continuing planter resentment.[1]

This, more than anything, though exaggerated by Sturge, alarmed the anti-slavery public in Britain. Brougham and Buxton, previously committed to apprenticeship, were convinced of its evils, and helped in the parliamentary fight for repeal, which was finally achieved in August 1838, two years ahead of the schedule fixed by the Emancipation Act.

The decline in West Indian production which followed was a serious embarrassment to the B.F.A.S.S.—sugar exports from Jamaica, for instance, where nearly half the West Indian apprentices had been located, dropped only slightly before 1838, but almost halved between 1838 and 1840. Overall exports from the West Indies dropped by almost 40 per cent during the same period. The average working day was cut from at least ten hours during slavery to as low as five hours in Antigua. Encouraged by abolitionist literature, many women refused to work, turning to household duties and sending their children, where possible, to school. Labour being scarce, wages were high, which hit the planters. The Select Committee of 1842, set up by Parliament to examine the effects of complete freedom, could not conceal the worrying economic condition of the islands, the testimony of abolitionists Scoble, Candler, and Knibb notwithstanding.[2]

Immigration schemes, seized upon by the planters as the answer to the labour shortage, were regarded with suspicion by philanthropists pledged—through the Aborigines Protection Society—to oppose disguised slavery, in the form of contract or indentured labour, obtained mainly from India. Although imported labour was costly, fair success was enjoyed with it in Mauritius, Trinidad, and Guiana (and to a lesser degree Jamaica), and between 1842 and 1870 the total number of Indian emigrants was 533,595. However, the agitation against the system carried on in anti-slavery papers like the *British Emancipator*, and by Scoble, Buxton, and

---

[1] Coupland, op. cit., pp. 143–5; Mathieson, *British Slavery and its Abolition*, pp. 167, 249, 257–73; and Harris, op. cit., pp. 54–5.

[2] Temperley, op. cit., pp. 167–8; Mathieson, *British Slave Emancipation*, pp. 104–5.

Brougham (whose views were largely supported by the Sanderson Report of 1840) helped to keep it in check, although indentured labour was not completely abolished until the First World War.[1]

The planters were also attacked on another front, this time by an alliance of abolitionists and commercial interests. Reference has already been made to the opposition, both before and after 1833, to the West Indian sugar monopoly. From 1838 the position became more complicated, for West Indian sugar was now 'free-grown', thus meeting abolitionists' early objections to it. But the hostility of other sugar producers increased, supported by free traders. Opponents of the monopoly were further encouraged by partial success: Mauritius gained entry into West Indian preserves in 1826; the East Indies had a similar success in 1836.[2]

Sturge and his colleagues were naturally reluctant to identify themselves too closely with the planters, and in any event seem to have been slow to grasp that the welfare of the West Indian freedmen depended largely upon the prosperity of their former masters. An added difficulty was created by the fact that failure to support free trade made abolitionists more than usually open to accusations of indifference to domestic suffering.[3]

At a conference leading to the formation of the B.F.A.S.S. in 1839 it was unanimously resolved 'to recommend the use of free-grown produce, as far as practicable, in preference to slave-grown, and to promote the adoption of fiscal regulations in favour of free labour'.[4] But free-grown produce was not necessarily the cheapest available, and the ideal solution for the London society would have been the admission of foreign *free*-grown sugar at colonial rates, but treaties with Brazil and other sugar producers, entitling them to most favoured nation treatment, made this impossible.[5]

It became fashionable to point out that Britain admitted slave-grown coffee, cotton, and tobacco, and there are signs that by the 1840s anti-slavery sentiments were losing ground both in Parliament and the country at large. The Peel administration continued the trend of whittling away the West Indian monopoly, but the reduction in duties on sugar from Java, Manilla, and Cochin

---

[1] Harris, op. cit., p. 67; Coupland, op. cit., p. 146.
[2] G. R. Mellor, *British Imperial Trusteeship, 1783–1850*, London, Faber & Faber, 1951, p. 139.
[3] J. E. Ritchie, *Thoughts on Slavery and Cheap Sugar. A Letter to the Members and Friends of the British and Foreign Anti-Slavery Society*, London, 1844, p. 28.
[4] Mellor, op. cit., p. 140
[5] Mathieson, *British Slave Emancipation*, p. 144.

China not having proved a success (because a shortage in Cuba raised the European demand for foreign free-grown sugar), the Russell ministry introduced a bill allowing importation of all foreign sugars at a uniform rate of 23*s*. and providing for the gradual reduction of this rate to the colonial level over five years.[1]

This was a real defeat for the abolitionists. The most they could claim was to have slightly delayed the advance of free-trade ideas, with regard to sugar. And it has been suggested that while the central leadership—Sturge, Lushington, Gurney, Denman, Brougham, Inglis, and Acland—remained steadfastly protectionist, carrying the boycott of slave-grown produce into practice, in Glasgow, Liverpool, Manchester, and Birmingham, anti-slavery men were converted to free trade.[2]

The effect of the 1846 Act on West Indian production was as expected—an immediate decline in island sugar prices and a gradual loss of a position in the British sugar market long threatened.[3] By 1851 over one-third of the sugar retained for use by Britain was of foreign origin. Economic and political crises continued to afflict many of the islands over the next two decades, in spite of the postponement of the equalization of duties on colonial and foreign sugar until 1854, and the relief and development grants paid out by the British government.

By 1860 perhaps the only encouraging development, from the abolitionists' point of view, were signs of 'the slow, but steady, formation of a middle class of inhabitants, chiefly coloured, independent of manual labour, and occupied in various branches of commercial industry'.[4] (It is interesting to note at this stage that the industrial schools for the freedmen favoured by successive British committees on colonial education—as self-supporting, inexpensive, and likely ultimately to alleviate labour shortages where they occurred—were opposed by the B.F.A.S.S. because it was feared such schools might prevent the Negro rising above the station in which he was born, namely that of agricultural labourer. By the 1860s abolitionists in Britain had completely reversed their attitude on this issue.[5])

The other main problems facing the B.F.A.S.S. in the years

[1] Ibid., pp. 147–9, 154–5.
[2] Ibid., pp. 158–9; Richard, op. cit., pp. 384–97. The evidence is, however, slender.
[3] See B. Hildrith, *The 'Ruin' of Jamaica*, New York, 1955, p. 177; L. M. Penson, *The Colonial Agents of the British West Indies*, London, University Press, 1924.
[4] Mellor, op. cit., pp. 144–6, 162.
[5] Ibid., pp. 147–51; and see below, pp. 130–1.

before 1860 were the suppression of the foreign slave trade and—closely connected with this—relations with American emancipation societies.

During the 1820s and 1830s successive British governments built up a network of treaties against the slave trade; these allowed Britain and the contracting countries, Spain, Portugal, Brazil, and eventually France, a mutual right of search of ships suspected of participating in the traffic, and laid down rules for the forfeiture of such vessels. By 1839 only the United States remained outside the system. But the slave trade still flourished, for only Britain was prepared to take positive steps to see that legislative prohibitions were observed. Furthermore the provisions of various anti-slave trade treaties simply made the traders more callous; thus, until 1822 the Spanish slavers, who could only be seized if they actually had their human cargo on board, often threw the slaves over the side if sighted and pursued, while the fear of cargoes being confiscated by Britain led to even tighter packing than before.[1]

American resistance to the British Africa Squadron was damaging but can be partly explained in terms of the peculiar sensitivity in the United States—dating from the Napoleonic Wars—on the question of interference with neutral shipping. The right of search was almost granted in the early twenties, but negotiations finally failed; from this point British patrols could only 'visit' and not stop suspected vessels, and the American government proved incapable of enforcing its laws of 1807 and 1819 against the trade. Only moderate aid was given to the Africa Squadron, even after the Webster-Ashburton treaty had been agreed in 1842, and indeed from 1839 onwards many slavers found their greatest safety—and only immunity from search—under the American flag, albeit often fraudulently assumed. No satisfactory agreement was reached between the two nations until the crisis years of Civil War, when the right of search was at last yielded by the United States.

The long struggle of the British government to suppress the slave trade brought disillusionment at home as the traffic grew. 'Twice as many human beings are now its victims as when Wilberforce and Clarkson entered upon their noble work', wrote Thomas Fowell Buxton in *The African Slave Trade and Its Remedy*, published in 1839. He maintained that about 150,000 Negroes were shipped out annually from West Africa, and that preventative measures had cost Britain approximately £15 million over the past thirty

[1] Coupland, op. cit., pp. 164, 176.

years. Coercion alone as a policy was a failure. Buxton, though in favour of retaining a strengthened Squadron, felt it was more important to call out the resources of Africa, both moral and economic; to make treaties with the chiefs of the coast and the interior; to encourage legitimate commerce through sending out trading ships and founding trading posts and factories; and to help the Negroes to help themselves by providing intellectual, agricultural, and medical education.[1] This was the programme of the Society for the Extinction of the Slave Trade and for the Civilization of Africa, which became the dream of Buxton's last years; but as his biographer puts it, the 'lofty vision that enabled him to brush aside much irrelevant detail now served him ill'.[2]

The Niger Expedition mounted by the Society in 1841, as the first part of its grand design, was grotesquely inadequate, ill-equipped, and dogged by bad weather and bad luck. The majority of the company of 145 whites were soon struck by fever, and forty-three eventually died of it; the model farm founded near Mount Palten was soon abandoned; negotiations with native chiefs proved abortive; and the expedition which had left with government blessing and support returned to Britain to be condemned as the work of senseless fanatics. The Africa Civilization Society was wound up in 1843 despite the protests of its influential patrons —in fact it died of its own dignity, as Sturge said of the earlier, equally unlucky, Africa Institution.[3]

After this fiasco the whole idea of a 'positive policy' for the redemption of Africa was dimmed and disparaged.[4] The arguments of free traders—that the Africa Squadron impeded the growth of legitimate trade on both sides of the Atlantic—were again favourably heard; and while some abolitionists such as Denman and Lushington successfully pressed for the retention of the Squadron, members of the Quaker dominated B.F.A.S.S., founded to fight slavery 'by the employment of those means which are of a moral, religious, and pacific character', opposed the use of force on principle.[5] Although very often their motives were unimpeachable, many contemporaries agreed with the cynical verdict of the M.P. from Manchester who remarked, 'The slavery delusion has been discovered to be a hypocritical protest; the Anti-Slavery Society itself would not support it; they were against the system of having

---

[1] Published in London, especially pp. 502–25; Mottram, op. cit., p. 117.
[2] Ibid., p. 128.   [3] Richard, op. cit., p. 78.   [4] Coupland, op. cit., pp. 174–5.
[5] Klingberg and Abel, op. cit., pp. 26–7; Richard, op. cit., p. 206.

war cruisers on the coast of Brazil, and they would rather see their doctrines spread by the spirit of religion than at the point of the bayonet—by commercial intercourse than by hostile negotiations.'[1]

As we know, however, the coercionists led by Palmerston and Russell won the day against the abolitionists, and appeared to be vindicated by the Lords Select Committee of 1850, which reported that the slave trade had been expelled from all its haunts north of the equator except the Bight of Benin.[2] The East African trade, supplying mainly South America, Arabia, and Persia, was also attacked through naval patrols, supplemented by treaties with the rulers of the state of Oman, through which much of the traffic passed. Again Buxton—and later Livingstone—urged the inadequacy of blockades alone, and the desirability of British occupation of African territory, this time at Mombasa. But like early schemes for the settlement of West Africa, these arguments were unacceptable to most British statesmen and free traders, though in the event it was only by occupation of East Africa that the Arab slave trade was to be finally abolished at the end of the century.[3]

One of the incidental reasons why the B.F.A.S.S. opposed the cruiser system was that it involved the nation in unwelcome conflict with the United States. Sturge always maintained that the stronghold of slavery was America, and deplored what he felt to be the declining interest of Quakers throughout that country in abolition.[4] This was one of the reasons for his visit to the United States in 1841, following the precedent set by George Thompson, whose mission of 1834–5 to the Northern states had led to the accumulation of a vast amount of information on American conditions, which was used in British anti-slavery propaganda for many years.[5]

But Thompson's mission also revealed the difficulties in the way of Anglo-American co-operation in this sphere. The Englishman's trip was condemned by the President himself, aroused hostility in the North and in the South against outside interference, and

[1] *Hansard's Parliamentary Debates, Third Series, Commencing With the Accession of William IV* (in future simply *Hansard*), LXXIII, 1844, 655.
[2] W. L. Mathieson, *Great Britain and the Slave Trade, 1839–65*, London, Longmans 1929, pp. 90–114, 191–9.
[3] Coupland, op. cit., pp. 200–2.
[4] Richard, op. cit., pp. 205, 221–2; J. Sturge, *A Visit to the United States in 1841*, Boston, 1842.
[5] Duncan Rice, op. cit., p. 29; Klingberg and Abel, op. cit., p. 24.

helped to give the anti-slavery movement an alien character (already emphasized by the heavy attack of the North on a primarily Southern institution). As an observer put it later, during a visit by Thompson to America in 1850,[1]

> The appearance of a Foreigner in the field in an occasion of peculiar excitement gives the advocates of slavery the opportunity to change the issue, . . . crying out against foreign interference and covering up the great question itself with clamour—so that truth is not lighted and progress for the time halts. The name of 'Agitator' adds to the odium of 'Foreigner' in the matter of 'interference'—and the American John Bull gives up to his natural propensity to antagonism as well as to his jealousy.

The world anti-slavery convention of 1840, at which American delegates expressed themselves as anxious for British support, was in fact the highpoint of co-operation between the two nations.[2] Thereafter the frustrations experienced by the American abolitionists and their English counterpart, for whom no direct action over slavery in the United States was possible, inevitably led to intermittent strain and ill will. From the very formation of the B.F.A.S.S., some Americans in the field—such as Lewis Tappan—were opposed to asking for financial aid, and this opposition grew with the passage of years.[3] And since the British societies took sides in the quarrels of the American movement, it is scarcely surprising to find rivalry and bitterness developing. Charges of interference might not have been made so often, had abolitionists in the United States been as outward looking and ambitious as those in Britain, but while so much remained to be accomplished in their own land, this was impossible.[4]

We should not assume, however, that because co-operation was difficult it was non-existent. Abolitionists on both sides of the Atlantic worked assiduously against the annexation of Texas by the United States on the grounds that it might lead ultimately to the seizure of Cuba and all Mexico, and the extension of slavery into each area. Since Britain had interests in Texas, there was scope for action on the part of the B.F.A.S.S., which, encouraged by advice and information from America, argued for British recognition of Texas on condition that slavery be abolished in the new state,

---

[1] Joseph Sargent, London, 6 December 1850, to Dr. Estlin, 24.125(51), Estlin Papers.
[2] Temperley, op. cit., p. 94; Thistlethwaite, op. cit., pp. 113, 118.
[3] Klingberg and Abel, op. cit., p. 45; letters in Estlin Papers, 24.122 (37), (40).
[4] Klingberg and Abel, op. cit., p. 10–11.

which would then be eligible for loans from Britain. Even though the issue finally went against them, the memorials presented to the government by the abolitionists say much for their perseverance and depth of knowledge of American affairs.[1]

English and American anti-slavery groups alike condemned colonization as a means of solving the Negro problem in the States, for once sinking the policy differences which normally beset them. Thus Thompson and his followers in Britain, as well as members of the B.F.A.S.S., were critical of the Liberia experiment (and the support of Dr. Hodgkin and Buxton was discredited after the disastrous failure of the Niger Expedition). Again, over the need to persuade the churches to take a stand against slavery and the necessity of suppressing the Atlantic and coast-wise slave trade, the two movements were as one.[2]

A most serious threat to their delicately balanced relationship was presented, however, by the American Civil War. The close ties between British and American abolitionists meant that at its outbreak the former had a fair appreciation of the complexities involved, and consequently found it difficult quickly to adopt a clear cut policy towards the war. Garrison and his British followers had for years been arguing that disunion was the swiftest road to emancipation. (Without the economic and political support of the North, so the theory went, the Southern States would soon collapse and be forced to rid themselves of slavery as the price of readmission into the Union.) Then, too, the Republican party in 1860 seemed as committed to protectionism and other economic policies untenable to Britons, as to freeing the Negro.[3]

These and many other problems raised by the war, which we must now consider, brought about a gulf between abolitionists in Britain and America (and a crisis between the two nations), which the British freedmen's aid movement developing in the sixties finally and fortunately went some way to bridge.

[1] Klingberg and Abel, op. cit., pp. 12–20.
[2] Ibid., pp. 25–32.
[3] Ibid., pp. 35–40.

CHAPTER II

The Civil War, Jamaica, and the Abolitionists

'Since the beginning of the civil war ... the interest of American politics has never permanently flagged. Both in domestic and foreign affairs there is always occasion for hope, for fear, for excitement, or at least for curiosity.'

Saturday Review[1]

By 1860 the causes of Anglo-American governmental antagonisms —such as British claims to Nicaragua, American territorial expansion, or the right of British ships to search, in peacetime, vessels suspected of taking part in the slave trade—were virtually all at an end.[2] The close ties which had long bound the two countries, a common history, language, and people, were further strengthened by massive British immigration to the United States and steadily improving communications.

The ignorance and confusion which is said to have characterized British opinion on American politics in 1860 may therefore come as a surprise.[3] Interest in the United States, it seems, did not produce accurate observation. Writing in 1865, Sir Leslie Stephen noted that:

The name of America five years ago called up to the ordinary English mind nothing but a vague cluster of associations, compounded of Mrs. Trollope, *Martin Chuzzlewit*, and *Uncle Tom's Cabin*. A few flying reminiscences of disputes about territory, and a few commonplaces about democracy, made up what we were pleased to call our opinions.[4]

Ignorance, not to say prejudice, is clearly reflected in much British comment on the American Civil War, but, equally clearly,

---

[1] 5 May 1866, p. 524.
[2] E. D. Adams, *Great Britain and the American Civil War*, London, Longmans 1954, 2 Vols., Vol. I, pp. 4–16.
[3] Ibid., Vol. I, pp. 42–5; D. Jordan and E. J. Pratt, *Europe and the American Civil War*, London, 1931, pp. 84–5.
[4] *The 'Times' on the American War: a Historical Study*, London, 1865, pp. 4–5.

not all observers were similarly misinformed. Thus, as we have seen, the hesitant attitude of British abolitionists towards the North in 1861 was due to an excess of knowledge about the United States rather than to ignorance, and the intensity of British interest in the war must be accepted, on press evidence alone.[1] As the London *Economist* put it,

The tidings from what we can no longer call the United States bid fair, for some time to come, to surpass all others in interest and importance. The relations of this country with America, commercial and political, are so intimate, that every transaction on the other side of the Atlantic has its echo and vibration here. Nothing that passes beyond our shores can affect us so powerfully or concern us so much as the proceedings and condition of the great Federal Republic.[2]

Unfortunately, however, it was the shortcomings and ambivalence of much British comment which impressed the majority of Americans, wherever their loyalties lay. After the war, said Henry Cabot Lodge, 'The North was left with a bitter sense of wrong and outrage, and the South with a conviction that they had been uselessly deceived and betrayed.'[3]

The attitudes and policies of the British government and people during the American Civil War have already been very fully analysed by historians.[4] In brief, after a period of uncertainty about the motives and combative strength of North and South, following the secession from the federal Union of the latter, British humanitarian sentiment gradually rallied and led to a fairly widespread sympathy for the North. However, disillusion followed after the fall of Fort Sumter and President Lincoln's emphasis on the preservation of the Union as his main purpose; the right of Republicans to wage war for such a cause, as well as their ability to win, was questioned.

Instead of overtly taking sides in the conflict, the British government issued a Neutrality Proclamation in May 1861 (attacked in the North as hasty and unfriendly, with its implied recognition of the belligerent status of the rebels), and endeavoured to adhere to a policy of strict neutrality for the duration of the war. But the anti-slavery interest became increasingly warm in its support of the

[1] Jordan and Pratt, op. cit., p. 123.
[2] 12 January 1861, pp. 29–30.
[3] Quoted in H. C. Allen, *Great Britain and the United States: a History of Anglo-American Relations (1783–1952)*, London, Odhams, 1954, p. 501.
[4] See especially Allen, op. cit., Chapter 13; Jordan and Pratt, op. cit., pp. 3–188; and Adams, op. cit.

Union after Lincoln's 1863 Proclamation freeing the slaves (or at least those of them in rebel controlled areas), and the mounting military successes of the North from this point onwards convinced even those unsympathetic to the Union that the cause of the South was lost.

However, hopes of obtaining foreign support were at first high in the Confederacy. The greatest misgivings were entertained by the British government about the future of trade with the South. In March 1861, Lord Lyons, the British Ambassador to Washington, confided to Secretary of State Seward, as he was to do many times, that 'if the United States determined to stop by force so important a commerce as that of Great Britain with the cotton-growing States, I could not answer for what might happen'. It was not until the war was nearly over, with Britain's persistent neutrality before them, that Southerners began to doubt their earlier, confident assertions that 'Great Britain will make any sacrifice, even of principle or of honour, to prevent the stoppage of the supply of cotton'. This confidence was based not just on occasional apparent breaches of the neutrality policy, but on the important fact that, according to a *Times* estimate, approximately one-fifth of the entire English population was dependent, directly or indirectly, on the prosperity of the cotton districts, and thus on the Confederate South from which something between 78 and 84 per cent of the English cotton supply was drawn.[1]

British policy pleased neither section, but in view of the outcome of the war, the resentment of the North became of paramount importance. The inability or unwillingness of the British government to check the activities of Southern agents, or close its ports to Confederate ships, was understandably much resented by the Union, as was the building in British ports of the *Alabama*, *Georgia*, *Florida*, and *Shenandoah*, vessels bound for the Confederacy, in whose service they did tremendous damage to Northern shipping.

As well as producing new problems, the Civil War revitalized a number of complex, older grievances: the San Juan boundary dispute between Canada and the United States; the rights of Americans to fish off the Canadian coast, confirmed by the Reciprocity Treaty of 1854 and withdrawn in 1866; and the claims of the inhabitants of the Ohio valley and Great Lakes region to free navi-

[1] Adams, op. cit., Vol. I, p. 64, Vol. II, p. 67; and Consul Bunch of South Carolina quoted in Vol. II, p. 5.

gation of the Lakes and the St. Lawrence. (All these difficulties had to wait for solution until 1872, when the Alabama claims negotiations finally culminated in the Treaty of Washington and the Geneva arbitration award, a settlement which heralded a long period of tranquillity in Anglo-American relations.)

Englishmen kindly disposed towards the North sometimes deplored the American tendency to assume that everyone in Britain thought alike about the Civil War.[1] Although it is possible to see something like unanimity in British rejoicing over the final Northern victory in 1865, or mourning for the assassination of Lincoln earlier in the year, many voices were raised initially both for and against the Union cause; Americans chose to generalize from the latter, with unhappy results.

Thus John Lothrop Motley expressed the common view of Northerners when, in 1862, he wrote to his old friend J. A. Froude, the English historian, that a 'vulgar and ignorant prejudice' had 'characterized nearly the whole of the English press and the great majority of English public speakers' on the Civil War. It was the American's opinion that 'you and I will never live to see anything more than the most cold and formal relations between our two countries'.[2] A pro-Union newspaper, the London *Daily News*, reported American correspondents as saying that Britain could 'never be to us again what you were—neither your liberal parties, nor your philanthropists, nor your religious world. We believed in you as no people ever believed in another before, and terribly have we been undeceived'.[3]

The tone of the British press, the attitude of the aristocracy, and the speeches of public men were all condemned. *The Times*, still the most powerful paper in Britain during the 1860s, thundered against the Union cause to the end; many other journals in London followed its lead, among them the *Morning Post*, the *Standard*, the *Herald*, the *Saturday Review*, and *John Bull*, while the *Index*, which first appeared in May 1862, was soon recognized as the

---

[1] See Goldwin Smith to Charles Eliot Norton, Oxford, 7 November, 1863, Goldwin Smith Papers, No. 14/17/134, Cornell University Library, Ithaca, New York; C. W. Dilke, *Greater Britain: a Record of Travel in English-Speaking Countries During 1866 and 1867*, 2 Vols., London, 1868, Vol. I, p. 303.

[2] Vienna, 8 April 1862. Quoted in W. H. Dunn, *James Anthony Froude. A Biography*, Oxford, 1861–3, 2 Vols., Vol. II, pp. 339–40; for a similarly embittered Northern view see H. Adams, *The Education of Henry Adams*, Boston, 1918, pp. 114–93; J. Bigelow, *Retrospections of an Active Life*, New York, 1909–13, 5 Vols., Vol. II, pp. 455, 474, 531; Vol. III, p. 602.

[3] 16 June, 1865.

British mouthpiece of the Confederacy.[1] Among the names gracing the publicity sheets of the London Southern Independence Association (whose activities were duplicated by clubs throughout the country) we find some ten members of parliament, in addition to the Marquis of Lothian, the Marquis of Bath, and Lords Robert and Eustace Cecil.[2]

Both in and outside Parliament the speeches of Arthur Roebuck, Sir John Ramsden, Gladstone, and Lord Russell particularly offended Northern sensibilities. And S. Van Auken has shown that, although Englishmen entertained a distorted picture of both North and South, many became convinced that the Confederates were engaged in a romantic fight for freedom. A number of factors encouraged such a view—the belief that democracy on the American pattern could and should not endure, an economic interest in the South, dislike of Northern protectionism, and fears of American strength, both real and potential.[3] Furthermore, there were Southern supporters in plenty even among the much scrutinized working men of Lancashire and Yorkshire.[4]

The North was not, of course, totally without sympathizers in Britain. Prominent Radicals like Cobden, Bright, and Mill, Professors E. S. Beesly and Goldwin Smith, Thomas Hughes, and the Duke of Argyll lent support to the Union. So too did a number of newspapers in London and the provinces—notably the London *Daily News, Star,* and *Spectator,* the *Manchester Examiner, Newcastle Chronicle,* and *Birmingham Post.*[5] There were also some powerful metropolitan journals, such as the *Economist* (edited and dominated at this time by Walter Bagehot) and the *Telegraph,* which preserved a fair degree of impartiality on American affairs. Goldwin Smith, the Oxford historian who was soon to make his home in the United States, assured an American correspondent in 1863:[6]

[1] J. Grant, *History of the Newspaper Press*, London, 1871–2, 3 Vols., Vol. II, pp. 36–7; Jordan and Pratt, op. cit., pp. 56–7, 80–4, 86–7; Adams, op. cit., Vol. II, p. 33.
[2] *Index*, 14 January 1864, p. 23.
[3] *English Sympathy for the Southern Confederacy*, B. Litt. thesis, Oxford, 1957, see especially pp. vi, 12–13, 20–3, 46 f., 74, 78, 83f., 100–6.
[4] Ibid., and R. Harrison, 'British Labor and American Slavery', *Science and Society*, Vol. XXV, no. 4, December 1961, pp. 291–319; 'British Labour and the Confederacy', *International Review of Social History*, Vol. II, Part I, pp. 78–105; and Harrison, op. cit., pp. 40–77.
[5] See F. J. and W. P. Garrison, op. cit., Vol. IV, pp. 71–4.
[6] Letter to C. E. Norton, op. cit., for similar views, see also his *The Civil War in America*, London, 1866.

You have a strong party of friends here, and they have done you some service. . . . a good deal of the intellects, the more religious part of the middle classes, the Ministers of most of the Free Churches, and the great mass of the intelligent lower classes are on your side. This has been the case at least since the great issue between Free Labour and Slavery was fairly tendered: you could hardly expect that it should be so before.

Although slavery played a crucial part in influencing British opinion and policy during the Civil War, for two years abolitionists in Britain presented neither a united front nor a clear attitude towards the Union. This was partly the result of confusion over Northern war aims and dissatisfaction with Northern policy regarding the emancipation of the Negro, partly the consequence of strained relations with American abolitionists, and partly a reflection of the declining interest in anti-slavery work noticeable in Britain by the 1850s.[1] In a study of slavery published in 1864 one observer suggested that 'all that remains of . . . old abolitionist zeal is a decent protest'.[2] The caution of their fellow-workers before Lincoln's 1863 Emancipation Proclamation deeply offended Northern abolitionists, even though veteran agitators like George Thompson, F. W. Chesson, and others of the London Emancipation Society assured American friends that 'On the vital question of slavery, *the heart of the people is sound*'.[3] (Thompson, however, in 1862 noted and deplored the inaction of the British and Foreign Anti-Slavery Society; and at least one Garrisonian organization in Britain, namely the Glasgow Emancipation Society, was similarly hesitant.)[4]

Once the Emancipation Proclamation was issued, and the predicted servile revolt failed to materialize, British anti-slavery leaders rallied behind the North, rejoicing—in the earlier exuberant words of Thompson—that 'the "base, brutal and bloody" scribes of a venal and profligate press have been foiled in their hellish design to make us the allies of the child-stealing, women-

---

[1] See Jordan and Pratt, op. cit., pp. 127–9; J. Bright to C. Sumner, 6 September 1861, *Proceedings of the Massachusetts Historical Society*, 1912–13, Vol. XLVI (in future simply *Proceedings*), p. 95; C. N. Hall, *The American War*, London, 1862, pp. 22–3; Rev. G. G. Lawrence, *Three Months in America in the Summer of 1863*, Huddersfield 1863, pp. 51–6; Temperley, op. cit., pp. 316–26.
[2] A. Rooker, *Does It Answer? Slavery in America, a History*, London, 1864, p. 3.
[3] See Maria Weston Chapman to Mary Estlin on American feelings, in Estlin Papers, 24.122 (35), (36), (40); F. J. and W. P. Garrison, op. cit., Vol. IV, p. 67.
[4] Ibid., Vol. IV, p. 65; *Glasgow Emancipation Society Minute Book IV*, Smeal Collection.

whipping demonocracy of those doomed Southern States'.[1] The British Anti-Slavery Society, having in 1861 contemplated recognizing the Confederacy in return for co-operation in suppressing the slave trade, began from 1863 to publish a series of pamphlets on the war, maintaining that the North was fighting against slavery, and the South 'to fasten upon the civilization of the nineteenth century, a barbarism more intense in wickedness, cruelty, and depravity, than any to be paralleled in the darkest days of the history of the human race'.[2]

Although their efforts after 1863 to make amends to the North were not entirely successful, British abolitionists found in the next two years the opportunity of improving relations through co-operation with American societies organized to help the newly emancipated slaves. But the freedmen's associations which were being established in Britain even during the Civil War, offshoots of the Anti-Slavery Society and its local branches, were quickly faced with rivals for their attention in the British colonies. The operations of these societies occupy the main part of this study, and we may begin with their initial trial over the freedmen involved in the Jamaica Revolt of 1865.

Freedmen's aid associations were formed in London and the provinces, in Scotland and Ireland, with the express purpose of helping the American Negroes freed by the Civil War. By the time the conflict ended, approximately four million slaves had been emancipated. During the twelve or so years of Reconstruction which followed, Southern whites and Negroes alike were in need of help, but, partly because of their previous condition, partly through the need of the Republican party for their support, and the sincere anti-slavery sentiments of a vociferous minority within the party,[3] the freedmen received immediate assistance from both the federal government and a host of voluntary agencies.

Under these circumstances it is reasonable to suppose that—during such a crucial period of social readjustment, when the

[1] Thompson to G. Wilson, 11 January 1862, John Rylands Library (English Ms.), Manchester; E. D. Adams, op. cit., Vol. II, pp. 101–15; Jordan and Pratt, op. cit., pp. 140–2, 145, 151.

[2] *Chronological Summary of the Work of the Anti-Slavery Society During the 19th Century*, London, 1901, pp. 10–11, and *What the South is Fighting For*, London, 1863, Tract No. 1, pp. 1–2.

[3] For a sympathetic treatment see J. M. McPherson, *The Struggle for Equality: Abolitionists and the Negro in the Civil War and Reconstruction*, Princeton, University Press, 1964.

intervention of the North in Southern affairs was bitterly resented
—interference from outside the United States, and especially from
Britain, might have seemed both impertinent and ill-advised.

Nor, on the face of it, was the appearance of freedmen's societies likely to be welcomed in Britain, where they were competing
for funds with innumerable good causes of more obvious domestic
concern—poor relief, education and law reform, temperance,
factory reform, and care for the sick and aged.

British humanitarians, however, often dispirited and disillu-
sioned by the early sixties, had found a new cause of challenging
dimensions: the opportunity, at last, not only in a practical fashion
to help American abolitionists, but also for a gesture of goodwill
towards the United States, deeply resentful of British conduct
during the war. In addition, through freedmen's aid something
might be done to combat the increasingly hostile British attitude
to coloured, especially Negro, races. (As well as its organization
and actual campaign, all these aspects of the British movement
will be examined at length elsewhere.)[1]

Although on the issue of Reconstruction—the post-war reconstruction of the Southern economy and politics, in which the
Negro freedman was the central figure—British governmental
sources, almost without exception, are silent, popular interest was
considerable. This was largely the outcome of the unique attention focused on America during her four years of Civil War. Supporters of both North and South were curious, sometimes anxious
to see whether an enduring peace settlement could be made. By
1865, the early ignorance about American politics had been
banished by the newspaper correspondents who flocked to Washington and New York throughout the war, and by a flood of propaganda literature of all kinds.

The British freedmen's societies hoped to benefit from this
greater understanding; but while the degree of knowledge exhibited, especially in the press, about Reconstruction and the United
States generally marks a break with the past, in other respects the
pattern of British interest remains the same. Thus opponents of
American democracy can be found and Radical advocates too;
critics of United States commercial policy and admirers of her
economic might; abolitionists anxious for the Negro and men of a
frankly racist outlook. The strength of this last group was, however, growing rapidly, and was to be a serious embarrassment to

[1] See below, Chapters III–V.

the freedmen's associations, not only in 1865, when the needs of the Jamaica freedmen were dramatically brought to their notice, but in their work for the American Negro during Reconstruction.

The chief concern of freedmen's aid was obviously the Negro, though idealism might demand consideration for the white as well as the coloured population of the South.[1] Just as before the Civil War the destruction of American slavery had been the main aim of British abolitionists, so the outcome of the experiment in racial equality in the States after 1865 was held to be of vital importance to the progress of anti-slavery activities elsewhere in the world.[2]

But the race problem of the South was equally interesting to those whose attitude to the Negro was far from benevolent. With the triumph of free trade, imperialism in Britain had come temporarily under attack; the value of colonial possessions was further questioned following the series of shocks to Victorian sensibilities administered by the Indian Mutiny, and endemic native wars in South Africa and New Zealand. In consequence, attitudes towards colonized peoples also suffered a change, and racist views became increasingly common. British abolitionists, like most dedicated minorities, were extremely vocal, but, having lost some of their early fire, found themselves condemned as 'Nigger-Philanthropists',[3] and 'moral ghouls',[4] or, far worse, accepted as respectable and ignored. The freedmen's aid societies aimed to disturb middle-class complacency, but faced the unpleasant fact that the old concept of Anglo-Saxon (or Anglo-American) kinship was being transformed into one of white, Anglo-Saxon supremacy.

The lectures of Herman Merivale on 'Colonization and Colonies', first delivered at Oxford between 1839 and 1841, and republished with additions twenty years later, plainly illustrate the changing British attitude to race. In the original version of his

---

[1] See letter of B. Cadbury, Secretary of the Birmingham and Midland Freedmen's Society, to T. Phillips, Assistant Secretary to the Anti-Slavery Society, 1870–1, and a secretary of the National Freedmen's Aid Union of Great Britain and Ireland, in Anti-Slavery Papers, Rhodes House, Ms. British Empire S18, C39/27 (in future A.P. C. . ./. . .).

[2] John Hodgkin, London barrister and Quaker, prominent in freedmen's aid and anti-slavery work, to Aspinall Hampson, a London Congregational clergyman and first secretary of the N.F.A.U., 24 July 1865, A.P. C118/95.

[3] T. Carlyle, *Shooting Niagara: And After?*, reprinted from *Macmillan's Magazine*, August 1867, London, 1867, p. 14.

[4] Letter from J. H. Elliott, a friend of Carlyle, who sent the letter to the press, to the *Spectator*, 22 September 1866, pp. 1042–3: moral ghouls were defined as those who 'love and relish bad people'—such as the Jamaica Negroes who rebelled in 1865.

eighth lecture Merivale had advocated the immediate amalgamation of native races with the colonists, 'as master and servant, as
fellow-labourers, as fellow-citizens, and, if possible, . . . by inter-
marriage'. Each native was to 'be regarded as potentially a citizen,
to become such in all respects as soon as possible'.

By 1861, the unfortunate experiences of South Africa and New
Zealand had tarnished this ideal, and it was felt that 'natives must,
for their own protection, be placed in a situation of acknowledged
inferiority, and consequently of tutelage'. 'It has been in later
years', Merivale added, 'too much the fashion to rely on phrases;
to imagine that by proclaiming that all fellow-subjects of whatever
race are equal in the eye of the law, we really make them so. There
cannot be a greater error, nor one more calculated to inflict evil
on those classes whom it is intended to benefit.' Amalgamation was
now condemned, since coloured people could 'only meet with the
whites in the same field of hopeful industry on the footing of in-
feriors, and that if such subordinate position is not recognized by
law, and compensated by legal protection, it will be enforced, at a
heavy disadvantage to them, by the prevailing sentiment of the
conquering race.'[1]

Writing in the *Daily News* in 1865, an American Negro abolitionist, Sarah Remond, although she paid tribute to the work of
the British anti-slavery movement, suggested that 'there is a change
in the public opinion in Great Britain in reference to the coloured
race'. The planter interest, always hostile, had lately increased its
strength, and, since 'the civil war in the United States the Southern
Confederates and their natural allies, these former West Indian
planters, have united together to endeavour to neutralise the interest felt for the oppressed negroes, and to hold them up to the scorn
and contempt of the civilised world.'[2] The *News*, strongly sympathetic towards the American North, explained apologetically that
the Civil War had been a 'time of strange reaction in the public
mind of this country against the generous sympathies which the
anti-slavery movement in the United States had always excited'.[3]

In an article published in 1866, the *Saturday Review*, liveliest and
most popular of the Victorian weeklies,[4] took a humorous tilt at
the once fashionable preoccupation with philanthropy. 'Of the

---

[1] H. Merivale, *Lectures on Colonization and Colonies Delivered Before the University of Oxford
in 1839, 1840, and 1841*, New ed., London, 1861, pp. 510–11, 513–23.
[2] 22 November 1865.   [3] 27 February 1868.
[4] See A. Ellegard, 'The Readership of the Periodical Press in Mid-Victorian Britain',
Göteborgs Universitets Arskrift, Vol. LXIII, 1957, (3), pp. 22, 24.

many contrivances devised by good and kind-hearted people for adding to the stock of human discomfort and misery', it declared feelingly, 'their public conversaziones are the most severely intolerable. An Exeter Hall[1] meeting is bad. A meeting of the council or committee of a philanthropic society is also a hard thing to endure. The fussiness and egotism and gross disproportion between talk and action on such occasions are hugely wearisome, and the proceedings are as dust and ashes in the mouth.'[2]

A similar attitude can be seen in other sections of the press. The *Daily Telegraph*, in some ways a liberal paper, complained bitterly in 1865 about the 'professional philanthropists' and 'theological disputants' who always took the part of the Negro. (Most abolitionists, it will be remembered, viewed their work as essentially religious in character, and many were Nonconformists.) 'Nothing delights them more', alleged its leader writer, 'than . . . trading upon sectarian prejudice';[3] 'Willing, though perchance unconscious, slaves of a single preconceived and dominant idea [namely, the Negro is always right], they are blind to every fact which contradicts their theory . . . we English of 1865 must decline to entrust the control of public affairs to Dissenting ministers, just as emphatically as our ancestors protested against similar encroachments on the part of the Church of Rome.'[4]

That the freedmen's aid movement succeeded against such a background of hostility bears witness to the stubborn strength of the humanitarian, anti-slavery tradition in nineteenth-century Britain, among the rich, the religious, and the radical; while the opposition which the societies encountered is a vindication, if one were needed, of their existence amid a multitude of domestic benevolent concerns. This opposition was greatly and unexpectedly increased as a result of the Jamaica Revolt of 1865, which divided the Victorian literary and political world and brought odium upon the Negro and his defenders.

In October 1865, there took place an uprising of Negro peasantry upon the island colony of Jamaica in the British West Indies. The uprising was speedily suppressed by troops under the direction of the colonial governor, Edward Eyre. In the course of the pacification of the island by the army, nearly five hundred Negroes

---

[1] A famous meeting place in London used by various charitable organizations, especially the Anti-Slavery Society.
[2] 26 May 1866, pp. 616–7.   [3] 9 December 1865.   [4] Ibid., 11 December 1865.

were killed, and more than that number were flogged and tor-
tured. While restoring order, Governor Eyre managed to secure
the court martial and execution of a personal and political enemy,
one George William Gordon, a mulatto member of the Jamaica
House of Assembly.[1] The story of the insurrection and its repres-
sion was broadcast throughout the civilized world during the last
months of 1865, but its causes were by no means easy to determine.

After the Emancipation Act of 1833, freedmen left the plantations in great numbers to live in their own villages and cultivate
their own provision grounds. The early enthusiasm of the Negroes
for education faded, and with it the zeal of their largely missionary
leaders. Attendance at Christian churches fell sharply, while from
the 1840s revivalism, obeahism, and myalism converged to form
the basis of an independent Jamaican folk religion and culture.[2]
Cultural dualism in turn contributed to, though it did not alone
account for, the island's economic decline.

The planters' difficulties have already been touched upon—an
unreliable, badly distributed, and inadequate labour force; loss of
protection for sugar in the British market and the rise of foreign
and colonial competitors (which also affected the coffee estates);
an unhealthy reliance upon one crop and soil exhaustion, combined with excessive dependence on credit; and absenteeism,
leading to the draining of excess profits from Jamaica.[3] In spite of
similar economic difficulties, most of the other sugar colonies succeeded in adapting themselves to the exigencies of emancipation,
and then of free trade; Jamaica, however, was further hampered
by its system of government.

A chartered colony, administered by a Governor, Council, and
Assembly (the last named often split between a Town and Country
Party), the island suffered from constant friction and sometimes
deadlock among these three bodies, in spite of amendments to the
constitution in 1854. The result was chronic maladministration,
especially in the sphere of finance. Emancipation had been resisted
to the last in Jamaica, thus increasing racial friction, and, with the
encouragment of the island missionaries, the Baptists especially,
the Negroes were encouraged to take what was, to their old masters, an unwelcome interest in independent labour and in politics.

---

[1] B. Semmel, *The Governor Eyre Controversy*, London, McGibbon & Kee, 1962, p. 13.
[2] O. Patterson, *The Sociology of Slavery. An Analysis of the Origins, Development and Structure
of the Negro Slave Society in Jamaica*, London, McGibbon & Kee, 1967, pp. 182–215,
287.
[3] Semmel, op. cit., pp. 29–55.

(Though it should be noted that in fact there were far more white and coloured electors than black, and too few of any group for the effective operation of parliamentary government.)

The appointment of Edward Eyre as temporary governor in 1862 did not promise well, as by the very nature of his commission he did not at the outset enjoy complete authority. The Governor also immediately ran foul of the Assembly over finance, making in particular an enemy of Gordon, a magistrate for many years, whose dismissal he approved on the grounds of false accusations by Gordon against the supervisor of the prison at Morant Bay. The whole incident highlighted the position of the Jamaican stipendiary and unpaid magistrates—their inadequate numbers and performance, as well as offending the dismissed man's considerable following. One of the chief difficulties with the magistrates was that, being mostly planters, their judgements with regard to wages and squatters' rights were often suspect; Gordon, as a mulatto, might be expected to incline towards his own race, though he was himself a proprietor.

By 1865 then, the island of Jamaica suffered from long-term economic stagnation, together with judicial and political mismanagement; it was also in the grip of a religious revival, personal feuds, drought, and high prices for imported food and cotton, resulting from the disruptions of the American Civil War. These conditions in turn produced crime and physical hardship, aggravated by the improvident habits of the Negro population. The final impetus to revolt came from the wild rumours circulating in 1865 that slavery was to be reintroduced; the inflammatory speeches and campaigning of Gordon and the genuinely concerned Baptist misssionary Underhill; and the misconstrued efforts of Governor Eyre to restore order among the discontented peasantry.[1]

The Jamaica rebellion, though brief in itself, was destined radically to affect the attitude of the Victorian public towards coloured races, dividing its great men, and also to change the course and nature of freedmen's aid in Britain.

As soon as news of the uprising was received, a committee was formed to demand an official inquiry into what it considered the excessive cruelty and illegal use of martial law on the part of

[1] See W. L. Mathieson, *The Sugar Colonies and Governor Eyre, 1849–1866*, London, Longmans, 1936, pp. 106–12, 121–7, 153–5, 168–225; and Semmel, op. cit., pp. 29–

Governor Eyre. It has recently been observed that among the officers and rank-and-file of this committee 'we find virtually all of the leading figures in the two principal pro-Northern [Emancipation] societies. Having triumphed in their support of one struggle for democracy and against slavery across the seas, these gentlemen were willing to fight for the same principles at home.'[1] They were determined to 'make effective use of the events in Jamaica to further their overall political principles and objectives'.[2] For the same reasons most of the prominent British advocates of the North and opponents of slavery lent at least their names, and in many cases their active support, to the cause of the American freedman. The Jamaican Negro, as a fellow citizen of the Empire, and more directly the responsibility of the British government, was a creature of far greater emotional impact and political utility.

Thus, although they did not desert their old protégé, Victorian Radicals had now to consider his claims along with those of the 400,000 ill-used Negroes of Jamaica. Of the 301 original members of the Jamaica Committee, thirty-four held office in either the National Freedmen's Aid Union of Great Britain and Ireland (formed in 1866) or the London freedmen's society (founded three years before).[3] Many of those who thus divided their energies were M.P.s; invariably they were the 'men of name and position' whose support the Duke of Argyll and others considered vital to the success of freedmen's aid.[4]

The economist and philosopher, John Stuart Mill, at this time Liberal M.P. for Westminster, was one of the earliest Jamaica Committee members, and also acted as Vice-President of the freedmen's aid Union. John Bright, a committee member of the London society and Vice-President of the Union, was quick to join the critics of Governor Eyre, as were Thomas Hughes, barrister, author, and Liberal M.P. for Lambeth, and his fellow Christian Socialist, the barrister J. M. Ludlow; in addition, the former was a Vice-President of the Union and a London committee member, and the latter served on that society's council and executive committee. Charles Buxton, M.P., the first Chairman of the Jamaica

---

[1] Semmel, op. cit., p. 62; see also G. Ford, 'The Governor Eyre Case in England', *University of Toronto Quarterly*, April 1948, pp. 222-3.

[2] Semmel, op. cit., p. 65.

[3] For the committee members, see the *Jamaica Papers, No. 1*, London, Jamaica Committee, 1866, pp. 94-7.

[4] Argyll to Gladstone, 31 January 1866, Gladstone Papers, British Museum, Add. Ms. 44100, Vol. XV.

Committee, was involved in both freedmen's organizations, as was his brother, Sir Thomas Fowell Buxton, M.P., a fellow member of the Jamaica Committee. Thomas Potter, Cobden's successor as M.P. for Rochdale, and staunch friend of the American North; the Radical, Edward Baines, M.P. for Leeds; and Edmond Beales, barrister leader of the Reform League, also served the cause of the freedman in America and Jamaica.

Goldwin Smith, admirer of all things American (except protection), played a leading role on the Jamaica Committee, in addition to supporting the freedmen's aid movement, addressing many of its meetings. Smith was at pains to show that the race problems of America and Jamaica could not be separated. He felt that the Jamaica uprising was 'A sort of corollary of the question between slavery and freedom in America',[1] 'and the one cause no less worthy than the other'.[2] In a speech at the final meeting of the Manchester Union and Emancipation Society, over which he had presided, Smith described the task of Reconstruction in the States as 'perhaps the hardest ever undertaken by statesmen. Jamaica tells us with terrible emphasis what are the perils of a community composed of the ex-slave owner and the ex-slave.'[3]

Other prominent figures who bestowed their patronage alike on the Jamaica Committee and the two main freedmen's organizations, were Jacob Bright, M.P. for Manchester (and brother of the Radical leader); Henry Fawcett, political economist and Liberal M.P.; Peter A. Taylor, M.P. for Leicester and Treasurer of the Jamaica Committee; Frederick W. Chesson, Secretary of the Aborigines Protection Society; and the non-conformist M.P. and philanthropist, Sir Francis Crossley. The Duke of Argyll, one of the most steadfast supporters of freedmen's aid, was deeply concerned about the Jamaica affair; writing to Gladstone at the end of 1865 he declared the latest accounts from the island to be 'indeed lamentable. How bloody we are when we are roused and frightened—and impelled by hatred of race.'[4]

This dual allegiance sometimes brought problems. Benjamin Scott, Chamberlain of the city of London, a prominent Congregationalist and temperance advocate, and the Vice-President of the London freedmen's society, also joined the Jamaica Commit-

---

[1] G. Smith, *Reminiscences,* New York, 1910, p. 357.
[2] E. Wallace, *Goldwin Smith, Victorian Liberal,* Toronto, University of Toronto Press, 1957, p. 23.
[3] Smith, *The Civil War in America,* op. cit., p. 69.
[4] Argyll to Gladstone, 2 December, 1865, Gladstone Papers, Add. Ms. 44100, Vol. XV.

tee. By 1866 he felt obliged to decline an invitation to become a vice-president of the national Union, because of the latter's reluctance to involve itself with Jamaica. Shortly afterwards, Scott declined to help the movement any further, on the grounds that Jamaican affairs occupied all his time.[1]

The freedmen's associations in London soon received news, from various parts of the country, of the impact of the Jamaica uprising. In November 1865, speaking for the Union, Thomas Phillips had declared it to be 'most seriously affecting us'.[2] A member in Leicester confirmed that operations were being hampered by 'the claim of Jamaica' upon public concern,[3] while a Bristol worker wrote, 'I am truly grieved with affairs in Jamaica— the accounts are so conflicting that I am as yet unable to form a judgement, but I have no doubt that it will have an injurious effect on our efforts for the American freedman.'[4] Reports came in from the Birmingham secretary, who spoke of being 'at present greatly embarrassed by the sad tidings from Jamaica'.[5] A similar state of affairs was reported in Leeds.[6]

It was the nature of the public reaction to trouble in Jamaica which began to prove an embarrassment to the freedmen's societies. When the first news filtered back to England, condemnation of the Governor's actions was widespread and violent—temporarily drowning dissenting voices, such as that of *The Times*.[7] But before too long, the character of the Jamaica Committee was giving cause for alarm in certain quarters. It was formed just when agitation for political reform had reached its final and most violent phase, and it soon became clear that 'the leadership of the suffrage fight—Bright, Beales, Hughes, Mill—and the leadership of the Jamaica Committee was the same. What could be more natural than to identify the two causes? It was a thing easily done since the underlying principle of both was identical', namely the defence of liberty, law, and democracy, at home and abroad.[8]

---

[1] Benjamin Scott to Aspinall Hampson, 3 and 6 January 1865, A. P. C120/2 and C117/141. Scott did not, however, resign as Vice-President of the London Freedmen's Aid Society.

[2] T. Phillips to A. Hampson, 24 November, 1865, A.P. C119/101.

[3] Edward Brewin to A. Hampson, 27 January 1866, A.P. C117/100.

[4] Joseph Davis to A. Hampson, 23 November, 1865, A.P. C118/16.

[5] William Morgan to A. Hampson, 30 November, 1865, A.P. C119/62.

[6] Thomas Harvey to A. Hampson, 5 December 1865, A.P. C118/88.

[7] Semmel, op. cit., pp. 22–5; see also Mathieson, *The Sugar Colonies and Governor Eyre, 1849–66*, p. 232.

[8] Semmel, op. cit., p. 85.

In his *Autobiography*, John Stuart Mill wrote, 'There was much more at stake than only justice to the negroes, imperative as was that consideration. The question was, whether the British dependencies, and eventually, perhaps, Great Britain itself, were to be under the government of law or of military licence.'[1] The Radicals felt that 'either the terms under which the Empire was held were bound to change the character of the British constitution or the spirit of the constitution was bound to change the character of the Empire', and committed themselves to the defence of liberty against 'administrative massacre, rule by terror', whether this took place in Britain or her colonies.[2] Goldwin Smith justified the Committee in its attempt to establish that 'all British subjects, black or white, were under the protection of British law';[3] he argued 'that the ancient securities for public liberty had largely lost their value' and should at all costs be renewed.[4]

The members of the Jamaica Committee soon found themselves abused for their Radical views, and 'denounced by conservative imperialists as traitors to the Empire'.[5] Mill countered with the accusation that the supporters of Governor Eyre were 'the same kind of people who had so long upheld negro slavery'; who were willing to let pass 'without even a protest, excesses of authority as revolting as any of those for which, when perpetrated by instruments of other Governments, Englishmen can hardly find terms sufficient to express their abhorrence.'[6]

We have already seen that during the 1850s and 1860s, as Britain's colonial possessions became increasingly troublesome, there was a perceptible hardening of middle- and upper-class attitudes towards the Negro. The old, somewhat patronizing view of the peaceful 'child of nature' was now disturbed by fear. A contemporary journalist, Justin McCarthy, noted at the time of the Jamaica crisis the growth of 'the "damned nigger" principle; the principle that any sort of treatment is good enough for negroes, and generally speaking serves them right'; this, he felt, was common 'among considerable classes of persons', even though it was not allowed to make its appearance much in public debate.[7] It was clear, in fact, that 'to bring English functionaries to the bar of a criminal court for abuses of power committed against negroes

---

[1] J. S. Mill, *Autobiography*, London, 1908, pp. 169–70.
[2] Semmel, op. cit., pp. 178, 179.   [3] Smith, *Reminiscences*, op. cit., p. 358.
[4] Wallace, op. cit., p. 23.   [5] Ibid., p. 24.   [6] Mill, op. cit., p. 169.
[7] J. M. McCarthy, *A History of Our Own Times*, London, 1882–97, 5 Vols., Vol. III, p. 275.

and mulattoes was not a popular proceeding with the English middle classes.'[1]

There was considerable agreement among the press, after the uprising, that the Negro was still an essentially barbarous creature. *The Times* wrote:

It seems impossible, to eradicate the original savageness of the African blood. As long as the black man has a strong white Government and a numerous white population to control him he is capable of living as a respectable member of society. He can be made quiet and even industrious by the fear of the supreme power, and by the example of those to whom he necessarily looks up. But wherever he attains to a certain degree of independence there is the fear that he will resume the barbarous life and the fierce habits of his African ancestors.[2]

The *Daily Telegraph* stated bluntly: 'Events have proved that the negro is still a savage', and concluded that 'we must rule the African with a strong hand, since we are bound to continue the thankless task of ruling him at all.' Similarly aggrieved, the *Morning Post* observed: 'we have done all that could be done for the negroes in our colonies; we cannot change and raise their nature from Africans to Englishmen, and as Africans we must deal with them.'[3] Jamaica was, in fact, as Wesleyan missionary William Arthur complained, 'exhibited as a specimen of a country under negro ascendancy, as the pet, model government of philanthropists and Missionaries, as brought to ruin in spite of great advantages by the natural tendency of the negro, when free, to sink and drag down those who try to save him. The original baseness of his race, its incurable meetness for a servile condition, and the folly of attempting to raise it, are ostentatiously assumed to be proved by late events.'[4]

The largely Radical Jamaica Committee was affected by this change of attitude. The boisterous proceedings of the Reform League unfortunately provoked unhappy comparisons between the black rabble of Jamaica and the white rabble of London. 'Like the Negro, the white rabble was tainted from birth and irredeemable, their unhappy condition an inevitable result of laziness,

---

[1] Mill, op. cit., pp. 170–1.   [2] 13 November 1865.

[3] Quoted in *Jamaica: Who is to Blame?* Reprinted from two articles in the *Eclectic Review* by a Thirty years' Resident, London, 1866, p. viii; see also *Daily Telegraph*, 14 December, 1865.

[4] *The Outbreak in Jamaica. A Speech by the Rev. William Arthur, M.A., Delivered at the Anniversary of the Folkestone Auxiliary to the Wesleyan Missionary Society*, 21 November 1865, London, 1865, pp. 3–4.

drunkenness, and want of thrift. And, like the whites of Jamaica, the "respectable" classes felt themselves a small and exposed and fearful minority.'[1]

In this hostile climate of opinion, Argyll lamented that he had 'heard the hanging of Gordon [the so-called (mulatto) leader of the Jamaica rebellion] defended and rejoiced over',[2] and the Leicester Freedmen's Aid Society opposed meetings in the area for a time, 'such is the prejudice against the Negroes, strengthened by the Jamaica outbreak[.] *Wrong* as this is, we have to contend with it.'[3] Englishmen had family as well as commercial ties which could be threatened by the rebellious Negroes. A correspondent in Bath reported to the Union Secretary that the 'last appeal to the Bath public has been but very coldly responded to and [I] think in a great measure owing to the Jamaica question[.] There being a great many . . . friends and relatives of the planters in Bath the Influence has gone the wrong way.'[4] A little later Edwards suggested that 'when that sad and bloody business is settled we may do something again';[5] but the business was not to be settled until the next decade.

The violence of Carlyle's description of the Jamaica Committee as 'a small loud group, small as now appears, and nothing but a group or knot of rabid Nigger-Philanthropists, barking furiously in the gutter'[6] may have offended some, but there was considerable sympathy for his belief that allowing the colonies too much rope left 'nine-tenths of them full of jungles, boa-constrictors, rattle-snakes, Parliamentary Eloquences, and Emancipated Niggers ripening towards nothing but destruction'.[7] This sympathy led naturally to a conviction that the generous attitude of the American North towards the Southern freedmen—an attitude supported by the freedmen's aid movement—offered a by no means ideal solution to the race problem.

Thus *The Times* commented:

At this moment, when the negro question is the great problem of the United States, it will certainly not dispose the minds of the Americans towards treating the black race more kindly to know that in one country, at all events, they have been capable of a wanton insurrection

[1] Semmel, op. cit., p. 83.
[2] Argyle to Gladstone, 2 December 1865, op. cit.
[3] Edward Brewin to A. Hampson, 27 January 1866, A.P. C117/199.
[4] R. P. Edwards to A. Hampson, 13 March 1866, A.P. C118/52.
[5] Ibid., 12 April 1866, A.P. C118/53.
[6] T. Carlyle, *Shooting Niagara: and After?*, op. cit., p. 14.   [7] Ibid., p. 19.

against a Government from which they had received nothing but benefits, and under which they possessed almost every right that even the
extreme Abolitionists would confer upon them.[1]

On another occasion it was suggested that the lesson of the Jamaica
revolt 'comes at an important time, and shows how cautious the
American States should be in dealing with their great population
of Africans. . . . we are convinced that it is for the benefit both of
the white man and the negro that the latter should remain essentially under the tutelage of the former.'[2]

Similar comparisons between the race problems of the two
countries may be found in all sections of the press, and, as author
and missionary David Macrae observed, 'the comparative failure
of emancipation in the West Indies was greedily seized upon as a
strong argument against a similar experiment in the States'.[3] Nor
were gloomy views simply confined to conservatives and racists.
Liberal M.P., Sir John Kennaway, for instance, argued against
political rights for the American freedmen because of their failure
in Jamaica—'All races and all classes are entitled to justice', he
wrote, 'but all are not ready for self-government'; while the
Duchess of Argyll made the same point in letters to Charles
Sumner.[4]

There was, to aggravate these feelings, a certain amount of impatience with the enthusiasm of anti-slavery groups for the under-
privileged of foreign lands, and dissatisfaction with the prospect
Carlyle held out of 'beautiful Blacks sitting there up to the ears in
pumpkins, and doleful Whites sitting here without potatoes to
eat'.[5] In 1866, Carlyle was an old man, just recovering from the
death of his wife. His friend and disciple, John Ruskin, was however, very willing to take upon himself 'the cause of order' and
good sense,[6] and soon after the Jamaica uprising sent a letter to the

[1] 3 November 1865; see also 4 November 1865.
[2] *The Times*, 13 November, 1865; see also 10 November 1865, 31 January, 10 April and
20 June 1866.
[3] *Daily News*, 18 and 27 November, 1865; *Manchester Examiner and Times*, 3 January
1866; *Irish Times*, 4 July 1865; *Edinburgh Evening Courant*, 16 February 1866; *Manchester Courier*, 7 March 1866; *Daily Telegraph*, 23 June and 12 September 1866; *Pall
Mall Gazette*, 17 February 1866, p. 5; and *The Americans at Home*, Edinburgh, 1870,
2 Vols., Vol. I, p. 373.
[4] *On Sherman's Track; or, the South After the War*, London, 1867, pp. 76–7; and *Proceedings*, op. cit., p. 106.
[5] T. Carlyle, *Occasional Discourse on the Nigger Question*, London, 1853, p. 6.
[6] E. T. Cook, *The Life of John Ruskin*, London, Allen & Unwin, 1912, 2 Vols., Vol. II,
p. 112.

Daily Telegraph in which he argued that the emancipation of white men from enslaving labour and conditions should and would precede that of the Negroes, and accused the Radicals of indifference to the hardship on their own doorsteps.[1]

In addition to meeting increased signs of colour prejudice following the Jamaica rebellion, the freedmen's aid societies were themselves divided by it. At this time negotiations for a national union were in progress between all the local and Quaker organizations. This union, it was hoped, would steer clear of comment on American politics. By taking under its wing the Jamaica Negro, the centre of a political storm in Britain, it would risk being labelled as a political organization, both at home and in the States. When the first step towards unity was taken in May 1865, with the formation of the National Committee, the Duke of Argyll had pointed out the very real drawbacks attaching to such a label in the public mind.[2] And in the prevailing atmosphere of suspicion of the Negro, the movement could not afford to be controversial.

A Manchester friend of John Bright reported him as saying 'that he thought we should do very wisely to keep the Jamaica freedmen's affairs quite distinct from those of America', adding, 'and I think he is right'.[3] This view was supported by the Friends' Central Committee for the freedmen, the Birmingham association, and the National Committee—opposed with great determination by the London Freedmen's Aid Society. Arthur Albright, the Birmingham secretary, was convinced that 'the Jamaica Will of the Whisp' was just another indication of 'the great practical unwisdom that guides the affairs' of the obstinately independent London society.[4] and feared that the issue would bring his plans for a union to a halt, especially since J. M. Ludlow and Thomas Hughes favoured helping the Jamaica Negroes.[5] Albright described the attempts of the London society to enlarge the scope of the movement as 'shameless pranks with a great cause'; and 'As for the separatist lot being in "honour" bound to work their new fields what sort of honour did they ever display?'[6] He felt sure that

[1] 20 December 1865.
[2] *Speech of . . . the Duke of Argyll . . . May 17, 1865*, London, 1865, pp. 4, 6.
[3] Joseph Simpson to A. Hampson, 19 January 1866, A.P. C120/28. The strong freedmen's society in Glasgow led by William Smeal supported this view, see A.P. C121/125.
[4] A. Albright to A. Hampson, 30 December 1865, A.P. C117/22.
[5] A. Albright to A. Hampson, 25 December 1865, A.P. C117/19.
[6] A. Albright to A. Hampson, 25 January 1866, A.P. C117/25.

the main reason why 'the separatist lot' had adopted Jamaica was to enable themselves to maintain autonomy on grounds of principle—and that their stand would split the whole movement and diminish the chances of success in either field.[1]

Pride was certainly involved;[2] but so, too, was principle. Albright held America particularly dear, and was always something of a Hotspur, often at loggerheads with his own avowed supporters. (In this case one of them feared that he might 'soon be prostrated with "Union on the Brain"!'[3]) The freedmen's movement did not collapse in a cloud of ill humour,[4] and several local secretaries were at one with the London society in thinking that charity should begin at home.

The secretary of the Bradford society suggested, that, for humane and practical reasons, any future plans should 'include the freedmen in our own colonies and not leave these to separate efforts— The multiplication of Societies for kindred objects is a nuisance which people will not countenance or tolerate—If it be announced when funds are solicited that they will be apportioned to the relief of urgent distress amongst the coloured races where it may be found to exist as the result of the former existence of slavery that ought to be sufficient—As to the squeamishness about not offending the scruples of people excessively attached to impartiality in the Jamaica question (—which means no partiality for the weak and oppressed) we can afford to throw it overboard.'[5]

In Manchester the feeling was the same. 'I am very strongly of opinion', wrote the local secretary, and 'it is also shared by other members of our Committee that . . . the base [of the movement] should be sufficiently widened to enable us to assist the Freedmen in Jamaica and if need be in any other part of the world . . . If there is any good to be done in Jamaica or elsewhere pray dont [*sic*] let us be throttled by red tape [;] the local societies I am sure

---

[1] A. Albright to A. Hampson, 23 February 1866, A.P. C117/29.

[2] See letters of Frederick Tomkins to A. Hampson, 17 August 1865–2 February 1866, A.P. C120/54–68, and also C120/70, J. H. Tuke, Hitchin, to A. Hampson, 9 September 1865.

[3] John Hodgkin to A. Hampson, 10 January 1866, A.P. C120/19.

[4] J. M. Ludlow speaking for the London society (*Freed-Man*, 1 January 1866, p. 134) acknowledged the sincerity of views on both sides, and John Hodgkin for the Union (*Freed-Man*, 1 May 1866, p. 235) wished the London society well in its efforts, once it had adopted the Jamaican cause. The Tomkins/Hampson correspondence is not unfriendly (see n. 2).

[5] W. S. Nichols to A. Hampson, 5 January 1866, A.P. C119/72; also C121/118.

would sanction a widening of our base and to advocate the claims of *Freedmen Everywhere* would entitle us to more sympathy and I think would obtain it.'[1]

At Mere in Wiltshire, the local freedmen's society felt it only just to consider the plight of the Jamaican Negro. The report of a meeting held there in December 1865 began:[2]

> In consequence of the sum of £87 having been collected in this Town for the relief of the Black Freedmen of America, and within the last four or five months remitted great interest was excited by the rumours of the terrible and murderous doings of the Blacks of Jamaica. It was feared by many that after all our estimate of the Black Man's Character was too high. As subsequent reports were received which made it apparent that such rumours were untrue and that the merciless shedding of blood had been done by the white man, a desire for a [protest] meeting was generally felt.

There was unanimous indignation about the 'unpardonable and savage like' actions of the military against these 'hardworking sons of the soil', and a 'strong conviction . . . that the English love of fair play and justice had been grossly set at naught'; the assembly therefore united in a Memorial addressed to Lord John Russell, asking the government to 'do what may be necessary to restore the sullied honor and justice of England.'[3]

The group least concerned with political angles and most with humanity, the Quakers, also aimed—through their local monthly meetings—to help the Negroes of many lands. During the 1850s and early 1860s the Gloucester and Nailsworth Monthly Meeting maintained a general 'Negro and Aborigines Fund', and in 1865 raised money specifically for Negro education in the West Indies.[4] The following year collections were made to alleviate suffering in Jamaica, and a fund was also set up 'in aid of freedmen of North

---

[1] R. Longdon to A. Hampson, 4 January 1866, A.P. C1 19/32. The Leeds society under the influence of Wilson Armistead—he had always favoured helping the Negroes of every land (see his *Five Hundred Thousand Strokes for Freedom*, London, 1853)—took a similar line.

[2] Report of a meeting held at the Lecture Room, Salisbury Street, Mere, on 12 December 1865, Rutter Papers. (John Farley Rutter, 1821–99, was a prominent local Quaker and solicitor.)

[3] Ibid., and from a handbill advertising the meeting.

[4] See the Minute Books of the Gloucester and Nailsworth Monthly Meeting, Society of Friends, Book 1854–67: reports of Monthly Meetings at Cheltenham, 8 January 1857, 10 October 1861, 9 January 1862; at Cirencester 12 February 1857, 12 September 1861, 14 November 1861, 10 May, 10 August 1865; and at Nailsworth, 12 July 1865.

America'.[1] (A 'Negro Education Fund' was still soliciting contributions in 1870.)[2]

But by far the strongest impetus for taking up the Jamaican cause came from the London society, and its journal the *Freed-Man*, both of which were directly influenced by certain prominent members of the Jamaica Committee, including Jacob Bright, F. W. Chesson, Thomas Hughes, and J. M. Ludlow (who gave the proceeds from his book, *President Lincoln Self-Portrayed*, to help the society). These men had a strong practical reason for wishing to see the Jamaica Negroes prosper. Hughes, together with Lord Alfred Spencer Churchill, who now became the London President in place of Sir Thomas Fowell Buxton (the latter henceforth devoting his energies solely to the Union), John Hart Estcourt of Manchester, Chairman of the London society's finance committee, and Peter Taylor, M.P., Treasurer of the Jamaica Committee and a Vice-President of the Union, was a Director of the Jamaica Commercial Agency Company, whose capital financed a cooperative venture among the Negroes of Cornwall County, exporting the produce of their small-holdings and importing British goods in return. It seems fair to say, however, that the Europeans involved in this Company regarded it largely as a means of 'helping those who are already helping themselves', and introducing into the island improved agricultural methods and machinery.[3]

Far beyond commercial motives however, the London society, like the Jamaica Committee, was inspired by the legal and democratic implications of the rebellion. 'This is not a question of party', wrote the *Freed-Man* in 1865—though it soon became so; 'it is one of freedom and of humanity. Mr. Gordon was as much under the protection of our law, as the hand that writes this, or the eye that reads it, and his sham trial and violent death is an invasion of the Great Charter. . . . Shall the honour of the British name be vindicated before the world, or shall this stain upon our nation and our Queen remain?'[4] A month later, there followed an article condemning the illegal use of martial law by Governor Eyre, which, if allowed to pass unchallenged, could establish at home or abroad

---

[1] Ibid.; for Jamaica, Monthly Meetings at Cirencester, 14 March 1866, 9 May 1866; Cheltenham, 11 April 1866; for America, Cheltenham, 10 October 1866; Cirencester, 14 November 1866, 13 November 1867; Gloucester, 5 December 1866.

[2] Book for 1868–79: Monthly Meeting at Gloucester, 8 October, 1870; Cirencester, 14 September 1870; Cheltenham, 12 October, 1870.

[3] *Freed-Man*, 1 December 1866, p. iv.

[4] Ibid., 1 December 1865, p. 110.

the undesirable 'precedent that the executive may, on its own alle-
gation of public danger, take the lives of subjects, at its will and
pleasure.'[1]

It was felt that justice was due alike to the Negroes of Jamaica
and America. 'We could not help the Freed-men of America', said
Jacob Bright, 'in any way so well as by helping them through the
Freed-men of the West Indies. If it were shown that justice was
done there between white and black, an example would be set
which would extend to all future times.' Bright argued that 'The
questions affecting the Freed-men of America and Jamaica could
not be seperated [*sic*], and he did not believe we should be found
deserting our friends in the former country because we were attending to our own people in the latter.'[2]

Even a staunch member of the Union, a prominent Hitchin
Quaker, Frederick Seebohm, stressed the similarity of the race
problems of both countries, and hoped that the Jamaica rebellion

may teach *us* and *America* that the policy of keeping a race in a low
moral and social position in order to maintain the supremacy of another
race over them, *will not work* even in a purely selfish point of view. Just
as the old English policy of keeping the peasantry in a sort of serfdom
under the higher classes in England ended in chartist riots and the
burning of ricks and mills and almost in Revolution, so must the same
policy in Jamaica or in America produce the same results in the case
of the negro. The world and its laws are not so framed as to permit such
a policy to be pursued with safety for long. Let us hope that the painful
condition of Jamaica will teach both England and America this lesson.

Like Bright, Seebohm hoped that England would not lag behind
America in coping with her own particular task of 'reconstruction'.[3]

In a lengthy article in the *Freed-Man* on 'What "Freed-Men's
Aid" Means', J. M. Ludlow pleaded the cause of the Jamaica
Negroes on grounds of kinship and humanity; 'as . . . our own
fellow-subjects', he believed they had 'a right to claim our first
attention over any inhabitants of a foreign country'. This was a
potent argument. The work of the Jamaica Committee was to be
'the purely political one of enforcing justice for the Jamaica Freed-
man'; 'the purely social one of providing for his necessities was to
be left to the Freed-Men's Aid Societies.' In theory an admirable

---

[1] Ibid., 1 January 1866, pp. 131–2.
[2] *Freed-Man*, 1 January 1866, pp. 142–3.
[3] F. Seebohm to A. Hampson, 12 December, 1865 A.P. C120/9.

arrangement; in practice this nice division of labour was scarcely appreciated by the general public. Both Ludlow and the London society felt that true philanthropy could not be confined within arbitrary limits, and that it would be particularly bizarre and heartless to exclude the suffering of one's own dominions. This broad outlook, it was urged, would not abate 'one jot or tittle of their sympathy for the American Freed-men ... or their hearty admiration of the efforts of the American Freedmen's Aid Societies.' Ludlow believed the latter would understand and applaud the new policy, and hoped that ultimately British and American organizations would co-operate on behalf of the freedmen of the world. The initiation of such a scheme belonged by right to 'England, the mother of Freedom'.[1]

F. W. Chesson also supported these views, adding the practical suggestion that:

To form another association would unwisely and unnecessarily multiply societies; create confusion out of doors; and embarrass those who, whenever work in this cause has to be done, find that they have to do it, or it remains unaccomplished. If another society were established it would consist, for the most part, if not entirely, of the same men who have already given abundantly of their time and labour and money to the Freed-men's Aid Society.[2]

The Jamaican activities of the London Freedmen's Aid Society, supposedly purely 'social', did not pass unnoticed. In 1867, an anonymous pamphlet was published by the planter interest,[3] intended as an exposé of the activities of the Baptist Missionary Society and the London society on the island, with the latter taken to represent the whole freedmen's aid movement. This society's '*ostensible* object', said the pamphlet, was 'to afford relief to the emancipated blacks, and to promote their material and religious interests by educational and other means'; its ulterior motive was far different. 'The most prominent enemies of Southern [American] Independence, of the planters, and other white inhabitants', it was stated, 'were the leaders in the movement. Their real intention was to use this organization for the purpose of creating disaffection in the minds of the negroes—encouraging a feeling of

---

[1] *Freed-Man*, 1 January 1866, pp. 132–4
[2] Ibid., 1 February 1866, p. 155.
[3] *Jamaica: Its State and Prospects. With an Exposure of the Proceedings of the Freed-man's Aid Society, and the Baptist Missionary Society*, London, 1867, pp. 8–9.

animosity against their former masters, and in this, and in every other way using the occasion to subvert and ruin the planters.'

In particular, alleged the writer—and perhaps worst of all—the London freedmen's society, together with similar American organizations, had urged the Negro not to work, though in Jamaica, as in the Southern States of America, work was readily available.

The invincible hatred towards the West India planter which had slumbered—but had never died out, now developed itself towards the Southern proprietor. The worst of tyrants, and the most unscrupulous of partizans themselves, the opposition of these people to slavery, and to real or imaginary oppression, was a specious theme on which they might . . . dilate. Falsehood and misrepresentation were small matters to them, so long as they might gain their point, and make use of the credulity of the simple and the sympathy of the humane. Thus, one of the results was the formation of the 'British and Foreign Freed-man's Aid Society', [the London society adopted this title along with the Jamaica Negro, intending to parallel the British and Foreign Anti-Slavery Society,] whose office it was to make a great show of philanthropy, and while *pretending* to be the friend of the negroes, to make this the channel for ruining, if possible, the planter.

It is hard to assess how far these views represented or influenced those of the British public, but it seems clear, in the light of modern research into the Jamaica rebellion, that by the late 1860s there was considerable sympathy among the upper- and middle-classes for the white planter interest, epitomized by Governor Eyre. Justin McCarthy admitted that 'The Jamaica Committee were denounced by many voices, and in very unmeasured language, for what they had done', but felt that their activities had so publicized the issues and dangers involved, that nothing similar could occur again.[1] He was wrong. It is apparent today that 'what had seemed so extraordinary to John Stuart Mill and his comrades—administrative massacre, rule by terror—has become a commonplace in the imperial history of our century: Amritsar, the Black and Tans in Ireland, Cyprus, Nyasaland.' 'Race prejudice . . . was the principle underlying the acceptance of the deeds of Governor Eyre . . . by the British public. As we now see, it was a principle capable of indefinite extension.'[2]

The freedmen's aid movement was undoubtedly affected by this prejudice, just as the earlier anti-slavery movement had felt the

[1] McCarthy, op. cit., Vol. 3, pp. 279–80.
[2] Semmel, op. cit., pp. 178–9.

prejudice of its time. It is difficult to see how, in fairness, the claims of the Jamaica Negroes could have been ignored, but by adopting this new cause, the majority of the local freedmen's societies felt they were treading on dangerous ground, since Jamaica introduced 'many questions of a political nature not contemplated in the original . . . *philanthropic aim*'.[1] For this reason, at a special meeting on 22 December 1865, a motion thus to broaden the scope of freedmen's aid was finally defeated.[2]

The violence and political implications of the Jamaica debate to some extent obscured the original aims of the movement as a whole—namely, the making of a practical gesture of goodwill towards America and a contribution to the work of relief and education among the Negroes in the South. Neutrality had at first been urged on all other issues. The involvement of the London society with Jamaica, however well meant, appeared in conservative eyes only to confirm the existence of an unworthy political campaign against the propertied whites of both countries. The *Daily Telegraph* observed sharply that while dissenting clergymen and wayward philanthropists could not be prevented from dabbling in politics, sensible men knew how to regard their activities; 'Exeter Hall is strong', it conceded, 'but Exeter Hall is not England; and assertions which pass unchallenged on its platform are much more rudely dealt with out of doors.'[3]

However, the records of the British and Foreign Freedmen's Aid Society have not been discovered, and its activities can be only partially traced through its magazine the *Freed-Man*. Those of the Union remain (and it is with the operations of this body that the next chapters are concerned) to show how it successfully subordinated political issues to the more important—because, as far as Britain was concerned, the more realizable—aspects of the work.

[1] J. C. Gallaway, London, to A. Hampson, n.d., A.P. C118/71.
[2] Ibid.
[3] 11 December 1865.

CHAPTER III

Freedman's Aid in Britain: Organization (I)

> 'Whoever may be to blame for the recent war, and its disastrous
> effects, the negro is innocent. He neither originated the strife
> nor took advantage of the opportunity it gave him of inflicting
> revenge for past wrongs; and by his patience under injury, and
> readiness to respond to calls of justly requited labour, has won
> for himself a fair title to the sympathy, respect and assistance
> of the civilized world.'
>
> *Freed-Man*, 1865[1]

The British movement to help American freedmen during the
1860s is one of the more unusual products of mid-nineteenth century humanitarianism and its success has been allowed to go virtually unremarked. Previous discussion of British activities in this
sphere has been confined to an occasional paragraph or footnote
in the biographies of philanthropic Victorians, and works by or
about American participants in freedmen's aid.[2]

The strength of the movement lay in its connexion with the
British and Foreign Anti-Slavery Society. The freedmen's aid
societies formed during the 1860s, though organized separately
from this Society, were simply an extension of its activities in the
American field. The National Union founded in 1866 to help the
Negroes was, according to its secretary, 'made up mainly of earnest
Anti-Slavery Men', whose activities were aimed at involving those
Englishmen of leisure, means, benevolence, and religion, who had
previously lent money and support to movements for the abolition
of slavery and the slave trade.[3]

Louis Chamerovzow, champion of coloured races throughout the
Empire and Secretary of the Anti-Slavery Society from 1852 to
1870, and Frederick W. Chesson, Secretary to the Aborigines'

---

[1] 1 August, pp. 11–12.

[2] See, for instance, L. Coffin, *Reminiscences*, Cincinatti, 1876, pp. 651–712; O. O.
Howard, *Autobiography of Oliver Otis Howard*, New York, 1907, 2 Vols., Vol. II, p. 196;
W. P. and F. J. Garrison, op. cit., Vol. IV, pp. 233–4; E. Russell, *The History of
Quakerism*, New York, 1942, p. 416; R. M. Jones, *The Later Periods of Quakerism*,
London, 1921, 2 Vols., Vol. II, pp. 611–12.

[3] T. Phillips to O. O. Howard, 7 July 1868, A.P. C119/125.

Protection Society, attended freedmen's meetings, as did Charles and Thomas Fowell Buxton, sons of the leader of the parliamentary fight against slavery, and heirs to his generous spirit. Arthur Albright, William Allen, Samuel Gurney (Junior), Robert Alsop, George and Sarah Alexander, Thomas Phillips, and William Morgan also ranked among those who served both the Anti-Slavery Society and the freedmen's aid movement.

The remaining, old-established (and particularly the ladies') emancipation and anti-slavery societies, likewise co-operated in every way. The freedmen's association in Birmingham was formed in 1864 on the initiative of the Birmingham Ladies Negro's Friend Society, then some 40 years old.[1] During the same year the London Ladies Emancipation Society recorded contributions to freedman's aid and stressed the importance of the cause to its members;[2] and the Edinburgh ladies were busy collecting for the Negro in 1866 and 1867.[3] The personnel of the old anti-slavery societies of, for instance, Dublin, Leeds, Glasgow, and Birmingham was virtually the same as that of the new freedmen's associations of those cities.

Within the broad plan of helping the Negro and the anti-slavery cause, philanthropists in England and America entertained a clear set of priorities: first, physical hardship must be relieved; then education, industrial training, and (where necessary) Christian conversion should follow. To these four practical aims, the British freedmen's aid societies added a fifth, namely the improving of Anglo-American relations.[4] To this end they linked themselves not only with the anti-slavery movement at home, but also with the voluntary freedmen's groups in the United States; these in their turn were similarly indebted to abolitionists for moral and practical support.

Although a few Englishmen were inspired to go out as teachers to the Southern States, the practical and unpopular interference in Southern affairs was, in fact, left almost entirely to their American co-workers. Had this not been the case, it seems unlikely that British help would have been accepted. Any significant invasion

[1] *Annual Report of the Birmingham and Midland Freedmen's Aid Association, to May 19th, 1865*, Birmingham, 1865, pp. 4–5, John Rylands Library.
[2] *The Second Annual Report of the Ladies' London Emancipation Society*, London, 1865, pp. 10, 11, 24, John Rylands Library.
[3] *Annual Report of the Edinburgh Ladies' Emancipation Society, and Sketch of Anti-Slavery Events and the Condition of the Freedmen During the Year Ending 15th February, 1866*, pp. 6–18, and Ibid., for . . . *The Year Ending 1867*, Edinburgh, 1866 and 1867, pp. 6–18, John Rylands Library.
[4] See below, Chapter V, for details about how these aims were put into practice.

E

by British missionaries and teachers would have aroused a justifiable storm of opposition from the Southern whites, and (though sectional feelings were probably still stronger than national) no doubt in the North as well.

It is clear that the American voluntary societies for the freedmen (the Freedmen's Bureau, established in 1865, was financed by the Federal government and generally operated independently) though happy enough to receive foreign donations, were not always lavish in their acknowledgements, and the public impact of British aid, though not its usefulness, was in this way greatly diminished.[1]

The importance of the ancient link between the British and American anti-slavery elements to the cause of freedmen's aid in Britain cannot be over-emphasized. The two movements had kept in the closest touch from the early 1830s, but, as we have seen, relations had not been entirely tranquil. Freedmen's aid presented an opportunity for anti-slavery workers on both sides of the Atlantic to renew amicable relations, for although some American abolitionists virtually abandoned their interest in the Negro at the end of the Civil War, many others, including J. M. McKim, Wendell Phillips, O. B. Frothingham, J. M. Walden, Thomas Wentworth Higginson, R. P. Hallowell, George Whipple, James Freeman Clarke, and Levi Coffin continued to labour on his behalf. Even William Lloyd Garrison, who resigned from the American Anti-Slavery Society in 1865, believing its work to be done, lent his support to four of the societies which helped the freedmen in the 1860s.[2]

Since the ties between the British and American freedmen's movements were so close, and the former would scarcely have existed without the latter, we may, with advantage, pause to look briefly at the situation in the United States.

Long before the creation of the Freedmen's Bureau in 1865, and even before Lincoln's Emancipation Proclamation, attempts were being made in America to help the Negroes adjust to a life of freedom. Schemes for colonization were, however, a signal failure, and while by the end of the war the army had absorbed some 186,000 Negro soldiers, three main problems still presented themselves: the need for physical relief, employment, and education.

---

[1] See letters complaining of this in A.P. C39/14, 24, 109a.
[2] See McPherson, op. cit., and H. L. Swint, *The Northern Teacher in the South, 1862–1870*, Nashville, Tennessee, 1941, Appendix I, pp. 143–70.

Temporary camps were set up to care for the unemployed and serve as government-operated employment agencies, and the freedmen were re-employed on plantations and special colonies, under government supervision.[1]

Freedmen's aid societies were numerous and active—there were, in fact, over fifty of them, including the religious associations. Those at New York, Boston, Philadelphia, and Baltimore pooled their resources in 1865 to become the National Freedmen's Relief Association with more than 150 teachers and agents in six Southern states, and distributing large quantities of supplies. Similar work was being done on a somewhat smaller scale by the Western Freedmen's Aid Commission at Cincinatti, the North-Western Freedmen's Aid Commission with headquarters in Chicago, and a host of church organizations. Nine of the secular societies were supporting in 1865 a total of 307 schools, with 773 teachers and 40,744 pupils. Money and supplies collected in 1865 by ten of these organizations amounted in value to more than $770,000.[2]

The Commissioner of the Freedmen's Bureau, General Oliver Otis Howard, naturally approved of the operations of such societies, while deploring the duplication and rivalry which their multiplicity sometimes involved. The Freedmen's Aid Union Commission did unite many of the voluntary societies in 1865; not all, however, and most of the church bodies continued to work independently,[3] with the Society of Friends playing a leading part, as it had done in the anti-slavery movement. Even so, the Freedmen's Bureau and the benevolent organizations generally managed to work well together, especially in the field of education. Howard recollects (his policy affording perhaps one of the earliest American examples of matching grants) :[4]

I early came to the conclusion that our school work was best promoted by placing one dollar of public money by the side of one of voluntary contribution. The Bureau gave to any benevolent society in that proportion. The society which undertook the most in that manner received most.

The normal practice was for the Bureau to furnish the land and the freedmen's societies to erect their own buildings.

[1] See G. R. Bentley, *A History of the Freedmen's Bureau*, Philadelphia, University of Pennsylvania Press, 1955, Chapter II; also W. L. Rose, *Rehearsal for Reconstruction: the Port Royal Experiment*, Indianapolis, Bobbs–Merrill Co., 1964.
[2] Bentley, op. cit., p. 63.   [3] See Bentley, op. cit., p. 64.
[4] O. O. Howard, op. cit., Vol. II, p. 271.

The activities of the various aid societies were not simply confined to America. Capitalizing on the international nature of the anti-slavery movement, agents from the American Missionary Association, the Western Freedmen's Aid Commission, the National Freedmen's Relief Association, and the American Freedmen's Aid Commission were dispatched to Europe on money raising tours, and generally seem to have found their most profitable field in Britain. In view of the wealth of the country and the British anti-slavery record, this success is not altogether surprising.

Charles C. Leigh, the European representative of the National Freedmen's Relief Association of America, in the middle of a tour through Germany, France, and Switzerland, declined an invitation to help with the work in England in the following terms.[1]

> I fear I will not be able to aid the friends in Great Britain, for I think that the time I have to spare may be better employed on the continent where they do not understand the needs and mode to relieve them as you do in happy, Christian, dear old England.

In his autobiography, Oliver Howard mentions only one freedmen's aid society outside America, and that was British.[2] Levi Coffin, the eminent American Quaker, has left a detailed account of his lucrative trip to England and Ireland in 1864, on behalf of the American Freedmen's Aid Commission;[3] during 1865 and the succeeding year, the Rev. J. C. Holbrook and the Negro preacher Sella Martin from the American Missionary Association, repeated his success;[4] and the papers of the American movement contain an interesting series of letters from the New England Quaker turned Southern teacher, William Forster Mitchell, on his profitable British tour of 1866–7.[5]

These visitors are just a few of the many Americans who canvassed Britain on behalf of the freedmen, during the Civil War and the years that followed.[5] Their presence and solicitations were both an incentive to the British movement, and a useful potential weapon against any charge of unwarranted interference in American affairs.

[1] Leigh to Aspinall Hampson, 4 September, 1866, A.P. C119/17.
[2] O. O. Howard, op. cit., Vol. II, p. 196.
[3] Coffin, op. cit., pp. 651–712.
[4] See Letters in A.P. C118/117, 120 (Dr. Holbrook), C119/44, 45, 46 (Sella Martin), and C121/79, 80.
[5] See series of letters from W. F. Mitchell to J. M. McKim of the American Freedmen's Union Commission, 1866–7, in the Anti-Slavery Papers, Cornell University.
[6] See the *Reporter*, December 1867, p. 21, for a list.

From the point of view of organization, freedmen's aid—as had the anti-slavery movement—followed a similar pattern in both countries, though naturally there was no British equivalent of the Freedmen's Bureau. Operations began in England with President Lincoln's Emancipation Proclamation. In his *Reminiscences*, Levi Coffin claims to have encouraged in London, in 1864, the formation of the first freedmen's aid society.[1] In fact, the Prospectus of the London society was issued on 2 April 1863, and its inaugural meeting held in St. James's Hall, Piccadilly, on 24 April.[2] A new committee was formed the following year, under the inspiration of the American leader, but after a short while the two associations agreed to unite.[3] In June 1864 came the foundation of the Birmingham and Midland Freedmen's Association, and smaller societies began to spring up throughout the country.

Prompted by the American societies' attempts to achieve closer union, and in an endeavour to enlarge the scope of the movement, a National Committee of British Freed-Men's Aid Societies was formed on 17 May 1865. When this proved too weak, a formal union of some forty or fifty associations, under the title of the National Freedmen's Aid Union of Great Britain and Ireland was agreed, in April 1866;[4] only the London society—the oldest—held aloof, mainly through pride, and an inability to agree over general aims.[5]

Careful arrangements were made for coping with the money and goods raised in England. If they wished, donors could specify some particular project or association in America to receive their contributions;[6] sometimes these items were even sent direct to the States.[7] Generally, however, local societies sent their donations to the Birmingham or London associations, or to the London Friends; after 1866, the National Union exercised an overall supervision of

---

[1] Coffin, op. cit., p. 664.
[2] *Prospectus*, Freed-Men's Aid Society, London, 1863; also the *Freed-Man*, 1 August 1865, pp. 1–3. John Bright noted in his journal, 'L.C. comes here to try to interest us in the condition of the Freedmen, and I hope he may succeed. Unfortunately he does not speak well, and his object might be more powerfully advocated.' Quoted in *John Bright and the Quaker*, by J. T. Mills, London, 1935, 2 vols., Vol. II, p. 223.
[3] *Freed-Man*, 1 August 1865, p. 3.
[4] See *Reporter*, May 1866, p. 1, 5, 6; also correspondence relating to the formation of the Union and testing out provincial reactions in A.P. C117/5–33, C118/64–8, 75–6. 98, C119/93–107, C120/7a, 31, 70, and C121/48, 168–9, 172, 191.
[5] See letters of Frederick Tomkins (a London barrister and secretary of the London society) to Aspinall Hampson, 17 August 1865–2 February 1866, A.P. C120/54–68
[6] Thomas Phillips to William Rowntree, Scarborough, 18 August 1868, A.P. C119/126.
[7] See letters of Samuel Bewley, a Dublin Quaker, to Hampson, A.P. C117/74, 76.

this part of the work.[1] The American agencies which benefited regularly from British benevolence were the National Freedmen's Relief Association; the American Freedmen's Union Commission and the Western Freedmen's Aid Commission; the Friends' Freedmen's Association of Philadelphia and the Freedmen's Committee of the New York Society of Friends; the American Missionary Association; and the Baltimore Association for the Moral and Educational Improvement of the Coloured People.[2] By thus apportioning their donations, the British societies hoped to avoid the charge of favouritism and to make their influence widely felt. Unfortunately, since the American associations were as quarrelsome and jealous of one another as some of the principal groups in Britain, a degree of bad feeling from time to time was inevitable.

Thanks mainly to the efforts of Arthur Albright, the affairs of the freedmen's movement were handled in a creditable manner. Care was taken to draw up regular lists of subscriptions from the various societies and interested individuals, and these were published, to ensure accuracy and encourage givers, in local newspapers, the Union's *Reporter*, or the journal of the London society, the *Freed-Man*.[3] The most outstanding achievement in the administrative field was a series of agreements reached with various British shipping and railway lines, and with the American government, for preferential treatment of goods bound for the freedmen.

For the London association, the (Quaker dominated) house of Barclay, Bevan, Tutton and Co., received and forwarded contributions free of charge; the same service was performed for the Union by Alexander, Cunliffes and Co. The firm of Johnson, Johnson and Co., accepted and sent free to Liverpool packages of clothing and other articles for the Negro; the railways charged no freight to the port, and a commission house in Liverpool, on the same terms, received and conveyed such consignments to the docks.[4] A number of steamship lines agreed to give free transport to America, among them the firms of Inman and Co., Guion and Co., Rathbone Brothers and Co., the Cunard Company, and the National Steamboat Company.[5] The generosity of these various

[1] See letters of Arthur Albright on the subject in A.P. C117/6, 7, 10, and C121/171.
[2] See draft of a letter from Thomas Phillips to General Oliver Otis Howard, 7 July 1868, A.P. C119/125.
[3] See letters mentioned above, n. 1, for difficulties involved; sample lists in *Reporter*, February 1867, pp. 111–2; *Freed-Man*, 1 March 1866, pp. 204–11 and 1 April 1866, pp. 230–2; and A.P. C118/29.
[4] Coffin, op. cit., pp. 676–7.   [5] *Reporter*, May 1866, p. 11.

companies, especially in Liverpool, traditionally regarded as sympathetic to the American South,[1] is commented on with gratitude but no show of surprise by the freedmen's movement. No doubt the prosperous Quaker businessmen involved in its activities were able to exert influence in high places, but the facilities afforded are a striking confirmation of anti-slavery and pro-American sympathies existing in unexpected quarters.

Nor were such generous impulses confined to one side of the Atlantic. In 1864, John Bright was asked to inquire whether clothes and books collected in Britain might not be shipped to the United States duty free, and promptly wrote to Charles Sumner to enlist his aid.[2] Levi Coffin, when in England, put the same request to the American Ambassador; Adams, who had been sorely tried by his wartime experiences in Britain,[3] gladly reported this friendly request to Secretary Salmon P. Chase, and wrote to the President of the Birmingham association, who had also approached him:[4] 'I have no doubt that everything possible will be done to facilitate . . . so benevolent a purpose; and the feeling of kindness the act will create will be worth far more than all.' Permission was granted, and everything possible was done. At the final meeting of the National Union in December 1868, it was estimated that approximately £20,000 had been saved as a result of the concession to its goods of duty free entry into the United States.[5]

The response to freedmen's aid in Britain varied enormously, though from the foundation of the Union in 1866, the movement claimed to be truly national in scope. Certainly there were a great many societies in England, often in towns of no real size; fewer details are available about activities in Scotland, Ireland, and Wales. A report published by the Birmingham and Midland Association in 1865 noted the existence of forty-five societies, of which thirty-nine were in England,[6] three in Scotland (at Edinburgh, Glasgow, and Dundee), and three in Ireland (at Dublin,

[1] See Van Auken, op. cit., p. 93.
[2] Bright to Sumner, 3 September 1864; *Proceedings*, op. cit., p. 132.
[3] See *The Education of Henry Adams: An Autobiography*, pp. 110–23.
[4] Copy sent by A. Albright to T. Phillips, A.P. C38/101a.
[5] *Friend*, 1 January 1869, p. 13.
[6] Accrington, Banbury, Bath, Birkenhead, Bowdon, Bradford, Bridgwater, Brighton, Bridport, Bristol, Canterbury, Carlisle, Cheltenham, Darlington, Derby, Evesham, Gloucester, Halifax, Hanley, Hertford, Kendal, Leeds, Leicester, Lincoln, Liverpool, London, Malton, Manchester, Margate, Mere, Newcastle, Nottingham, Peterborough, Reading, Rochester, Sheffield, Southampton, Worcester, York.

Belfast, and Waterford). Wales was not represented.[1] However, interest in the freedmen was not confined to those places which supported a society, and the Birmingham report acknowledged contributions from individuals in another thirty-three towns and cities throughout Britain.[2]

An organizational analysis of freedmen's aid confirms the strong connexion with the British anti-slavery societies which we have already observed: the personalities involved in the former often sustained the latter, while the social, economic, religious, political, and regional structures of the two movements corresponded closely.

Because of their ambitious hope of improving, through philanthropy, the relations between Britain and America, the freedmen's societies aimed at capturing 'the mind of England',[3] and Albright was constantly fretting at anything which might prevent the cause securing 'public favour' and 'a National character'.[4] Throughout the country organizers advised the 'exciting of an interest among the public at large',[5] and welcomed the formation of the Union as a means of arousing 'national sympathy for the Freedmen',[6] of making 'the movement in the Country really National;—and really of the British name'.[7]

The first issue of the *Freed-Man* described one of the main purposes of the National Committee (formed in 1865) as being 'so to combine the sympathies of our countrymen in general with the views and feelings of those already interested in the cause of the Freed-man, as to impart a national character to the entire work'.[8] When Levi Coffin came to Britain on behalf of the freedmen, he recognized 'that much depended on the character and standing of those who gave countenance to and took part in the work'.[9] The English societies shared this belief, and claimed to enjoy the support of the 'aristocracy of virtue and of intelligence' in every part of society.[10] The vast majority of the active campaigners for the

[1] *Annual Report of the Birmingham and Midland Freedmen's-Aid Association to May 19th, 1865.*
[2] Ibid., p. 9.
[3] A. Albright to A. Hampson, 10 November 1865, A.P. C117/8.
[4] Ibid., to (not indicated), 27 January 1866, A.P. C121/172.
[5] J. Alexander, Sudbury, to A. Hampson, 16 May 1866, A.P. C117/54.
[6] J. S. Jones, Liverpool, to A. Hampson, 21 April 1866, A.P. C118/142.
[7] J. C. Gallaway, London, to A. Hampson, n.d., A.P. C118/71a.
[8] 1 August 1865, p. 10.
[9] J. Hodgkin, London, to A. Hampson, 24 July 1865, A.P. C118/95.
[10] *Freed-Man*, 1 August 1865, p. 7.

freedmen were, however, drawn from the more religiously minded of the upper middle class; crusaders whose unflagging enthusiasm for good causes prompted Carlyle to describe them as 'sunk in deep froth-oceans of "Benevolence," "Fraternity," "Emancipation-princ ple," "Christian Philanthropy," and other most amiable-looking, but most baseless, . . . baleful and all bewildering jargon'.[1]

We find among them many seasoned abolitionists. In Leeds, the work was largely in the hands of Wilson Armistead, a Quaker and close friend of William Lloyd Garrison; the author of a number of remarkable books on the Negro, of which the most influential was probably *A Tribute for the Negro*, published in 1848. Freedmen's aid could call upon, in Scotland, the services of two veteran anti-slavery crusaders: William Smeal of Glasgow, who was also a life-long friend of Garrison and editor of the Quaker journal, the *British Friend*; and Eliza Wigham, an Edinburgh Quaker, who had lent vigorous support for many years to the temperance and women's suffrage movements. Throughout the North, invaluable assistance was given by the Pease family of Darlington, prominent among whom in this connexion were Joseph Pease, the first Quaker M.P. and an active member of the British and Foreign Bible Society and the Peace Society, and John Pease, an early champion of Bible schools and innumerable charitable projects, and possessed of a first-hand knowledge of American conditions.

But by far the dominant personality of the British freedmen's aid movement was Birmingham Quaker Arthur Albright, Secretary of both the Midland association and the National Union. Albright, whose impatient energy earned him the nickname of 'The Steam Engine', in partnership with his brother-in-law Edmund Sturge, conducted a highly prosperous chemical works near Birmingham. His commercial success soon afforded him considerable leisure time, which he devoted, together with much of his wealth, to a variety of worthy projects including the anti-slavery and peace movements. From 1861 Albright concerned himself privately with helping slaves escaping from the Confederate States, and went to America during the war on their behalf. At home, driven on by an overpowering sense of mission, he addressed meetings, throughout the country, gathered publicity material, checked subscriptions, recruited speakers, and organized a host of fund-raising ventures.

[1] T. Carlyle, *Occasional Discourse on the Nigger Question*, pp. 5–6.

He was not an easy man to work with, expecting from his colleagues a similar dedication, and prone to outbursts of impatience and self-reproach; but his dedication was total, and the achievements of the movement were largely his own. Albright remained an officer of the Anti-Slavery Society long after freedmen's aid activities had to come to an end.

The career of many Friends followed a similar pattern. G. W. Alexander was sufficiently successful (having inherited a bank) to be able to retire early and apply himself to social work. His interests included the Aborigines Protection Society, the B.F.A.S.S., and the temperance and freedmen's aid movements.

Also involved in the campaign were three other prosperous, members of the London banking fraternity; Frederick Seebohm, James Hack Tuke, and Joseph Gurney Barclay. Seebohm and Tuke, cousins and friends of John Bright, both lived in Hitchin, Hertfordshire, where they were partners in the banking firm of Sharples and Company. The former successfully combined banking—he eventually became a director of Barclays and President of the Institute of Bankers—with the careers of author and historian, and had ample means at his disposal. Tuke, similarly affluent, was able to devote time to various charitable missions on behalf of the Society of Friends, while Barclay laboured for the London City Mission, the Flounders Institute, the Bible Society, and the Bedford Institute and Foreign Missions.[1]

It is noticeable that these contributors to freedmen's aid had, in the main, reached middle age. This was, of course, partly inevitable—only at that point were the leisure and means necessary for philanthropy likely to be enjoyed. But it is also a reflection of the close connexion with the British anti-slavery movement which, by the middle of the century, was in terms of leadership an ageing organization. (Many of the great issues which had occupied abolitionists were successfully resolved: the slave trade had dwindled to comparatively small proportions; slavery was banished from the West Indies, Britain's Eastern possessions, and the colonies of France, Denmark, and Sweden. Race prejudice was growing in Britain. New blood, not surprisingly, was hard to come by.)

[1] See for these biographical details particularly R. M. Jones, op. cit., Vol. II, *passim*; Emden, op. cit.; *The Annual Monitor . . . or, Obituary of the Members of the Society of Friends in Great Britain and Ireland*, London, 1843–1908; and the *Bibliographical Catalogue*, London, 1888, Friends' House—which also holds an extensive type-written bibliographical catalogue.

Thus it is not surprising to find, on looking at the local organizers of freedmen's groups, that George Dixon, an abolitionist from Ayton, Yorkshire, who went out as a schoolmaster to the South, had retired from teaching in Britain; William Smeal was in his seventies; Samuel Bewley, the most active Irish Friend, was over 60, as were John Hodgkin of Lewes, Robert Alsop and Frederick Seebohm; William Collins of Northampton was over 70, Josiah Forster in his eighties, and even the dynamic Albright was past 50. In 1866 Levi Coffin recorded a typical donation from England as '£50 . . . given by Mrs [.] Ann Alexander of Ipswich now in her 84th year, whose good words of holy sympathy and prayer for the freedmen does one good to read'.[1]

While the practical work of aid was carried through by often little known members of the middle class, the freedmen's movement, partly because of its far reaching aims but also because it was customary, made a bid for the support of the titled, the famous, and the powerful. In 1865, a prominent member of the Union wrote to Lord John Russell giving him information about the freedmen; his letter explained that 'our object was to obtain [from the Government] a statesmanlike expression of joy at the termination of slavery in . . . America and sympathy with her in the arduous practical work which lies before her in connexion with emancipation.'[2] From the beginning it was planned to approach the Queen for 'her patronage to our work as a practical manifestation of "the sympathy and congratulation" which she has officially declared this Country to feel in the overthrow of Am[erican] Slavery'.[3]

Although these ambitious plans for securing Government and royal patronage came to nothing (not surprisingly, while the tricky Alabama negotiations occupied the attention of the administration), Joseph Simpson was able to remark, with reference to the Union's Vice-Presidents, that 'We seem at last to be getting *aristocratic* even over Carlyles [*sic*] hated Quashee!'[4] The Duke of Argyll, writing to Gladstone, whose interest was aroused, declared himself ready to 'support any effort which may be made in England to assist the Free Blacks', however small, since 'a little may go a great way in showing good will, and in conciliating good will there

[1] L. Coffin to J. M. McKim, Cincinatti, 24 November 1866, Anti-Slavery Papers, Cornell University.
[2] J. Hodgkin to A. Hampson, 6 July 1865, A.P. C118/94.
[3] Albright circular, 3 July 1868, A.P. C121/195.
[4] J. Simpson to A. Hampson, 6 April 1866, A.P. C120/31.

[in America]—especially when it comes from men of name and position in this country.'[1]

In addition to Argyll the Union enjoyed the patronage of the Duke of Sutherland, the Earls of Shaftesbury and Ducie, and Lords Cavendish, Calthorpe, Lyttleton, Brougham, and Romilly. (An American worker writing in the *American Freedman* commented that though 'Not many of the English nobility manifest an interest in the welfare of our American freed-people [,] a few of them, however, do show an active interest in this direction. Sir Thomas Fowell Buxton, the Duke of Argyll, and Lord Lyttleton give not only the use of their names, but to some considerable extent also the services of their personal attention and of their means for the promotion of the good work . . . and they are acknowledged representatives in high places of our freedmen's interests.'[2]

At the other end of the scale, however, there was some attempt to attract working-class support for the movement. The whole question of the attitude of British working men to the American Civil War is now in the melting pot, and it does seem that their sympathy for the North and the Negro was not so monolithic as Radicals claimed. Even so, some headway was made by the freedmen's societies through appeals on the free labour issue.

At a fund-raising meeting in Derby in March 1865, the Rev. W. Jones, a Canadian Methodist minister[3]

advised the working men who wished thoroughly to understand the questions involved in this great subject, to read the tract by Goldwin Smith, the regius professor of Oxford, who showed that this struggle was that of true democracy, against oligarchy all the world over, and that it was to the interest of the working man that there should be the victory of freedom over slavery.

Such a victory would be ensured only by helping the Negroes through the difficult transition period which inevitably followed emancipation, though as early as 1863 the British Anti-Slavery Society was asserting that 'free-labour has been fairly tested, and has most completely vindicated itself'.[4]

---

[1] Argyll to Gladstone, 15 September 1865 and 31 January 1866, The Gladstone Papers, Add. Ms. 44099, Vol. XIV, and 44100, Vol. XV.

[2] Vol. I., no. 8, 1866, p. 120.

[3] *Derby Reporter*, 10 March 1865.

[4] *The Twenty-Fourth Annual Report of the British and Foreign Anti-Slavery Society*, London, 1863, p. 13.

One of the Society's wartime tracts, *Labour and Slavery*, by journalist Edward Dicey, had been designed to show the struggle as
one of 'the weak against . . . the powerful. And in such a struggle
it would be enough to make one despair of England, if the sympathies of free English labour were with the champions of slavery.
This has not been the case.'[1] As a correspondent of the *Birmingham
Daily Gazette* put it, 'in these modern times slavery . . . is a question
affecting the independent rights and interests of labour generally
throughout the world. Take away all the slaves, and the value of
the free labourers would rise every where, *pro tanto*, to a higher
level. . . . Free labour is consistent with the dignity of man—digni-
fies him in fact. Slavery degrades him.'[2]

The only really active working men's auxiliary to a freedmen's
aid society appears to have been in Birmingham, a centre not
vitally involved in cotton manufacture, though some success was
also reported from Leicester and Bradford.[3] Appeals were made to
labour's 'well-known liberality'[4] and reminders issued that the
expansion of the British textile industry had 'caused a corresponding increase in the slave system of America'.[5] A pamphlet issued
by the Birmingham auxiliary made the same point, and suggested
that British contributions might help to give the 'freed slave the
first start for himself he has never had in his life.'[6]

In 1865 the annual meeting of the Birmingham's freedmen's
association was pleased to report 'how deeply the woes of the . . .
[Negroes] have affected the hearts of the poor as well as the
wealthy of our land'; 'not unfrequently the same post has brought
the large gift of the opulent, the shilling of the workman, and the
mite of the widow.'[7] Three years later the Union's executive
was still waiting to realize 'A Penny Subscription from Working men following an example set by the artisans of certain
quarters of Paris and by the Swiss peasants and partially by
Birmingham'.[8]

In attempting to stir up interest on economic grounds, however,

[1] Quoted in *The First Annual Report of the Ladies' London Emancipation Society*, p. 8.
[2] 25 July 1864.
[3] See letters in A.P. C117/106, 111, and C40/51.
[4] *Birmingham Daily Gazette*, 12 January 1865.
[5] *Birmingham Daily Gazette*, 30 March 1865.
[6] *Why Should Birmingham Workmen Help the Freed Refugees From Slavery? Who are in Great
Distress*, pamphlet in John Rylands Library.
[7] *Annual Report of the Birmingham and Midland Freedmen's Aid-Association to May 19th, 1865*,
p. 9.
[8] Circular to all societies, 3 July 1868, A.P. C121/195.

the freedmen's movement was not content simply to invoke idealism, or to apply for funds to the respectable but scarcely affluent
labouring section of the community. It operated rather on the
assumption that 'in works like this, those are the wisest who appeal
to all motives, and we know perfectly well that in a world such as
we move in, self-interest is most assuredly one of the strongest'.[1]

What did the average Englishmen want from America? Far
more than a fair deal for the Negro, he looked for cheap cotton.
This was the reasoning behind declarations that a donation to
freedmen's aid would be 'at once the best peace making act and
the most profitable investment England ever made for her own
material interests'.[2] A handbill put out by the Union for circula-
tion in the North, appealed for educational funds on the grounds
that 'Colored Schools are nearly synonymous with cheap cotton,
and that is the lifeblood of your community'.[3] The Bradford
Freedmen's Aid Society promised local working men that 'The
reward [of generosity] shall come back to you in orders for the
productions of your looms and workshops. Four millions of free
labourers, educated and provident, multiplying under favourable
circumstances, will demand ten times the amount of Bradford
goods which they would get under a degrading and exterminating
serfdom'.[4]

In Birmingham the cause of the freedmen was identified with
British commercial prosperity, for as the former were encouraged,
'as Wages are better than the Whip, and . . . *Cash* is better than the
Lash, then we shall have cotton-clothing far cheaper, and Lancashire far more thriving than ever'.[5] 'It is scarcely possible to
estimate', declared a circular in 1864, 'the enormous *interest which
the people of England have in the early development of the powers of the
coloured freed people, as cotton growers.*'[6] Such appeals did not fall on
deaf ears; local tradesmen, prosperous Quaker merchants, indus-
trialists, and members of the profession were, as we have seen, the
financial mainstay of freedmen's aid.

The success of the movement was also due in part to its support

[1] *Reporter*, May 1866, p. 8.
[2] A. Albright to A. Hampson, 10 November 1865, A.P. C117/8a.
[3] Handbill, A.P. C38/43.
[4] Appeal from W. S. Nichols of Bradford, 12 November 1867, A.P. C40/51.
[5] *Why Should Birmingham Workmen Help the Freed Refugees From Slavery In America? etc.*
[6] *The Birmingham and Midland Association for the Help of the Refugees from Slavery in America, by a Vessel to be Freighted with Stores*, Birmingham, 1864.

from the churches (whose role is the subject of the next chapter), in part to its having been launched just when growing agitation for parliamentary reform had focused attention as never before on the bonds uniting Britain and America. John Bright and the other Radicals who wanted a considerable extension of the franchise found a favourable example of their aims in the United States, and disillusionment with their idol was not to come for at least another decade.[1]

It was in keeping that those involved in the reform struggle—men like Bright, Goldwin Smith, John Stuart Mill, Edmond Beales, and Thomas Hughes—supporters of the American North and steadfastly opposed to slavery as one of the few flaws in its democratic system, should be willing to support a movement in aid of the freed Negro: in the words of one of the first appeals, 'loving gratitude to America demands it'.[2] A letter in the *American Freedman*, from a deputation visiting Britain, noted that Bright and Hughes were active supporters of freedmen's aid in the belief that 'freedom in the South means also freedom in the North—that freedom for the slave means also freedom for all classes, with freedom for the *press*, and freedom for the pulpit, and so has involved in it that, by and by, we shall all be "free indeed" '.[3]

But, as the Jamaica Revolt had proved, politics, whether domestic or foreign, were to be a serious problem for the freedmen's societies. In the first place, we know that the connexion between the leaders of the suffrage fight and those who supported the Jamaican as well as the American freedmen caused considerable uneasiness in the public mind, and plunged the movement into controversy at its outset. Then, during the turbulent years of Reconstruction, there was a real need to allow for the ill will on both sides of the Atlantic which resulted from the Civil War.

Benevolence and Christian zeal sustained freedmen's aid in Britain, but it aimed in addition to act as a vehicle of goodwill towards America and the American government. This was its chief appeal for someone like Bright;[4] but the problem was how to do so without seeming to meddle in American politics. For the freedmen's societies did not merely take a sympathetic interest in the Negro, they also sent out large sums of money to help him, and

---

[1] See Lillibridge, op. cit., Chapter III; H. Pelling, *America and the British Left. From Bright to Bevan*, London, A. & C. Black, 1956, pp. 10, 35–48.

[2] *Freed-Man*, 1 August 1865, p. 3.

[3] Vol. I, no. 8, 1866, p. 120.

[4] See, for instance, his speech in the *Reporter*, May 1866, p. 8.

directed how these should be used.[1] That not all Americans appreciated their efforts is clear from the correspondence of the English movement.[2]

The approach therefore adopted was ostensibly bi-partisan; or, better still, the Negro was to be divorced from politics and considered simply as a suffering human being. Thus an official circular put out in 1865 stressed that 'This appeal is made—not on political grounds, for our Association comprehends gentlemen of every shade of politics—but on grounds of humanity and Christian philanthropy.'[3] The support of M.P.s was welcomed no longer, as with the anti-slavery movement at the beginning of the century, because political action was entertained, but for reasons of prestige. Efforts to recruit Government support were unsuccessful: success, in fact would have confirmed many in their belief that freedmen's aid was a political stunt. (The Birmingham society admitted that 'It may not be deemed expedient for the British government to intermeddle; but we, the people of England, are bound to aid this enterprise by our duty to the negro, to ourselves, to America, and to the world at large'.)[4] But Gladstone gave the movement his blessing, and the Union was successful in recruiting the support of a large number of M.P.s from all parties—it counted some twenty-seven politicians among its Vice-Presidents, and the London society claimed the services of another eight.

The British freedmen's associations were not opposed to politics as such, as being a dirty game, or to American politics in particular, as were sections of the Tory press; simply to any political affiliation which might render them objectionable to potential supporters, whose own affiliations happened to be different. And in view of the outspoken comments of the British press during Reconstruction, if the wartime North–South division of loyalties was to be avoided at home and the bitterness engendered in the States allowed to die, prudence on the part of the movement was doubly necessary.

British criticisms, needless to say, were not well received by

---

[1] See letters in A.P. C39/14, 19, 56, 100, 120, C118/77, C119/37, C121/43, 104.

[2] There seems to have been on the American side a dislike of appearing to beg: see letter of L. Coffin to J. M. McKim, 5 January 1866, Cincinatti, Anti-Slavery Papers, Cornell University, as well as letters in A.P. C119/33, C120/27.

[3] Circular no. 15 of the Birmingham and Midland Freedmen's-Aid Association, John Rylands Library; see also A.P. C118/85 and *Derby Reporter*, 10 March 1865.

[4] *Four Million of Emancipated Slaves in the United States. An appeal to the People of England, from the National Committee of the British Freedmen's-Aid Associations*, pamphlet in the John Rylands Library, p. 2.

Americans. Charles Sumner complained to John Bright in 1866 (and again in 1867 and 1868) :[1]

> It is hard that the United States should be so misrepresented by the London press. The *Times* has a correspondent who sees through rebel spectacles and writes with a rebel pen. . . . But it is harder to bear the pretentious liberalism of the *News* correspondent, who is more mischievous than the other from his pretenses [sic].

Like other prominent men interested in freedmen's aid, Bright realized the need for caution. Soon after the Civil War he was entreated by one of his American correspondents, a Boston publisher, to make some public statement on Reconstruction. 'You must be aware', he was told, 'that the deliberate expression of your views will largely influence public opinion among our people—and through the people will be likely to act upon the government itself.'[2] The English statesman did not take up the invitation, and confided to Sumner, 'I abstain from writing or speaking in public on this matter, because I think as "outsiders" we are liable to mistakes, and also that interference and advice from England are not likely to be received in a very cordial spirit by a large portion of your countrymen.'[3]

In the same vein the Duke of Argyll, always a staunch friend of the abolitionists, and of the North during the Civil War, at a well-publicized freedmen's meeting in 1865 dismissed suggestions that 'taking part in the proceedings of these societies was in some degree a political demonstration'.[4] But Argyll, like Bright, was keenly interested in the problems of Reconstruction; the latter wrote often and impatiently to Sumner for the latest news, and was not alone in finding—as earlier, over the Jamaica crisis of 1865, that neutrality was easier to advocate than observe. This difficulty was experienced by those actively involved in the freedmen's aid movement and by the general public to whom they appealed; and it was inevitable.

All the British societies relied for information upon Americans involved in the work, with definite views on how the South should be 'reconstructed' (nearly all inclined to the policies of the Radical Republican section of Congress). It was unrealistic to expect people in either country suddenly to abandon their old sympathies and

---

[1] 13 August 1868, Bright Papers, British Museum, Add. Ms. 43390, VIII.
[2] Frank Moore to Bright, 10 August 1865, Bright Papers, Add. Ms. 43391, IX.
[3] 2 October 1865; *Proceedings*, p. 147.   [4] Op. cit., pp. 4, 6.

F

affinities with North or South, and a movement devoted to the welfare of the Negro was bound ultimately to favour whichever party in America seemed to promise him the best opportunities of intellectual, physical, and social advancement.

As early as 1865, William Morgan, an honorary secretary of the Birmingham Association, was complaining that 'The whole subject [of freedmen's aid] has grown upon us in a manner never anticipated at the beginning of the movement, and it has become inevitably complicated by political considerations . . . so that there is the utmost need for circumspection in all our proceedings'.[1] These political considerations affected the public response to canvassing tours on behalf of the freedmen.

Joseph Davis of the Bristol Society wrote to the Union secretary in some concern about the visit to Bristol in 1865 of an American deputation, outspokenly Northern in its sympathies. He explained that 'Bristol has during the War and still, strong Confederate feelings [.] All our papers have been in favour of the South—we are extremely anxious that American politics may not be at all touched on, and our Mayor would not have taken any part in the movement but on condition that we kept quite clear of them—we think it is sufficient to plead for an immense mass of human beings, in a state of great destitution, and to assist whom is a Christian duty, without criticizing the conduct of any party thro' whom they are brought into this state.'[2] The Recorder of Birmingham and Commissioner of the Bristol Bankruptcy Court, M. D. Hill, an 'Abolitionist of more than thirty years standing', declined to attend any more meetings of the society without an assurance that there would be no repetition of the events of the last meeting, when[3]

the Gentleman who came as a delegate from the United States assumed a tone and indulged in a course of observation calculated to introduce controversy of an irritating nature into an assembly met for a charitable purpose where above all things it was important that harmony of feeling and opinion should remain unbroken. . . .

Such an assurance—as far as it was possible—was given, but the problem it raised remained a very real one.

The existence of old wartime loyalties also inhibited the activi-

[1] William Morgan to Aspinall Hampson, 30 November 1865, A.P. C119/62.
[2] Joseph Davis to Aspinall Hampson, 31 August 1865, A.P. C118/11.
[3] M. D. Hill to the Bristol Freedmen's Aid Society Committee, A.P. C118/10.

ties of the Union in the Manchester area. Arthur Albright, the movement's most resourceful speaker and canvasser, hoped at first that a special Manchester or North of England society, on the lines of the Birmingham and Midland Association, might be formed.[1] 'I am sure there are good materials but no leaders at Manchester', he commented later, but added pessimistically, 'I do not expect great things. The nearer the slavery the deader the conscience.'[2] A fellow worker confirmed that Albright had 'not found the response from Manchester he had expected'.[3]

This hostility was explained by several local sympathizers. 'I have never considered Manchester much of [an] Anti Slavery Town', wrote one, 'the Manchester people [without constant prodding] are far too busy to give.'[4] A prominent Quaker member of the Union warned against the proposed visit of an American deputation, doubting[5]

whether . . . it would be at all wise for any American to appear at any of our Public Meetings as one *sent over to solicit sub[scriptions]* from this side for the freedmen. . . . It is astonishing how very sensitive our people are to aught like foreign influence on such subjects, and I am sure that (in this part of the country, at least) we can only hope for success by prominently setting forth that . . . we are sending [help] out to them voluntarily and without regard to creed or politics. . . .

Those working in the area on behalf of the freedmen complained of the slow progress to be made 'against the strong prejudices still existing here'.[6] Despite the wartime existence in Manchester of the most famous of the English Emancipation Societies, the sympathies of a large part of the business community, from whose support the movement stood to gain most financially, lay for co reasons with the South, while the sentiments of the working men to whom the Union also appealed, were in fact moreanti-aristocratic than pro-Negro.[7]

When the National Union was inaugurated, the speakers at that meeting disavowed all political intent, but concern for the Negro

[1] A. Albright to A. Hampson, 11 November 1865, A.P. C117/9.
[2] A. Albright to T. Phillips, 24 January 1868, A.P. C38/61.
[3] B. Cadbury to T. Phillips, 26 November 1867, A.P. C39/12.
[4] Thomas Clegg to A. Hampson, 7 January 1868, A.P. C117/145.
[5] Joseph Simpson to A. Hampson, 23 October 1865, A.P. C120/21.
[6] R. Longdon to A. Hampson, 22 November 1865, A.P. C119/24.
[7] See letters in A.P., C121/195 and C40/51; also M. Beloff, 'Great Britain and the American Civil War', *History*, Vol. XXXVII, p. 44. John Hodgkin complained that little had been accomplished in Manchester because 'the question had been made a political one there, which it should not have been' (A.P. C27/76).

soon brought concern with the politics which involved him. The Duke of Argyll had declared that 'The war is now over, and although the Americans are in the midst of a political contest involving great acrimony of feeling and great difficulties, I am sure we, in this country, take no interest in such contests', adding however, 'except so far as they are connected with the question of slavery. ... I dare say you will agree with me, that unless the negroes are assured of their civil rights, there has been practically no abolition of slavery; and that until the negroes are allowed to sue and to be sued, to enter courts of justice and give their evidence on the same footing as the white men, there will be no security whatever that the abolition of slavery is more than merely nominal.'[1] The Rev. W. Shaw, President of the Wesleyan Conference, though anxious not to be 'mixed up with any political questions on the other side of the water', felt hopefully that 'man everywhere should enjoy his natural rights, and perfect civil and religious freedom, and, these being secured, ... political rights will in due season come.'[2] Unfortunately, the American 'political contest'— discounting the somewhat arid constitutional issues—revolved round the question of whether the Negro should enjoy any or all such rights, how soon, and by whose authority.

It was part of Union policy to give, periodically, an encouraging picture of Southern conditions to British audiences, who must be convinced not only of the need to give, but also of the valuable effects of their generosity. Even so, at the very first meeting of the Union, its President, Sir Thomas Fowell Buxton, was expressing concern about what the South might do, if left entirely to its own devices. He noted uneasily 'the dreadful jealousy which exists between the old slave-owners and those who were their slaves,—not so much the jealousy between them because it exists only on one side, but that jealousy which exists in the minds of the old planters'. It was to be hoped that this feeling might diminish in time through self-interest and Northern influence.[3] John Bright also feared that the dispossessed planters would hardly look with charity upon the freedmen, whose new privileges were therefore highly precarious, while Thomas Hughes believed the Negroes to be 'in the most helpless condition in the world, and they had round them a population of planters who regarded them with the greatest possible hatred'.[4]

---

[1] *Reporter*, May 1866, p. 3.   [2] Ibid., pp. 10, 11.
[3] Ibid., p. 7.   [4] Ibid., p. 9.

Similar feelings of anxiety about the Negro were expressed by other Union members, who unwittingly acknowledged the necessity of Northern policies, if his welfare were to be secured. A Hitchin Friend, writing in 1865, felt that 'The prospects for the Negro have certainly not become more hopeful since we last met' and that the schools 'seem the one hopeful element in the present condition of things'.[1] Two years later, a Liverpool merchant, Josiah Thompson, wrote after a trip to America that 'The planters dont [*sic*] appear to like the [Freedmen's] Bureau or the Agents attached to it, but perhaps this may be one of the best arguments for their necessity',[2] and the Birmingham secretary complained that 'the old pro slavery spirit impedes and disturbs the work of the Freedmens Aid and Freedmens Bureau in America'.[3]

An appeal circulated among Bradford working men contained a telling passage on the plight of the Negroes. 'The evils under which they suffer', it ran, 'have been much aggravated, and the progress of amicable arrangements delayed, by the expectation of their oppressors that, under the retrograde policy of the National Executive [i.e. President Johnson] they might regain the power of exacting unpaid labour, and of preventing the education and elevation of the coloured people.'[4] A correspondent in Northampton confided that 'My fears for the freedmen in the early future have always kept ahead of my hope—' and admitted imperfections in both parties to Reconstruction:

The State Union [has] suffered such a dislocation and compound fracture too that it would require a Solon and a Lycurgus to reduce [it] to a state for sound harmonious working; having (as will surely be the case) to encounter the resuscitated *pro slavery* feeling of the South and the reviving anti colour prejudice of the North.

But he still felt that the only true policy was that which offered 'equal religious, political commercial and social rights recognized and secured'.[5]

When the Union circulated round its branches an address to be delivered to the American Ambassador, Reverdy Johnson, late in 1868, it was suggested that this should incorporate 'a few words expressive of our fears whether *the full privileges* intended by the

---

[1] F. Seebohm to A. Hampson, 2 November 1865, A.P. C120/7a.
[2] J. Thompson to A. Albright, 7 February 1867, A.P. C121/131.
[3] A. Albright to A. Hampson, 7 November 1865, A.P. C117/6.
[4] W. S. Nichols to T. Phillips, 12 November 1867, A.P. C40/51.
[5] William Collins to T. Phillips, 31 January 1868, A.P. C39/85.

Emancipation were being realized—and if not', would Johnson 'use his influence as far as he properly could, to impress upon the American Executive the anxiety which prevailed in England on this account—and the strong desire that the beneficent intentions of the U[nited] States Gov[ernment] and Executive might be faithfully carried into full effect.'[1] William Brewin of Cirencester wrote in like fashion to the Union secretary, hoping that 'you or others who are well acquainted with the position and condition of things in the S[outhern] States will . . . [lay] before his "Excellency" some points that may have a practical bearing on the future of the South'.[2] One of the Union's emissaries in America, he reported, could not 'point to anything that is satisfactory in the present or promising in the future—indeed where the people of any country [i.e. the South] are wrong *at heart*—it is very difficult for rulers to help'.[3]

As time passed, the freedmen's aid movement thus showed an increasing partiality for the policies of the Radical Republicans, who, whatever their motives, appeared to offer the Negro far more far sooner than the Southern Democrats and President Johnson. Arthur Albright admitted this preference openly in 1868, when commenting on reports in the New York *Nation*. They presented, he thought, 'a terrible picture of the South the only gain of which is that it seems to be stirring up the Republicans in the North to the needful effort on behalf of [President] Grant. I am glad to see that the Rep[ublicans] have carried Colorado and New Mexico by increased majorities and that the *Daily News* Correspondent writes so hopefully. The Southern Rascals have shown the cloven foot too plainly and too soon.'[4]

The two freedmen's newspapers at first tried to preserve a neutral attitude towards Reconstruction policies; much of their space was devoted simply to the Negro—his physical needs, his educational and moral progress. Reporting in 1865, Sir Thomas Fowell Buxton denied that the movement involved 'partizanship with the North as against the South'; 'Their object', he said, 'was totally different from any political purpose.'[5] This denial did not, however, impress the public at large, and two years later the *Freed-Man* again carried an article which again tried to explode the

[1] Joseph Thorp, Halifax, to A. Albright, 28 December 1868, A.P. C121/132.
[2] W. Brewin to A. Hampson, 30 October 1868, A.P. C117/116.
[3] Ibid.
[4] A. Albright to T. Phillips, 22 September 1868, A.P. C38/99.
[5] *Freed-Man*, 1 October 1865, p. 61.

imputed 'ulterior political object', pointing out shrewdly that 'those who are intensely absorbed in political questions have not the leisure nor the calmness of mind either to look dispassionately into the suffering condition of a neglected race or to devise means for their restoration. After the excitement of debate is over in reference to the wrongs of the Freed-men it has often happened that their condition has not only been left unchanged, but the conflicting parties, wearied by their own discussions, have rather felt in consequence great indisposition to look further into the subject.'[1]

Even so, the London society and its journal the *Freed-Man* found it impossible entirely to overlook politics. Thomas Hughes, in an article on 'American Re-construction' written in 1865, while admitting with respect the considerable support President Johnson's policies received in the States, and the need for caution on the part of England, owned that[2]

I for one have been quite confident that nothing but an immediate extension of the suffrage to the negroes would secure abolition in fact as well as in name. President Johnson's hesitation in the matter seemed to me like cowardice, or treason. I could not see the least reason why, when he was laying down his conditions of re-construction for the rebel states, he should not have added to the concession of civil rights, in the courts and elsewhere, the crowning political right of the ballot. Nor do I see the reason now. . . .

A leader on the Presidential veto of the Civil Rights Bill some time later, confirmed editorial opposition to Johnson. 'The President believes', it declared, 'that the Government of the United States is a Government of white men, and exists for white men alone. Congress believes that it is a Government of citizens without reference to the colour of its citizens. . . . The Civil Rights Bill . . . gives no new Article to the constitution, but . . . declares in relation to the freedom of the citizen and the protection of that freedom, only the fundamental law of the State. . . . It reserves the essential principles of citizenship from that destruction to which Mr. Johnson seemed to be willing to surrender them. It tells in unmistakable terms that the war having terminated in the defeat of the Southern oligarchs, an era of justice . . . alike for white and black, is to dawn upon those fair and promising Southern lands.' A tailpiece on the freedman declared him to be 'faithful, industrious and religious. God knows this is more than we can say for the whites. . . . We repeat for the hundredth time, that it is not the

[1] Ibid., 1 March 1867, p. 112.   [2] Ibid., 1 December 1865, pp. 85–9.

"irrepressible nigger" that makes the difficulty in the South, but the impracticable, ignorant and oppressive white man.'[1] A second article in the same issue underlined the hostile tenor of the leader.[2]

The following year, the leader columns of the *Freed-Man* again exploded indignantly against the drift of Presidential Reconstruction. Intense concern was expressed for the unfortunate freedmen, since 'Mr. Johnson does not love the black man, will not sustain him in his new rights, will not regard him as a "man and a brother." This is his great offence as a ruler, and leads to all the wrongs of which he is chargeable and all the scandalous and cruel oppressions and murders which the worthless among the late slaveholders perpetrate daily.' He not only did nothing to prevent offences against the Negro, but also openly tried to hamper the work of General Howard, head of the Freedmen's Bureau, 'than whom no truer christian, no wiser administrator, no firmer friend of humanity exists. It has been said of the President, and said with truth, "Southern disaffection looks up to him as its head, and bases its hopes on the sympathy of the man who ought to be its most stern and decided opponent."' The final pronouncement on Johnson was acid:[3]

He is, and we write the sentence with infinite pain, the enemy of the poor, the enemy of the nation and the enemy of God. What the end of such a man will be it is easy to divine, like the dreadful betrayer of the Saviour, he will in due time go to his own place.

In calmer mood, the President of the London society and editor of the *Freed-Man*, Frederick Tomkins, advised the Negroes 'to advance in knowledge, virtue and religion, and that in due time God would bring all things to pass', but he was forced to notice that 'Their old oppressors who strove to rivet on them indissoluble fetters are still at work striving hard to arouse prejudice against the coloured race. ... What does the present political battle cry— "That the United States government is a government for white men and by white men"—mean, except that the white man is to be the ruler and lord of the land, and the poor black is to be the helot?'[4]

The general condition of the South thus presented much cause for anxiety, with unchecked lawlessness prevailing among the whites, while the rights of the freedmen, who could not hope for justice, were curtailed. Under these circumstances the work of the

[1] *Freed-Man*, 1 June 1866, pp. 260–2.   [2] Ibid., p. 267.
[3] Ibid., 1 February 1867, pp. 101–2.   [4] Ibid., 1 January 1868, pp. 2–3.

Freedmen's Bureau was strongly upheld; segregated schools were condemned; and where the *Freed-Man* relied on American sources for news, it used papers with a similar bias towards Congressional Reconstruction.[1] It even ventured into combat with *The Times*, whose advocacy of the South, though less extreme than it had been, was still apparent.

An article on 'The condition of the South' complained that 'Elaborate efforts . . . are now made to show indirectly and inferentially that Emancipation has reduced both planters and negroes to a condition of absolute and almost hopeless ruin. The subject receives unwonted prominence, and the correspondent and editor return to it with unity of purpose and work with characteristic vigour. In a short time we shall find that the pro-Southern party in England will be quite convinced of the necessity of re-action, and the re-election of President Johnson. As a mere question of party politics this would give us no concern, but as a return to the old system of selfish injustice and oppression, it is most earnestly to be deprecated.'[2] The fears of Negro supremacy, sometimes voiced in the South, were dismissed as nonsense; the cry was raised by those elements of Southern society which depended for such lowly place as they enjoyed on the suppression of the Negro race. The freedmen had not revolted, nor shown any tendency to violence or dangerous ambition, although in all 'works of utility for the commerce of the world, [they] certainly have the "supremacy" '.[3]

If no word of praise could be found for President Johnson, a leader in 1868 vindicated in glowing terms the role of Congress in Reconstruction. After condemning those who, like the President, would 'deprive the Freed-man of those political rights which preeminently characterise modern society', it commended the striking 'persistency of the Congress of the United States in its defence of the rights of the Freed-man. Every possible means has been employed, not only by the disappointed enemies of the coloured race, but even by the President himself, to weaken the courage and break the spirit of the legislature at Washington'; but, steady 'in its purpose, the great Republican party has, with something like judicial impartiality, proceeded in its work of consolidating freedom. When in a future day the historian shall reduce to order the annals of this country during the last three years, we feel convinced

---

[1] Ibid., 1 February 1867, pp. 103–4, 107; 1 August 1868, pp. 9–10; 1 January 1868, p. 2; 1 October 1866, pp. 41–2; 1 January 1868, p. 16.
[2] Ibid., 1 February 1868, p. 21.   [3] Ibid., 1 January 1868, pp. 5–8.

that he will assign to the Fortieth Congress of the United States one of the highest places that any legislative body has at any time attained.'[1]

In February 1868, the *Freed-Man* had warned itself and its readers against 'superficial views, and partial representations'[2] on the question of Reconstruction; unity in the interests of the Negro was urged, but the policy line had already been decided.

The freedmen's aid *Reporter*, put out by the National Union, and guided by its desire to attract the widest possible support, managed fairly successfully to avoid overt political commitment. Even so, anxiety about the Negro, as the 'providential sine qua non of national harmonisation',[3] brought at least anxiety about the conflicting Reconstruction policies.

'Our American relatives are well able to fight their own political battles, and the true patriots will doubtless win the victory in the end', declared a leader in 1866, at the same time noting with concern that the Negro needed all the more help 'because of the degree in which these political battles, even battles about the Negro, absorb time, talent, and means, which otherwise would be largely employed for the negro's physical, industrial, moral, and social welfare'.[4] But while deploring, as the *Freed-Man* did, the effort wasted in political wrangles,[5] the same leader had cautious praise for the Civil Rights Bill, the Freedmen's Bureau, and the attitude of the North generally, on the grounds of

the iniquitousness of making mere colour a test of fraternity. On this point the vast majority of the North are sound—at any rate, up to the level of the Civil Rights Act; and there is a yearning desire, and an increasingly strong resolve, especially on the part of the North, to labour for the educational, social, and Christian elevation of the coloured people. We are at one with those engaged in this God-like work; and they are those who would have the Civil Rights Act a vital law of operation and experience, and not a mere statutory declaration. Those who oppose this act most strenuously are those who, in the past, wronged the negro most deeply.

'If the South will not act justly to the Negro,' continued the *Reporter*, 'how is it possible not to rejoice that the legislature has prolonged the existence of the Freedmen's Bureau for two years . . .?'[6]

[1] *Freed-Man*, 1 March 1868, pp. 41–2.   [2] Ibid., 1 February 1868, p. 20.
[3] *Reporter*, August 1868, p. 37   [4] Ibid., August 1866, p. 38.
[5] See also Ibid., October 1866, p. 57; February 1867, p. 101; March 1867, p. 113.
[6] Ibid., August 1866, pp. 37–8.

Its columns remained full of praise for General Howard, even when he and his agents came under fire in America.[1]

Like the *Freed-Man*, the Union journal borrowed news stories from papers—such as the *Daily News*—which were biased in favour of the North and Congressional reconstruction.[2] It, too, had occasion to criticize *The Times*. In January 1867, a leader welcomed its recognition of the distress prevailing in the South, but added, 'we should have been yet more gratified to read therein as faithful an account of what is, in its way, worse than mere famine (for famine can only destroy the body), viz., a state of bitterness, of deliberate and systematic cruelty, against the harmless and helpless negroes, such as may make civilization blush with shame'. *The Times* was grimly reminded that 'numerous crimes, including murders, are committed through the State [of Arkansas] against Freed-men, and the civil authorities almost universally neglect to take action, or to inflict punishment'.[3]

Again, in the case of some of the most serious rioting between the two races, in New Orleans in 1866, the Southern whites were held squarely to blame,[4] and the *Reporter* declared itself fearful of what might happen if the Democrats should regain their former political power. On one of the most bitterly contested issues of Reconstruction—that of Negro suffrage—it was of the opinion, unacceptable to many in the South, 'That whatever forms a condition of citizenship in any state, whether educational or pecuniary ought to have an impartial reference to white and black alike.'[5] The political commitment to the North, so long avoided by the freedmen's groups, could not in the end be denied.

Even the Quakers, who as a group showed little interest in the conflicting policies for Reconstruction, and in fact sympathized with both races in the South, from time to time expressed concern about the attitude of the Southern whites, who 'seem determined to annoy and discourage those who are endeavouring to instruct and elevate the Freedmen'.[6] An editorial in the London *Friend* urged the importance 'of fixing on a right basis the civil and political

---

[1] Ibid., June 1866, p. 17; January 1867, pp. 93-4.
[2] Ibid., September 1866, pp. 53-4; October 1866, p. 63; November 1866, pp. 71-2; January 1867, p. 93; January 1867, p. 97.
[3] Ibid., January 1867, p. 93. See also a letter in A.P. from Thomas Phillips to Aspinall Hampson, 24 November 1865, C119/101, in which he grumbles about 'the tone of the leading articles in the *Times* and the *Telegraph*'.
[4] Ibid., March 1867, p. 120.   [5] Ibid., December 1867, p. 14.
[6] 1 September 1866, pp. 189-90.

status of the American freedmen, and . . . the danger of withholding from them the rights enjoyed by all the white population. . . . The future maintenance of peace and freedom in the United States may depend on the manner in which the relations of the white and sable population are now determined.'[1]

In 1865 the Friends' Central Committee for the freedmen suggested that 'Whatever guards may be needful to prevent political power from falling into the hands of those incapable of using it rightly, we must all be agreed that the *test of colour* alone ought never again to be allowed to become the dividing line between those who are invested with the full rights of freedmen, and those who are not. And while so momentous a question seems to hang upon the balance, we surely ought not to rest upon our oars.'[2]

After two and a half years' teaching in the South, Yorkshire Quaker George Dixon reported himself as distinctly dubious about the good faith of the white population. The vetoing of civil rights legislation by President Johnson had 'made the late slave owners more bold and defiant', and it was feared that, without the success of General Grant in the 1868 presidential election, 'the Northern teachers and Friends of the Freedmen will be all driven from the South, and the Freedmen themselves will be terribly persecuted; and, for a time, their condition will be worse than it was in the days of slavery'.[3]

Although Dixon had gone out to America uncommitted, like so many other labourers on behalf of the freedmen, he eventually embraced the cause of the Radical Republicans; this decision, wherever taken, by the offence it gave among the Southern whites was to be a significant factor in the ultimate decline of the freedmen's aid movement, both in Britain and America.

We may now turn our attention to the last, and most important element in the makeup of the freedmen's aid movement—the religious element. Just as the anti-slavery crusade was essentially religious and evangelical in character, so the freedmen's societies approached their task with a missionary zeal, aiming at the conversion and elevation of the Negro, and drawing their personnel overwhelmingly from the Nonconformist sects and the Society of Friends.

---

[1] 1 November 1865, p. 231.
[2] *Report [II] of the Central Committee of the Society of Friends for the Relief of the Emancipated Negroes of the United States*, pamphlet in the John Rylands Library.
[3] *Friend*, 1 October 1868, p. 250.

CHAPTER IV

Freedmen's Aid in Britain: Organization (II)

'For fields of duty opening wide,
Where all our powers
Are tasked the eager steps to guide
Of millions on a path untried:
The Slave is Ours.

Ours by traditions dear and old,
Which make the race
Our wards to cherish and uphold,
And cast their freedom in the mould
Of Christian grace.'

JOHN GREENLEAF WHITTIER, Quaker poet[1]

Since a great many clergymen and Friends had been involved in the anti-slavery movement on both sides of the Atlantic, it was only natural, after emancipation, that they should continue to urge the benefit to the Negro of Christian aid and teaching. In America secular and religious societies for the freedmen soon found themselves in direct competition, with the latter—and especially the American Missionary Association—because of better resources, liaison with the Freedmen's Bureau, and connexions with the Negroes themselves, proving the more successful.[2]

The approach adopted by the freedmen's movement was, like that of the British Anti-Slavery Society, religious and evangelical. Emphasis was placed on the spiritual needs of the Negroes, and the Christian duty of their former masters (and all those who had any connexion with the products of slavery) to see that emancipation involved real progress. Philanthropy, it was argued, and especially Christian philanthropy, knows no frontiers; here was a work in which 'every one ought to take a part . . .—every one who values his own freedom, and who is thankful for the Gospel of Christ'.[3]

---

[1] 'Anniversary Poem', *The Complete Poetical Works of John Greenleaf Whittier*, Boston, 1895, p. 342.
[2] See A. F. Beard, *Crusade of Brotherhood. A History of the American Missionary Association*, Boston, 1909; McPherson, op. cit., pp. 401–3, 406–7; Swint, op. cit., pp. 37–40.
[3] *Reporter*, May 1866, p. 5.

In its ambitious, evangelical aspect—societies to help the freedmen were founded in France, Holland, Switzerland, and Germany as well as Britain and America—the freedmen's aid movement may be ranked alongside such contemporary bodies as the Evangelical Alliance, an international Protestant association formed in 1846, and the peace, temperance, and women's right movements, all of which can be considered Anglo-American ventures, and whose wide-ranging activities proved appealing to Victorians.[1]

The Christian connexion with freedmen's aid was stressed by London barrister and Quaker John Hodgkin, when the British associations were preparing an address to the nation in 1865. His first criticism of a passage relating to Negro education, was that

the work of evangelization—the civilizing effect of Christian instruction, is not sufficiently adverted to. And tho' this is a delicate question, and we do not want to give our operations a thoroughly missionary Character—(which might drive off . . . mere philanthropists whose aid we need, and possibly divide even some of the *Earnest Christians*, owing to sectarian differences)—yet a printed reference to the subject is both due to what is really going forward by the zeal of trusted men and women of different parts of the . . . Church—and is also a *sine qua non*, if the emancipated are to be both raised from *brutishness* and made peaceable, dutiful, loyal citizens.[2]

While Victorians concerned themselves with whether—or rather how—the instruction of their own children should include the Bible and the elements of religion, it was natural for them to regard Christian teaching as even more essential to the offspring of ex-slaves.[3]

Freedmen's aid workers in Edinburgh rejoiced to see that thousands of Negroes 'have flocked to the schools . . . that they may study the Bible, which they consider the charter of their freedom'; and the secretary of the London society noted during a trip to North Carolina that 'Many of them seem devout and Christian persons, and desire to learn to read the Bible from the purest and noblest motives.'[4] A prominent Belfast journal commented, '. . . Christians in heart, as most of them are already, to a degree which shames the better opportunities of their self-styled superiors, they

---

[1] See *National Freedman*, Vol. I, no. 3, pp. 160, 195–6, 273–4, 324–5, 355–6, 368–9, 378; Thistlethwaite, op. cit., pp. 92–102, 120–33.

[2] J. Hodgkin to A. Hampson, 24 July 1865, A.P. C118/95.

[3] See G. M. Young, *Victorian England. Portrait of an Age*, London, 1953, p. 115.

[4] *Annual Report of the Edinburgh Ladies' Emancipation Society, . . . 1867*, p. 7; and *Birmingham Daily Gazette*, 3 April 1865.

are eager to become, and their teachers are eager to make them, Christians also in understanding.'[1]

Under these circumstances, and given the naturally sweet disposition of the Negroes—'There was', declared, W. H. Channing, 'a moral sublimity in their patience and resignation to evil, . . . in their heroism and piety'—the freedmen's societies were confident that the evils superimposed by slavery could be removed. As Channing assured a Liverpool audience, 'under refined conditions . . . [the Negroes] would all develope after the most refined type of humanity'.[2] And the opportunities for missionary work were indeed enormous, for, as the London association observed, 'All the Southern white clergy, who have been compelled to submit to the Northern regime, stand aloof from this glorious movement.'[3]

In fact abolitionists in the United States made only moderate progress among church bodies of either North or South, nor were the various British sects (anxious to maintain good relations with their American brethren) in the van of the anti-slavery movement —in spite of its constant emphasis upon the sinfulness of slavery— although well represented by individual clergymen.[4] Once the slaves were free, and the responsibility of advocating their emancipation removed, the needs of the freedmen provided religious groups on both sides of the Atlantic with a new opportunity of doing their duty both to God and themselves. The British freedmen's aid societies accordingly presented the Negroes as '. . . Christ's poor, for whom, if we now render them no aid. He may ask of us, hereafter, an account', and their work as 'among the first of Christian duties and privileges'.[5]

Attempts were made to obtain donations from all the denominations in Britain, and the degree of success encountered was often determined by the attitude each had adopted towards slavery during the American Civil War.

---

[1] Quoted in *The Freedmen's Aid Commission*, reprint of an article in the *Belfast Northern Whig*, December 1864, John Rylands Library.

[2] *The Rev. W. H. Channing on the Freedmen of America*, circular no. 14 of the Birmingham association, John Rylands Library.

[3] *Birmingham Daily Gazette*, 3 April 1865.

[4] For details see for instance L. Filler, *The Crusade Against Slavery, 1830–60*, London, Hamish Hamilton, 1960; G. H. Barnes, *The Anti-Slavery Impulse. 1830–44*, Gloucester, Mass., 1957, pp. 88–99; *Glasgow Emancipation Society Minute Book I*, meeting of 1 March 1836, Smeal Collection.

[5] *Why Should Birmingham Workmen Help the Freed Refugees From Slavery in America?*; and *Annual Report of the Birmingham and Midland Freedmen's Aid Association, to May 19th, 1865*, p. 4.

The sympathies of the Church of England undoubtedly lay with the South. Writing to C. E. Norton in 1863, Goldwin Smith admitted that 'The clergy of the Establishment are against you, as a Commonwealth founded on Liberty of Conscience';[1] the most aggressive organ of the High-Church party defended slavery even after the Emancipation Proclamation; while prominent establishment clergymen like Bishop Wilberforce, and Bishop Whately of Dublin, and laymen like Lord Robert Cecil, the Earl of Shaftesbury, and Beresford Hope, supported the South, or slavery, or both.[2]

Under the circumstances it would be unrealistic to expect the Church to have shown great concern for the welfare of the freed Negroes. The records of its annual conferences make no reference to freedmen's aid, and there is no indication that deputations were received or allowed to plead their case. William Smeal, secretary of the Glasgow society, noted that although the 1866 Assembly of the Established Church of Scotland commended the plight of the freedmen to the sympathy of its members, no official collection was put in train.[3] Just before the Union was dissolved, two years later, an executive committee circular was listing among projects to be pursued 'An appeal to the Clergy and laity of the Ch[urch] of England through us to aid if not the A[merican] F[reedmen's] A[id] Commission then by transmission through us to assist the work of the American Episcopal Church[']s F[reedmen's] A[id] Commission'.[4] More surprisingly, perhaps, the annual accounts of the Church Missionary Society for the sixties have no record of any subscription to freedmen's aid.

This is not to say, however, that no Church of England clergymen took an active part, as individuals, in the movement. An American delegate touring Britain in 1866 noted that among the Negro's friends were 'a few of the clergy of the Church of England, and of the clergymen of other denominations, with a larger number of their people. They are becoming . . . better informed as to the real issues at stake here, and the greatness of the work we have to do, and the practical Christian spirit required in our labors.'[5]

The freedmen's societies invariably approached the prominent

[1] Smith to Norton, Oxford, 7 November 1863, Goldwin Smith Papers, Cornell University; also G. Smith, *The Civil War in America*, op. cit., pp. 71–5.

[2] Jordon and Pratt, op. cit., p. 133.

[3] W. Smeal to A. Hampson, 4 July 1866, A.P. C120/37.

[4] Circular d. 3 July 1868, A.P. C121/195.

[5] *American Freedman*, 1866, Vol. I, no. 8, p. 120.

men of their locality, and recruited the support of the local clergy.[1]
In this way the London association enjoyed the services of the Rev.
Samuel Garratt, and the Rev. Samuel Minton of Eaton Chapel,
Pimlico, served the national Union. The Rev. T. A. L. Greaves
was involved in Weymouth activities, the Rev. Mark Cooper,
Rector of St. Mary's at Southampton, and the Rev. Dr. Howson,
the Dean of Chester, lent his support. In the Leicester area the
freedmen's cause was assisted by D. J. Vaughan, Vicar of St. Mar-
tin's, Fellow of Trinity College, Cambridge, and founder and
President of the Leicester Working Men's College; James Noble
Bennie, Vicar of St. Mary's; and John Collier-Barker, Curate of
Hoby in Leicestershire, and later Vicar of Holy Trinity, Hinckley.
And in Belfast, Charles Seaver of St. John's Church and R. Hannay of Christ's also helped to organize local subscriptions, while
the Union counted several bishops among its patrons.

The record of the Nonconformist groups as regards slavery and
the Civil War is varied, but once the war was over, both churches
and ministers took part in freedmen's aid.

Britain's largest sect, the Wesleyan Methodists, included Northern and Confederate supporters in its ranks.[2] Even so the annual
conference in 1864 welcomed the return of a delegation to the
Methodist Episcopal Church of America, which had expressed
sympathy for its wartime sufferings and the fight against slavery.
The following year an address was drawn up rejoicing in emancipation and stressing the need 'to promote the spiritual and moral
improvement of the coloured race, millions of whom, . . . so long
in slavery, are now made free.'[3] In 1865 the Wesleyan assembly
was meeting at Birmingham, where Arthur Albright inspired the
most vigorous of the British freedmen's societies; on its initiative
a joint meeting was held during the Conference, at which over 200
Methodist ministers were present to hear about the plight of the
Negroes.

Among the speakers were the Rev. William Shaw, Conference
president, and ex-president Rev. George Osborn, Rev. William
Arthur, Secretary of the Wesleyan Foreign Missionary Society,
Bishop E. S. Janes of the American Methodist Church, and Robert
Dale, one of the most prominent dissenting ministers of the day.

---

[1] See letter of T. Phillips to A. Hampson, 14 November 1865, A.P. C119/100.
[2] Jordon and Pratt, op. cit., pp. 134–5.
[3] *Minutes of the Methodist Conferences*, London, Wesleyan Conference Office, 1868, Vol.
XVI, p. 130 and 369, see also pp. 151–3, 366–8.

Speeches stressed the ability of the freedmen, and Dr. Osborn hoped that '. . . Christians of every rank would join with him notwithstanding their old opinions . . . of North and South'.[1] The meeting was reported in the *Watchman* and the Birmingham press, and the Conference duly recommended Freedmen's aid to the Wesleyan Methodists for their financial and moral support.[2]

In December of the same year an article in the *Wesleyan-Methodist Magazine*, on the 'negro difficulty', urged that 'those organized efforts for the relief of American freed-men, which philanthropy has set on foot, should be encouraged and supported, and especially by those who advocated, and prayed for, the emancipation of the Southern slaves'.[3]

Beyond this, there is no record of official support, and it seems likely that the decision whether or not to contribute was left to individual members of the church, acting through the existing aid societies. It is difficult to establish the religious affiliations of the numerous obscure clergymen involved in the movement, but Methodist ministers do not appear to have been numerous in local associations. William Arthur, however, was an honorary secretary of the Union, the Rev. J. E. Hargreaves played an active part on the committee of the Carlisle society, while the Revs. James Donnelly and M. McCay served in the same capacity in Belfast.

The Congregational church adopted a cautious attitude to the American Civil War, although individual ministers, like Newman Hall, were among the most ardent supporters of the North, and at the close of 1862 a dissatisfied pro-Union group within its ranks formed themselves into a Congregational Committee of Correspondence on American Affairs, which distributed a considerable amount of anti-slavery propaganda during its brief existence.[4]

In 1865 the Congregational Union meeting in Bristol made up for its wartime stand by welcoming the efforts of the British freedmen's aid societies, and admitting a delegation composed of representatives from the English and American movements.[4] In response to their appeals the Union resolved to raise funds to help

---

[1] *Birmingham and Midland Freedmen's-Aid Association. The Speeches . . . Delivered in the Town Hall, Birmingham, on Wednesday Evening, August 2nd, 1865, at a Public Meeting Convened by the Above Association, More Especially in Connection with the Assembling of the Wesleyan Conference*, Birmingham, 1865, pp. 4–9.

[2] *Watchman and Wesleyan Advertiser*, 10 August, 1867, p. 257, and *Minutes of the Methodist Conferences*, p. 349.

[3] Vol. LXXXVIII, Part II, p. 1131.   [4] Jordan and Pratt, op. cit., pp. 135–6, 142–3.

[5] *The Congregational Year Book, 1866*, London, 1866, p. 401.

'elevate and evangelize the newly-enfranchised people of the Southern States', and ordered a collection to be made in all Congregational churches (some 2,000) on 14 January 1866.[1] A report was carried by the *Christian World*, which later gave account of the money raised.[2] The 1866 conference announced that over £3,000 had been received and sent out via the American Missionary Association, as a token of the Union's 'lively interest in the welfare of our American brethren, and in the efforts they are making to instruct and save an emancipated people'.[3]

Official interest was not further sustained; in 1868 Arthur Albright approached the Union's President for a donation, but was rebuffed, and wrote bitterly to a friend, 'What Dr[.] Raleigh means by "jaded interest" when his sect have begun and ended with a paltry £3,000 three years ago ... is rather hard to understand ... I did not suppose or give him to suppose he would make the Freedmen the subject of his Inaugural[.] I looked for a few earnest words from him on the subject[.] After his letter I dont [*sic*] expect even those.'[4] In spite of Albright's complaints, the Congregational church raised more for the Negro than any other religious sect with the exception of the Quaker's, and its clergymen and members were active in the various freedmen's associations.[5]

The Baptists, Presbyterians, and Unitarians were also approached for donations; like the Methodists they all afforded deputations a sympathetic hearing, and though the Baptist church also left the question to be decided by the generosity of its individual members, the other two bodies did try to organize—albeit not very successful—official collections.

At an autumn meeting of the Baptist Union in Birmingham in 1864, the Rev. J. H. Hinton, sub-editor of the Anti-Slavery Society's *Reporter* and member of the Evangelical Alliance, introduced a freedmen's aid deputation, and a resolution was duly

---

[1] Ibid., for 1867, pp. 35–6, and see also Circular to all Congregational clergymen, d. 12 December 1865, A.P. C120/38.

[2] 5 January and 2 February 1866.

[3] *The Congregational Year Book, 1867*, London, 1867, pp. 35–6.

[4] A. Albright to T. Phillips, 12 May, 1868, A.P. C38/92.

[5] For instance A. Hampson, first secretary of the Union; Dr. Raleigh himself was an Hon. Sec.; Rev. John Curwen of Plaistow, J. C. Galloway of Kilburn, Alexander Hannay of City Road, C. N. Hall of Surrey Chapel, and Dr. J. W. Massie of Islington were prominent members of the London society—its secretary Dr. F. Tomkins was also a Congregationalist. Others included Robert Dale in Birmingham, Richard Bulmer in Reading, Revs. G. McCallum and David Johnstone in Glasgow.

passed commending the cause as 'one for prompt liberal contributions throughout the Baptist Churches'.[1] During the June assembly of 1865, a second deputation was received, and its objects again commended; 'it should be the special care of the Christian Church', it was felt, 'to furnish the evidence that sympathy with freedom is not an empty boast, and that our concern for the enslaved is not a hypocritical pretence'.[2] And there, as far as the assembly was concerned, the matter rested, though individual Baptists continued to play a part in the movement.[3]

The English Presbyterians, a small group at this time, do not appear to have been involved in freedmen's aid, nor does the Irish branch of the church, though several prominent Irish Presbyterians—Drs. McCosh, Morgan, and Edgar, and the Rev. Hugh Hanna, all active philanthropists—were involved in the Belfast society.[4] A representative of the American National Freedmen's Relief Association reported preaching 'in the large presbiterian [*sic*] chapel' of Belfast, in 1865, and on his plans to approach the general assembly of the church then in session, but the outcome of such overtures—if indeed they were made—is not known.[5]

Deputations to the Scottish Presbyterians fared somewhat better. At the U.P. Synod of 1866 representatives of the American Missionary Association were sympathetically received, and a collection to help towards 'the physical, intellectual, and religious improvement' of the freedmen recommended. A cordial hearing was given to deputations in 1867 and 1869.[6] By 1 April 1867, the general secretary of the church reported, nearly £650 had been dispatched to the A.M.A.[7]

A similar pattern of events can be traced in the Scottish Free Church, which in 1866 welcomed an American delegation, expressed interest in freedmen's aid, and recommended generosity to its congregation.[8] By March 1867, about £500 had been raised

---

[1] *Baptist Handbook*, no details, 1865, p. 152.

[2] *Birmingham Daily Gazette*, 27 June 1865.

[3] For instance, J. P. Mursell of Leicester (President Baptist Union 1864); Rev. Francis Tucker of Camden Road Chapel, London, Hon. Sec. of the Union; Rev. J. Aldis of Reading (President Baptist Union in 1866).

[4] See Coffin, op. cit., p. 687.

[5] C. C. Leigh to A. Albright, 10 July 1865, A.P. C121/97.

[6] *United Presbyterian Synod Proceedings, 1864–70*, Glasgow 1870, pp. 269, 290, 429, 731.

[7] David Crawford to the Glasgow Freedmen's Aid Society, 9 April 1867, Edinburgh. Minute Book of the Society, Smeal Collection, p. 46.

[8] *Proceedings of the General Assembly of the Free Church of Scotland, 1864–8*, no details available, p. 258.

by the church and general public in the Dundee area, but no official collection had been ordered.[1] The 1867 assembly again drew attention to the need for helping 'the African race in the acquisition of knowledge, the discharge of the duties of citizenship and the development of Christian character', and in 1868 it was suggested that a collection should be made throughout the church in the autumn, but the outcome of this proposal is obscure.[2]

The comparative success enjoyed by freedmen's aid among church groups in Scotland was no doubt due in part to the strength of the anti-slavery tradition in cities like Edinburgh, Glasgow, and Dundee. Sella Martin, for instance, the Negro preacher, ex-slave and for some time minister of Westminster Church, Long Acre, who was in Glasgow at the beginning of August, 1865, remained in Scotland through to October, having by his success there secured an extension of leave from the States.[3] In May 1868, Martin was again working in Edinburgh. Dr. J. C. Holbrook, of the American Missionary Association was similarly enthusiastic; 'I find a great field here needing to be worked for the freedmen's cause', he wrote in November 1865, '—enough to occupy me all winter, probably.' By January there was still 'a month or more of work in Scotland'.[4]

The remaining sect, the Unitarians, as soon as the war was over sent an address to the American association rejoicing in emancipation and adding, 'If in preparing for their new condition the freedmen now for the first time introduced to the enjoyment of their natural rights, help from other lands is needed, be assured of our sympathy and our desire to join in the holy work of restoring a large and injured class of our fellow-men to the dignity and enjoyment of freedom.' By the time the general assembly met in May 1866, over £300 had been collected and forwarded to American Unitarians active in freedmen's aid.[5]

When due allowance has been made for the vagueness of both church and freedmen's society records, it seems fair to suggest that

[1] Letter from the Moderator of the Assembly to the Glasgow Freedmen's Aid Society, Minute Book, C324944, Smeal Collection, p. 45.
[2] *Proceedings*, pp. 325, 481. And see W. Smeal to A. Hampson, 4 July 1866, A.P. C120/37.
[3] See letters from Sella Martin to A. Hampson, A.P. C119/45–50.
[4] J. C. Holbrook to A. Hampson, 2 November 1865, A.P. C118/117; also 7 January 1866, A.P. C118/120.
[5] *The Fortieth Annual Report of the British and Foreign Unitarian Association, Wednesday, June 7th 1865*, London 1865, pp. 6–7, and *The Forty-First Annual Report of the British and Foreign Unitarian Association, May 23rd, 1866*, London, 1866, pp. 13–14.

the various religious groups in Britain raised between them in the region of £5,000 for the American Negro. In all cases examined, freedmen's aid deputations were given a friendly hearing; the Church plainly felt its duty in the matter, and contributions perhaps, in a small way, made up for the past neglect. But the success of the Congregational appeal shows what might have been achieved with better planning, and had all the recommendations which were made been carried through.

Arthur Albright, even in 1865, was sceptical of the value of a denominational approach to freedmen's aid. Although he appreciated the collections of the Methodists and Congregationalists as 'a mark of corporate sympathy on an extended scale', he asked himself whether they could ever 'realize anything like the proportion of *the whole* which the character [,] means and number of those two religious bodies would entitle us to expect.—[A]nd I have a fear that in a chapel collection a great many would give very small sums in comparison either with their means or with what they would do if they gave as citizens to some general collection and that they will hardly give both ways. . . . If all the religious people would set themselves to . . . act together . . . "to stimulate the community at large" . . . they *might* do ten times more than if they acted . . . denominationally and really imbue the mind of England with sound views not only of *our duty* in this crisis but of the exceeding interest that attaches to the issues working out in America —.'[1]

The problem of getting the different churches to co-operate over freedmen's work proved a tough one. William Forster Mitchell, superintendent of Negro schools in the South, viewed rather cynically (he was himself a Quaker) the competing sects which were 'pushing in' to the field, and once remarked, 'There are five [such] Sup[erintendents] of Colored schools in Nashville, . . . and call each other "Brother" but they are not ardent in their friendship for each other.'[2] In Britain the position was similar, even though the work was, by comparison, very small in scope, and the workers for the most part removed from all contact with the Negro. Albright commented with exasperation on a half-empty hall for a meeting in Bath, caused because a local committee member 'from Anti Unitarian prejudice had even avoided informing [Mr.

---

[1] A. Albright to A. Hampson, 10 November 1865, A.P. C117/8–8a.
[2] W. F. Mitchell to J. M. McKim, Nashville, Tennessee, 22 December 1866, Anti-Slavery Papers, Cornell University.

Edwards, the association's Unitarian chairman] . . . or other members of the Society [which included a Unitarian minister] of the Meeting [.] I do think the Meeting lost and the cause has lost by this narrowness.'[1]

It is interesting to find that the culprit here was a Quaker. The contribution of Friends to freedmen's aid in Britain was so important, far exceeding the efforts of any other religious group, that it deserves separate consideration; but the Society was undeniably clannish, an exclusive organization which—though for a time it joined forces with the freedmen's aid societies—preferred and was well equipped to operate charitably within its own ranks.

After a Quaker freedmen's meeting in Kendal in April 1865, a principal speaker commented that Friends 'had an old interest in the question of slavery. It was about 200 years since George Fox saw the effects of slavery in Barbadoes [*sic*] and groaned in spirit over the miseries he could not relieve; and from that time to this Friends had never been without a witness against slavery.'[2]

As we have seen, Quakers in Britain had played a central part in the emancipation struggle, also responding generously to the needs of the freedmen after the Jamaica revolt in 1865, sending out a two-man deputation the following year with over £2,000 at its disposal to help ease distress on the island.[3]

The Civil War in America brought fresh calls upon the British society, both on behalf of the newly emancipated slaves, and from Friends in the Confederate states who found themselves in distress —resisting an enlistment summons on pacifist grounds frequently led to heavy fines, confiscation of property, and even imprisonment.[4] From 1866 Francis King, a leading Baltimore Quaker, organized financial help for the needy Southern members, and of the £138,000 raised by 1891, £50,000 had been given by Friends in England and Ireland.[5]

That the American meetings needed financial support for so

---

[1] A. Albright to T. Phillips, 17 January 1868, A.P. C38/57; also 25 February 1868, A.P. C38/73 pressing for joint meetings which have obviously still to be achieved.

[2] Reported by W. Armistead to L. A. Chamerovzow, 3 April 1865, A.P. C27/76.

[3] *Minutes and Proceedings . . . 1866*, pp. 43–4.

[4] See *Friend*, 1 March, 1863, pp. 53–4; 1 October 1863, p. 243; 1 January 1864, pp. 2–4; 1 July 1864, pp. 155–6; 1 January 1866, pp. 4–5; 1 March 1866, pp. 45–6; *British Friend*, Glasgow, 1 November 1862, p. 270; 1 July 1864, pp. 161–3.

[5] *At a Yearly Meeting Held in London . . . 1861*, p. 317, for British sympathy; Russell, op. cit., p. 417, and *Minutes and Proceedings . . . 1867*, pp. 34–40 for details of part of the British subscription.

long was largely due to the strain imposed on their own funds by
the work of freedmen's aid, Quakers in Philadelphia, New York,
Baltimore, Washington, and Cincinatti being particularly active,
building schools for the Negroes and maintaining teachers throughout the South.[1] These efforts were observed with admiration and
concern on the other side of the Atlantic.[2] Kept in close touch with
American affairs by correspondence and exchange visits, British
Friends, far more than the public at large, recognized the magnitude of post-war racial problems.[3]

Almost as soon as the Emancipation Proclamation came into
effect, a report had been received from New York describing the
condition of the coloured refugees, and the Meeting for Sufferings
(an executive body which acted as a clearing house for information and for action on the basis of that information, and responsible in consequence for a variety of good works) declared that the
'Friends in this country are called upon to manifest their sympathy
in the efforts that are being made by Friends in America for the
relief of these distressed fugitives'.[4]

The following year, 1864, a visit to Britain by Levi Coffin,
though not aimed exclusively at members of the Society, excited
the imagination of Quakers throughout the country.[5] One of the
most successful of the many American fund raising tours on behalf
of the freedmen was undertaken by a Friend, W. F. Mitchell,
in the summer of 1867. During the course of his stay—almost a
year—he attended nearly half the quarterly as well as monthly
and particular meetings, and with three years' teaching experience
in Negro schools to draw on, was an affecting and financially
useful speaker.[6]

English Quakers who had visited the States during and after the

---

[1] See Jones, op. cit., Vol. II, p. 603; Russell, op. cit., p. 414.

[2] See *Letters Written During Joseph Crosfield's Second Journey in America From 19th Aug. 1865
—26th Jan. 1866*, Journal in Friends' House, London; Crosfield, who toured
Tennessee, Virginia, and North Carolina, is full of praise for the work of American
Friends, pp. 56, 67–8, 69, 85.

[3] See *Minutes and Proceedings . . . 1862*, p. 3, for epistles from the Y.M.'s of New York,
New England, Baltimore, Ohio, Indiana, and the Western region. In 1866 the
London Yearly Meeting welcomed an American deputation representing Iowa,
Indiana, Cincinatti, and New York—see *Minutes and Proceedings . . . 1866*, pp. 3–4;
the same Y.M. noted the return of three English Friends from tours in America,
ibid., pp. 18–19.

[4] *Minutes and Proceedings . . . 1863*, p. 56.   [5] Coffin, op. cit., pp. 651–712.

[6] For letters relating to this tour, see A.P. C118/114, C121/151; A. Albright to T.
Phillips, A.P. C38/7, 9, 13, 14, 18, 19, 21, 34, 37a, 39, 40a, 57, 61, 71, 73, 119a,
111; B. H. Cadbury to T. Phillips, A.P. C39/9, 10, 12, 13, 14, 24, 26, 29, 56, 57.

war were expected to report on the conditions and needs of the freedmen.[1] John Hodgkin, as being most familiar with American affairs, was commissioned to produce publicity material, and soon complained when he felt that a Friend similarly placed, cotton spinner Joseph Simpson of Manchester, was not putting his knowledge to good use. 'To *distribute* [information]', he felt, 'is as important as to collect' donations.[2] (In fact Simpson's impressions of America were ultimately published in the *Friend*, the *Reporter*, and in pamphlet form.) J. J. Neave's journal of his visit to the South in 1865 was published at some length in the *British Friend*, while Joseph Crosfield, a Liverpool tea merchant who had made a similar tour, testified in a series of letters home to the 'capacity and intelligence of many of the negroes', their eagerness to learn, and the difficulties placed in the way of progress by extreme physical distress.[3]

While Levi Coffin was in England he had helped to form a freedmen's association in Peckham, consisting mainly of Friends. When the secretary, John Taylor, wanted to stir up fresh interest in the area, he wrote for news, from an eye witness in the work. 'I have corresponded with him regularly', observed Coffin to a friend, and 'received a letter from him . . . requesting . . . some particulars and interesting items from our field of labor—which he said he could use from under my hand to good advantage.'[4] Coffin duly obliged and his letters, together with those of other American Friends, were published to effect in the various Quaker and freedmen's journals.

In February 1863 a freedmen's committee—the first of its kind—was established by British Quakers, and the first appeal to members of the Society issued from London. By May two issues of this appeal had been circulated, and over £2,000 received from meetings throughout the country.[5] A second appeal was printed in 1864,

---

[1] Albright took this in hand, see letter from J. Thompson of Liverpool to Albright, 7 February 1867, A.P. C121/151.

[2] J. Hodgkin to A. Hampson, 7 October 1865, A.P. C118/96.

[3] See *British Friend*, 1 July 1865, pp. 165–7, and Crosfield, op. cit., letter 7, p. 60, letter 9, p. 72.

[4] L. Coffin to J. M. McKim, Cincinatti, 22 November 1866, Anti-Slavery Papers, Cornell University.

[5] *Minutes and Proceedings . . . 1863*, pp. 56–8; Minutes of the Devonshire House Monthly Meeting for 1863, p. 124; 1864, pp. 213, 221–2; 1865, p. 338; 1866, p. 369; 1867, pp. 448, 470; Minutes of the Lewes and Chichester Monthly Meeting, Quaker Ms. 52/8, 132, 137, 141; of the Banbury M.M., 13 March 1863, Minute 4; 1 April 1863, Minute 2; of the Plymouth M.M., August 1866; of the Gloucester and Nailsworth M.M., 10 October 1866, Minute 2; 14 November 1966, Minute 2; 5 December 1866, Minute 1; 13 November 1867, Minute 3.

by which time subscriptions had passed the £3,000 mark.[1] In the meantime visits had been made by prominent Friends familiar with the situation to all but three of the twenty-two English Quarterly Meetings, and correspondence committees were in being at Dublin, Edinburgh, Glasgow, and towns throughout England.[2]

The cause of the freedmen was again urged at the Yearly Meeting of 1865, and during a meeting at the beginning of June it was reported that funds approached £6,000.[3] The following year, the Y.M. was able to claim that the Negroes 'continue to excite the lively interest of Friends in this country', and it hoped 'that efficient measures will be everywhere taken for raising Yearly subscriptions for the promotion of these objects, as long as the pressing need may continue'.[4] Most of the money raised by 1865 went direct to Friends' freedmen organizations in America, with the Friends' Central Committee established in London in March of that year handling operations.[5]

The response of Quakers to these appeals is a remarkable tribute to the respect felt by most members for the decrees and recommendations of their Society. (This was not altogether surprising, however, since failure to obey Society rules generally led to expulsion.) Arthur Albright once complained of this attitude, which made duty take precedence over intelligent interest.[6] But it would be wrong to question the zeal of those most involved in the work and the scale of the donations—whatever the motive of the givers —was certainly most gratifying. After a tour of Friends' meetings in the North, Wilson Armistead paid tribute to the generosity he had encountered, and emphasized 'the strong interest felt by some of those whose means are but small comparatively'.[7] Nor was this generosity without wider effect.

The *Birmingham Daily Gazette* felt that any movement unhesitatingly adopted by 'A class of persons [so] eminently benevolent; proverbially judicious in the application of charities; painstaking and conscientious in inquiries' deserved universal support.[8] A

[1] *Minutes and Proceedings . . . 1864*, p. 50.
[2] *Report [I] of the Central Committee of the Society of Friends, for the Relief of the Emancipated Negroes of the United States, etc.*, London, 1865, pp. 2–3.
[3] *Report of the Central Committee*, p. 2.
[4] *At a Yearly Meeting Held in London . . . 1866*, pp. 49–50.   [5] *Friend*, 1 July 1865, p. 140.
[6] A. Albright to A. Hampson, 10 November 1865, A.P. C117/8.
[7] W. Armistead to L. A. Chamerovzow, 3 April 1865, A.P. C27/76.
[8] 9 May 1864.

leader in the *Manchester Examiner and Times* drew attention to the
fact that 'The Society of Friends are, as usual, first in the field',
and hoped they would not be the last.[1] The *Kendal Mercury* likewise recommended any Quaker philanthropy, since 'The Friends
have a wonderful power of organizing such things, and what can
be accomplished they will accomplish. The question [of freedmen's
aid] is theirs in an especial way and they would be worthy al-
moners of the bounties of all societies—of all persons—who wish
to help the freed slaves of America.'[2]

Quakers welcomed such publicity, hoping to enlarge the scope,
and thus the benefit of their work, by 'inducing the co-operation
of their neighbours and the community at large'.[3] In 1865 the
Friends' Central Committee expressed a hope that they could stir
up interest 'in the different localities, and . . . reach the press in
every town in the kingdom'. But by the end of the year came the
admission that very little progress had been made in this direction.[4]
Such ambitious plans were doomed to failure, and the success
of the work ultimately depended, as with almost all charities, on
the labours of a dedicated few.

However, within the Quaker movement itself, success was
assured. It is difficult to make a completely reliable estimate of the
amount of money the Society raised for several reasons. In the first
place, of course, Friends were not alone in the work of freedmen's
aid. Although the formation of the national Union in April 1866
stirred up ill feeling between the London society and the other
principals, and the former ultimately refused to join, no opposition came from the Friends' Central Committee, which in fact
provided the Union with offices in London from which to operate.[5]

John Hodgkin wrote to the secretary of the National Committee, '. . . I do long that we may have nothing to impede our completely united action for the common good. The work is great, and
it needs the strength of the "faggot" instead of the feebleness of the
individual sticks.'[6] In March 1866 the last meeting of the Quaker
Committee was held in Devonshire House, London. After this
date, although many members of the Society still liked them to go

[1] 20 May 1865.   [2] 8 April 1865.
[3] *At a Yearly Meeting Held in London . . . 1867*, p. 99.
[4] *Friend*, 1 December 1865, pp. 258–9; for similar views see ibid., 1 November 1866,
   1 April and 1 July 1865; and *Minutes and Proceedings . . . 1864*, p. 50.
[5] See *Reporter*, May 1866, pp. 1, 11.
[6] J. Hodgkin to A. Hampson, 28 November 1865, A.P. C118/98; see also J. Simpson to
   A. Hampson, 10 January 1866, A.P. C120/19.

to Quaker projects, contributions from Friends were merged with the funds of the Union, and cannot be easily assessed.[1] It is clear, however, that gifts from wealthy Quakers continued to enrich the various freedmen's associations throughout Britain.

In addition, dedicated individuals like Albright, James Tuke, George Sturge, Joseph Pease, J. J. Neave, and William Pollard gave generously to a number of Society projects in America, without going through the aid societies in their own country, and continued to do so after the latter wound up their activities in 1868. The committee established in that year to correspond with groups in the States about the needs of the Negro was almost entirely composed of Friends, and the money raised by its efforts was contributed by Quakers.[2]

Other Friends responded to the appeals of American agents who toured Britain on behalf of the freedmen, and there is no complete record of their donations.[3] Nor is it apparent whether the various sums collected by the Society at particular meetings throughout the country automatically found their way to the central treasury in London.

Then, too, Quakers in Ireland were independently active, raising slightly more than £1,454 by the middle of 1865, around £1,773 in 1866, £1,673 in 1867, and £1,431 in 1868—a total of just over £6,330, which was sent direct to America.[4] In addition to these Irish efforts, and the £6,000 raised in response to the official appeals by 1865, the combined efforts of Friends throughout Britain appear to have brought in approximately £10,000 for educational purposes, and an appeal from the London Yearly Meeting in 1877 raised over £1,501.[5] At a conservative estimate, members of the Society probably contributed, through its machinery alone, in the region of £25,000 towards the relief and education of the American Negro.

The main reason for the success of the Society of Friends in freedmen's aid work—apart from considerations of discipline and the anti-slavery connexions already noted—was the affluence of

[1] *Friend,* 7 June 1866, p. 120.
[2] Ibid., 1 January 1869, p. 13, and 1 October 1869, pp. 241–2.
[3] See letters between Albright and Dr. J. C. Holbrook of the American Missionary Association, A.P. C121/79, 80, in which Albright tries to find out what the American has netted, and from which sources.
[4] See S. Bewley, Dublin, to A. Hampson, 21 October 1865, A.P. C117/74; also *Reports of the Proceedings of the Yearly Meetings Committees* [of Ireland] for 1866, 1867, 1868.
[5] *At a Yearly Meeting Held in London . . . 1878,* p. 51.

its members. Between 1840 and 1860 the anti-slavery movement was dominated by a comparatively small group of Quakers, highly respected and prosperous business men in London, the Midlands, and the North.[1] The Society of Friends was not numerically large; at the end of 1863 its membership was only 13,761; by the close of 1875 this figure had crept up to 14,253.[2] Its generosity to good causes was made possible not by size but by wealth. (In 1863 it was estimated that the annual gross income of the Society from individual members, legacies, property, and stock was between £2 and £3 millions.)[3]

Applying themselves to work with the same devotion that their religious activities demanded, Quakers generally prospered. Large fortunes, early retirement, and a faith which forbade personal extravagance encouraged philanthropy. Throughout the country they exemplified British humanitarianism—the Cadbury family in Birmingham, the Rowntrees of Scarborough and York, and dauntless individuals like William Collins of Northampton, Thomas Harvey at Leeds, John Rutter of Mere, and Samuel Bewley in Dublin.

Albright himself, when organizing an American fund raising tour on behalf of the freedmen, candidly advised his visitor to go to Essex, for 'in that County there are a large number of Friends Meetings with many *wealthy* people scattered among them from which we ought to get several hundreds'; the country would prove, he felt, 'to be a fat field for us'.[4]

Levi Coffin once wrote to an American friend that the Quakers 'generally manage their Society matters with very little expense to any body', and that the money from England for the freedmen, 'a large part of it from the Society of Friends', was raised 'without any cost of Agencies in collecting'.[5] The efficiency of the Society would certainly have been impaired without the gratuitous services of rich and charitable men like Albright, Charleton, and Tuke.

For all its wealth and international connexions, however, the British Society of Friends did not normally involve itself in conventional missionary activities, as did the Nonconformist sects

[1] Jordon and Pratt, op. cit., p. 126.
[2] *Minutes and Proceedings . . . 1864*, pp. 6–8; *1876*, p. 7.
[3] *Friend*, 1 October 1863, pp. 208–9.
[4] A. Albright to W. F. Mitchell, A.P. C38/13; to T. Phillips, 29 November, 1867, A.P. C38/24.
[5] L. Coffin to J. M. McKim, 7 February 1866, Anti-Slavery Papers, Cornell University.

on whom the anti-slavery movement also depended.[1] But freedmen's aid, because of the Quakers' historic concern for the Negro, was regarded as a 'great missionary work'.[2] As 'this is emphatically the work of the Church at the present time,' wrote one Friend, 'our own spiritual life and prosperity greatly depend upon our being faithful herein'.[3]

An address to the freedmen, prepared by the Meeting for Sufferings in 1868, welcomed the fact that 'many, perhaps most of you, regard this . . . blessing [emancipation] as a gift from God'. A list of duties set out for the Negroes' guidance placed at the top, with heavy emphasis, obedience to God.[4] While noting shortly after the war that moral and truthful conduct was still rare among the freedmen, an editorial in the *Friend* rejoiced that 'no coloured man can be found who is an unbeliever', a bold statement intended for home consumption, and rather more hopeful than truthful.[5] George Fox himself had instructed 'All Friends everywhere that have Indians or Blacks you are to preach the Gospel to them . . . to teach and instruct . . . them to live soberly, godly, and righteously'.[6] Under changed circumstances, his teaching still held good.

From the foregoing survey of the composition of the freedmen's aid movement in Britain, it would appear that three main factors influenced the geographical distribution of societies; these were the survival of old anti-slavery groups or individual abolitionists in certain areas; the presence of prosperous Quaker meetings or Friends; and the existence in any region of even one really enthusiastic supporter, with sufficient time, money, and influence to carry the movement in his locality. Also of importance was the survival of strong support for the American North in Britain, although lingering sympathy for the ex-Confederate states could equally prove a real embarrassment to freedmen's aid.

While it would be misleading to exaggerate the significance of regional differences, and a tempting but mistaken exercise to

[1] See Abel and Klingberg, op. cit., pp. 3–11, for details of overseas missions of Friends in the early nineteenth century.

[2] *Report of the Central Committee*, p. 4; see also *At a Yearly Meeting Held in London . . . 1877*, p. 657.

[3] *Friend*, 1 April 1866, p. 72.

[4] *Minutes and Proceedings . . . 1868*, pp. 54–5.

[5] 1 April 1866, p. 72.

[6] Epistle No. CCLV, Swarthmore, October 1679; *Selections from the Epistles of George Fox*, S. Tuke (ed.), London, 1848, pp. 205–6.

classify all British societies according to any one plan, the most
successful centres do appear to have combined at least two of the
above advantages; a few, like Birmingham and London, possessed
them all.

The Birmingham association was established in 1864 at the
instigation of a local women's anti-slavery society which had been
in existence since the twenties; by May a men's committee had
also been formed and appeals sent out to the public.[1] The city was,
as one of its leading journals remarked, in a leader publicizing the
work of freedmen's aid, 'linked, by a thousand sacred ties, with the
wrongs, . . . the liberation and the destiny of the negro, whose
cause she has so much helped to make, not merely national, but
cosmopolitan'. It was only fitting that the National Freedmen's
Aid Committee should, in 1865, 'be inaugurated, in the town
which is adorned by the statue, and which has charge of the
character and memory, of Joseph Sturge'.[2]

The Quakers involved in these early activities and the society
generally derived inspiration from the visit of American Friend
Levi Coffin, who divided his time between London and Birmingham, working almost exclusively with Quaker contacts.[3] Friends
came to play an increasingly important role in the Midland
society: all three secretaries—Albright, Benjamin Cadbury, and
William Morgan—were Quakers, and others among the committee included John and Joel Cadbury, Bedford Impey, Charles and
Edmund Sturge, A. J. Naish, and Thomas, William, and George
Braithwaite Lloyd. The pro-Union sentiments held by many freedmen's aid workers in Birmingham, for instance S. A. Goddard,
J. C. Gallaway, Morgan, and Albright were not without danger to
the success of the movement, and in a city the size of Birmingham
all shades of opinion on the American war could be found. However, the identification by partisans of the cause of the North with
emancipation accounts in part, it seems, for their sympathetic
view of Reconstruction and the plight of the Negro, which Southern sympathizers tended not to share.

---

[1] See *Annual Report of the Birmingham and Midland Freedmen's Aid Association to May 19th
1865*, pp. 5–6; *Birmingham Daily Gazette*, 31 March 1864, *Birmingham Daily Post*, 13
May 1864; the Local History Collection of Birmingham Reference Library contains
the Minute Book of the Society for 1864–5 (including circulars and newspaper cut-
tings; the entries themselves are not very informative) and annual reports for 1864–5,
1865–6, R. L. Catalogue nos. 361222, 129651.

[2] *Birmingham Daily Gazette*, 12 June 1865.

[3] For reports of his meetings see ibid., 1 and 28 July 1864; *Birmingham Daily Post*, 1 and
27 July 1864.

In London, freedmen's aid was able to draw on the wealth of the metropolis, and the patronage of M.P.s and public men gathered there, such as John Bright, J. M. Ludlow, W. E. Forster, Thomas Hughes, and Newman Hall, all prominent Northern supporters during the Civil War and involved in the work of the London Emancipation Society. Also, rather more important, living in and around the city were a large number of affluent Quakers, enjoined by their church to help the freedmen, among them Samuel Gurney, Benjamin Seebohm, and James Hack Tuke, John Hodgkin, J. B. Braithwaite and J. G. Barclay, William and Stafford Allen, Josiah Forster, John Pease, and Robert and Christine Alsop, all long familiar with anti-slavery work.

Levi Coffin wrote during his visit to England, 'I had become satisfied that if I succeeded in unlocking the heart of the British public I must get the key in London', and refers to two well-publicized meetings in the city attended by, among others, Cobden and Bright, Forster, the Buxtons, F. W. Chesson, and Samuel Gurney.[1] Since the London society declined to join the Union, the papers of that body are not very informative about its progress, though it was clearly a financial success.[2]

Mansfield in Nottingham affords a good example of a freedmen's association sustained largely by the enthusiasm of one man —Henry J. Wilson—working upon that section of the local community receptive to the Northern cause. Wilson corresponded widely on the subject of the Civil War and, later, freedmen's aid,[3] and a London acquaintance congratulated him in 1865 on his personal efforts and 'the glorious success attending the efforts to raise funds. Few if any Towns equal Mansfield in this—'[4] An American worker who toured Britain and visited the town acknowledged gifts of money which would, he felt, be 'enough to build a High School in Washington for the children', which might be called after Mansfield or Wilson himself.[5] Nottingham, though larger, was reported to have a preponderantly pro-Southern population—its 'Newspapers have for four years misrepresented

---

[1] Coffin, op. cit., pp. 660 f.

[2] See letters in A.P. C117/58, C39/10, 13; also *Reception of the Special Delegation to Great Britain of the United States National Freedmen's Relief Association*, Birmingham, 1865, in which the secretary of the London society reported having received £1,100 since Coffin's arrival.

[3] His correspondents included Neal Dow; see letter to Wilson in John Rylands Library English Ms. 741. no. 28(3).

[4] F. Apperson to Wilson, London, 28 April 1865, in ibid., 741, no. 7.

[5] L. M. Hayes to Wilson, London, 8 April 1865, in ibid., 741, no. 64.

the course of events' in America—who 'would contribute very little to the poor liberated slaves'.[1]

It would be wrong to say, however, that Southern sympathies automatically ruled out compassion for the Negro; philanthropy sometimes got the better of politics as the freedmen's movement hoped it would. In Mansfield, Wilson had originally been approached to do something by a draper of the same town 'although we differ very widely as to American politics'.[2] The *Birmingham Daily Gazette* printed and approved a letter from one of the city's M.P.s, William Scholefield, a Confederate supporter; the writer condemned President Lincoln's Emancipation Proclamation and was convinced that it should 'have been accompanied by more far-seeing arrangements for preventing the distress among the freed men which was sure to follow', but added, 'What little I am enabled to give I give with ungrudging pleasure'.[3]

Freedmen's aid gained a foothold in Liverpool, in spite of the presence of large numbers of Southern sympathizers. William Lloyd Garrison visiting Britain under the auspices of the movement after the war confided, 'it would be pleasant to ... take home a marked and hearty expression of good will to the United States from citizens of Liverpool, in view of the aid given to the Southern rebellion by the controlling influences of that great commercial mart', but did not anticipate the warmth of his reception in that city.[4] A freedmen's society was actually formed early in 1864, to which a number of substantial citizens lent their support, among them William Rathbone, Isaac B. Cooke, Andrew Leighton, a local shipbroker, and merchants David Stuart, Charles Edward Rawlins, Robert Trimble, Charles Robertson, John Patterson, and Charlton Robert Hall.[5] Levi Coffin, who visited Liverpool in the same year, records that his trip was successful, and that money raised there was sent out to the Boston Freedmen's Association.[6]

The Bristol society, although adversely affected by political questions, nevertheless continued to do good work; in this case an active secretary—Quaker Joseph Davis—and the strong local anti-slavery tradition probably ensured success. In any event, when the association dissolved in 1868, Davis was able to report 'We have raised altogether upwards of £4,000'.[7]

[1] Letters in ibid., 741, nos. 76, 69.
[2] Wilson to W. F. Webb, 27 February 1865 in ibid., 741, no. 129. [3] 12 June 1865.
[4] Letter d. 3 October 1867 from Frankfort on the Main, in A.P. C39/122.
[5] *Liverpool Daily Post* (Supplement), 8 March 1864. [6] Op. cit., p. 660.
[7] J. Davis to T. Phillips, 29 July 1868, A.P. C39/99.

H

Such sympathetic Friends were invaluable to the movement. During a tour of the north undertaken with William Foster Mitchell in 1867, Albright enjoyed a great success throughout Yorkshire where the Quakers and the cause of abolition were strong. At the county's Quarterly Meeting which he addressed, 'the expressions of interest and satisfaction were numerous and strong and came out spontaneously and incidentally met us wherever we went. We had nearly two days of the pleasantest canvassing work I ever undertook.'[1]

Albright was particularly successful in Leeds, which could call upon the services of the veterans Wilson Armistead and Thomas Harvey, for many years associated with the city's Anti-Slavery Society. (On this occasion £250 was raised. Levi Coffin records that at a meeting in Leeds after a Quarterly Meeting about £1,000 was collected for the freedmen, while on a trip to Leeds in 1866 Albright records raising £450. The same year the *American Freedmen* acknowledged receipt of £1,000 accumulated principally through the efforts of Armistead, following an appeal from the United States published in the London *Herald of Peace*.)[2]

Similarly lucrative visits were paid by the two men in 1867 to York (which yielded £500), where the freedmen's association was headed by a distinguished Quaker doctor, John Kitching, and to Bradford, whose society had an enthusiastic secretary in W. S. Nichols, and enjoyed the financial and moral support of W. E. Forster, M.P. (About £700 was raised in the city during 1865 alone.)[3] Two well-organized public appeals in Sheffield in 1865 raised nearly £700, which was unusually high for such affairs, while even a small village like Ayton was able to collect almost £65 for the freedmen, through the efforts of a local committee led by Quaker George Dixon.[4] Albright and Mitchell were encouraged to extend their tour into Essex simply by the knowledge that local Friends were both interested and active.[5]

In Scotland and Ireland, interest in freedmen's aid appears chiefly in areas where the old anti-slavery societies had operated

[1] A. Albright to T. Phillips, 3 November 1867, A.P. C38/7.

[2] Coffin, op. cit., p. 690; A.P. C119/106; *National Freedman*, Vol. II, 1866, p. 88.

[3] See W. S. Nichols to A. Hampson, 28 October 1865, A.P. C119/75, on Forster's promise of an annual subscription of £50; see A.P. C119/74, also C31/4, 10, C119/77, C120/25 on fund raising in the city.

[4] J. Baker, Sheffield, to A. Hampson, 25 November, 1865, A.P. C117/696; G. Dixon to A. Hampson, 28 September 1865, A.P. C118/29.

[5] See letters in A.P. C38/13. 14, 24, 34.

(though canvassers went much further afield), namely the large commercial centres—Glasgow, Edinburgh and Dundee, Dublin, and Belfast.

As far as Glasgow is concerned, records have survived which show that on the committee of the freedmen's society, formed after a visit from Levi Coffin in 1864, there were at least eleven former Emancipation Society members (founded in 1833, the Society wound up during the American Civil War). The wives of these men provided the nucleus of the ladies' committee which was also established. William Smeal, the well-known Glasgow abolitionist, became secretary and treasurer of the new association. Attendances at committee meetings were not large, but during its four years of activity Dr. Storrs and Sella Martin were entertained from America, and £200 raised for the freedmen, most of which came from the regular subscriptions of faithful followers.[1] This sum, however, scarcely did justice to a city the size of Glasgow, and both Storrs and Martin complained of their poor reception (though, as we have seen, Dr. Holbrook and Sella Martin did well there).[2]

It has been said, to digress briefly, that 'Ideological factors, rather than the direct operation of economic considerations, governed British opinion in relation to the Civil War. If, as a result of that conflict, Yorkshire and Dundee gained much of what Lancashire and Glasgow lost, there is little evidence to show that this had any appreciable effect on opinion about the rights and wrongs of the American struggle.'[3] As regards the reaction of those areas to the freedmen's aid movement, it is noticeable that economic considerations, as a direct result of the war, were important. Thus appeals were far more successful in Yorkshire than in impoverished Lancashire, and in the same way Edinburgh and Dundee contributed far more for the Negroes than did Glasgow. Also, we know that the freedmen's societies made a direct bid for support on economic grounds—reasoning that it was in the interest of businessman and working man alike to promote the well-being and diligence of the cotton-cultivating Negroes of the South.

It is unfortunately almost impossible to tell how far the strength of the movement in say Birmingham, Leicester, and Bradford as

[1] See *Minute Book*, 1864–7, p. 1, C 324944, Smeal Collection; also ibid., 2–3, 19, 21–3, 30–7, 48–9.

[2] See Storrs to A. Hampson, 27 September 1865, A.P. C120/46; and Martin to A. Hampson, 28 September 1865, A.P. C119/48.

[3] R. Harrison, 'British Labor and American Slavery', p. 313.

opposed to Manchester and Liverpool, relates not only to the economic attitudes of the working class but also to the broadening of the franchise in 1867, after which, in the former cities, radicals were drawing working men into the political parties. No doubt in seeking to establish working men's auxiliaries freedmen's groups were relying on the sort of interest in political questions evinced in the North of England during the Civil War, and the special interest taken by some sections of the labour movement in the progress of American democracy.

When we come to look at the Negro suffrage question during Reconstruction, however, we shall see that although conservative commentators were keenly interested, often arguing from the American experience with Negro voters against an extension of the vote in Britain, working men's newspapers like the *Beehive* (vociferous in its comments on the Civil War) were disappointingly silent.[1] Even British Radicals like Bright and Mill tended to regard the concession of the vote to the freedmen with disapproval.

But because working men's auxiliaries only existed, it appears, in three cities, and the wartime interest in American politics was not sustained in the labour press during Reconstruction, we should not assume conclusively that the working class was moved simply by economic considerations. The correspondence files of the London society, the most politically motivated of all the freedmen's groups, may one day shed more light on this difficult subject. While the movement drew its personnel and regular subscriptions from the prosperous and leisured members of society, organizers certainly paid tribute to the generosity of the humble; and it is also of course impossible to determine the class backgrounds of those who gave generously at large town meetings, where donations were anonymous.

To return to Scottish affairs—in the autumn of 1868 Sella Martin, touring on behalf of the American Missionary Association, reported a highly successful meeting in Dundee, as did Dr. Storrs, there about the same time, while in Edinburgh Eliza Wigham was exhorting the public to think of those labouring for the freedmen 'with grateful affection for their work's sake, and [to] grant them their aid, if it may be; and, at all events, their sympathy and prayers', and helping to organize shipments of clothes

---

[1] For Conservative views see for instance *Dublin Evening Mail*, 9 April 1866, 8, 11 January, 8, 22 February, 2 April, 7 December 1867; *Edinburgh Evening Courant*, 11, 17 April, 2 June 1866; *Manchester Courier*, 29 April 1867.

for the Negroes from the city.[1] Local correspondents record that over £500 was collected during the visit of Dr. J. C. Holbrook (also representing the A.M.A.) in 1865, and that the society was still raising money in 1868.[2]

In Ireland the work appears to have been almost entirely in the hands of the Quakers, though it may be that the records of other groups have simply disappeared. Although the Irish in America were regarded by contemporaries as prejudiced on matter of race —they 'cherish a traditional hatred of the blacks' wrote the *Spectator* in 1865, a charge hotly disputed by the Dublin *Freeman's Journal*—the Negro, both slave and free, was not without friends in Ireland itself.[3]

The Dublin anti-slavery movement had long enlisted the support of Richard and John Webb, Richard and Henry Allen, the Pims, the Bewleys, and the Wighams, and these Quaker families, which had helped so many good causes in the city, soon formed themselves into a freedmen's aid committee.[4] Levi Coffin visited Dublin in the autumn of 1864, when he held a public meeting for the cause presided over by the Mayor, and reported in the *Daily Express*. Coffin also went to Cork, Waterford, and other towns in Southern Ireland. The visit was a financial success and was repeated at the turn of the year.[5] Dr. Haynes and his son, representing the A.M.A., made a rewarding trip to Dublin in 1865.[6]

The arrival of Levi Coffin in Belfast in December of that year stirred up interest in the freedmen, and a committee was formed which included, in addition to Quakers, the Mayor, eight clergymen, and a professor.[7] The last named, Dr. James McCosh of Queen's College, followed American affairs particularly closely, ultimately leaving Belfast to become President of Princeton. In November 1866 the *Banner of Ulster* gave prominence to McCosh's report of a recent trip to the States, in which he urged the need to help the freedmen in every way, suggesting that 'If we [in Britain] had deliberated on these topics in time, perhaps we might have

---

[1] See S. Martin to A. Hampson, 28 September, 1865, A.P. C119/48; Storrs to Hampson, 27 September 1865, A.P. C120/46; E. Wigham, *The Anti-Slavery Cause in America and its Martyrs*, London, 1863, pp. 157–9; J. C. Holbrook to A. Albright, 18 May 1865, A.P. C121/79.

[2] See letters in A.P. C40/40, C119/56, 70.

[3] 2 September 1865, p. 977, and 29 February 1868, Leader, respectively.

[4] See Wigham, op. cit., p. 14, and *A Sketch of the History of Friends in Ireland*, London, 1896, pp. 29–30; also A.P. C117/77.

[5] Op. cit., pp. 682–3, 688.

[6] S. Bewley to A. Hampson, 1 October, 1865, A.P. C117/74.   [7] Op. cit., p. 687.

been saved that terrible outbreak in Jamaica and these distressing trials'.[1]

Ultimately, however, in spite of the close ties between the Irish and Americans, through immigration, and memories of American aid during the potato famine of the forties, the work appears to have remained in the hands of Friends, dutifully responding to the succession of appeals which issued from London. Albright at least seems to have doubted the enthusiasm of the rest of the community, for having visited Ireland himself wrote that, outside the Society, 'I dont [*sic*] know a soul that will really interest himself about the collecting'.[2]

Only Wales remains an enigma—for no immediately apparent reason, virtually untouched by freedmen's aid. The Rev. Thomas Phillips and Arthur Albright undertook a tour at the end of 1865, in co-operation with Dr. Holbrook, but its organization was poor, and although Merthyr, Newport, Aberdare, Abergavenny, Neath, and Hereford were visited, and Phillips reported 'There is an abundance of Virgin Soil to break up',[3] nothing further, according to the papers of the movement, was attempted. Possibly as one of the less wealthy regions of Britain it was deliberately neglected. No prominent Friends or abolitionists are referred to as operating in Wales, and the Union only had a limited number of experienced canvassers to send round the provinces. Albright admitted this difficulty to Phillips when discussing activities in the West of England; '. . . I feel sure the soil there is not so barren', he wrote, 'if it were worked and the people who may be moved were set in motion'.[4]

The success of freedmen's aid throughout the country was, then, determined by a number of factors—local attitudes to the Civil War and the Jamaica revolt, the location of anti-slavery societies, Quakers, and interested individuals, and, to some extent, economic conditions; though associations also prospered where circumstances were not auspicious in any obvious way. (Thus by 1868 Leicester had succeeded in raising more than Manchester and Glasgow, in spite of reported distress in the area.)[5] But if we try to assess how the movement fared as a whole, this wide geographical distribution of freedmen's groups becomes misleading.

In 1868 Arthur Albright gave as one possible reason for winding

---

[1] 8 November 1866.   [2] A. Albright to T. Phillips, A.P. C38/37a.
[3] See letters in A.P. C119/95–100.   [4] A.P. C38/78.
[5] See E. Brewin to A. Hampson, 2 July 1868, A.P. C38/143.

up the Union 'the small amount of *public* interest in the question', for 'beyond a limited circle of warmly interested and fairly interested friends it has already been difficult to move even the Christian public to active beneficence in behalf of the Freedmen'. The various affiliated societies were asked for their views on dissolution, and although when the matter had been raised in the autumn of 1867 it 'elicited expressions of surprise and dissent' in some quarters, many local workers were in favour, while a few had lost interest as early as 1865.[1] By the summer of 1868 even the vigorous Birmingham association had recognized that the movement could not survive much longer.[2] The Union was finally dissolved at the end of the year.

The reasons given by local societies for this slackening of interest vary, but many are obvious, and apply to the whole movement. Both in England and America, some people contributed initially because the war had stirred their sympathies and because freedmen's aid was a new and deserving charity, rather than from any particular wish to elevate the Negroes.[3] It was inevitable that such contributors would ultimately transfer their allegiance to some new object. As B. H. Cadbury put it in 1868, 'the time is gone by to produce any effect in raising more money for this cause[;] there are so many fresh ones now afloat that will be more acceptable to the mind of the public', however much dedicated workers might urge that 'the Freedmen will require the sympathy and help of all who love the oppressed, for years to come'.[4]

Other factors of importance in the decline of freedmen's aid were the sharp contraction both in numbers and influence of British abolitionists from the end of the decade, and the difficulty experienced by any charitable organization of penetrating the ignorance or inertia of the masses—in the absence of modern means of communication this might be done through propaganda, public meetings, canvassing tours, and the like, but such methods required money and efficient organization. Problems were also created by the split in the movement (resulting from events in Jamaica), by petty squabbles among members, and by the attitude to the Negro of the British workers themselves.

[1] Circular d. 3 July 1868, A.P. C121/195.
[2] A.P. C39/54 and 64; for other letters noting declining interest see A.P. C39/26, 98, 99, C117/103, C118/44, 54, 55, 139, C119/73, 77, 85, 143.
[3] See McPherson, op. cit., p. 403.
[4] Cadbury to T. Phillips, 28 October 1868, A.P. C39/66; and J. J. Brown to A. Hampson, 3 January 1866, A.P. C117/119.

George Thompson, touring Britain in 1863 on behalf of the Union, wrote to Garrison 'This Anti-Slavery movement is assuming gigantic proportions . . . . It will read a salutary lesson to our public men. It will mould the decisions of our Government. It will neutralize the poison diffused by our journals. It will enlighten and stir up our ministers of religion. It will create the anti-slavery sentiment of the new generation. In a word, it will put England in her old and proper position.'[1] The old abolitionist exaggerated the significance of his reception; although there was an undoubted resurgence of anti-slavery feelings in Britain during the Civil War, it was not sustained.

In fact as early as 1866 local freedmen's aid society secretaries were deploring 'the great indifference of the public generally to the sufferings of their fellow men', the fact that 'the British Public have not felt more sympathy' for the Negroes, and the difficulty of interesting the 'inert masses' in their cause.[2] A correspondent in Evesham wrote 'there is a *great deal* of apathy on the subject and in fact very little is thought about it', while in Essex and elsewhere friends regretted 'the great want of information on the subject even amongst respectable people, many of whom appear to have *no* knowledge of the existence of so gigantic an evil, and as a consequence, are not prepared to assist in relieving it'.[3] This state of affairs was aggravated by a variety of organizational problems.

Just as the American Freedmen's Union Commission was hampered by defections from its ranks and competition from the evangelical associations,[4] the British movement was disturbed from the end of 1865 by arguments between those who wanted to confine themselves to helping American freedmen, and a group which favoured the inclusion of freedmen in all parts of the world. Prior to this the decision of the London society not to join the national Union had caused considerable bad feeling. The correspondence relating to these matters is not particularly edifying, a fact ruefully admitted by Union secretary Thomas Phillips, who declared himself 'most anxious that we should avoid written—especially printed, public controversy. . . . My strongest fear and

---

[1] F. J. and W. P. Garrison, op. cit., Vol. IV, pp. 74–5.

[2] See letters from J. Neave, 11 March 1867, A.P. C119/67; W. Pollard, 3 December 1866, A.P. C119/130; and A. Albright, 3 May 1867, A.P. C117/49.

[3] W. Brown to A. Hampson, 13 November 1865, A.P. C117/122; and letter from J. Shewell, 12 November 1866, A.P. C120/14; (see also A.P. C38/150, C118/85, and C121/127).

[4] See McPherson, op. cit., pp. 402–4.

regret are that the poor Negroes have been—are—the chief
sufferers—and may suffer yet more—if these gross irregularities—
as they are deemed—be allowed to continue. I fear the ill odour
may generate suspicion—contagion—death!'[1]

John Hodgkin feared that the history of the Union proposed in
1866 might turn out to be 'a story of our troubles, and (the ill
natured might add) of our squabbles', and upon receipt of a letter
from J. M. McKim 'in which he speaks of the anticipated destitution as colossal and appalling and affecting hundreds of thousands',
Albright wrote, 'How miserable that our efforts to do our little to
relieve this should be thwarted and impeded by struggles of the
pettiest intestine kind.'[2] The lack of one directing force undoubtedly led to duplication of effort, feuding, and the publication of
two journals when one would have been enough.[3]

Also within the Union clashes of temperament were frequent.
Albright especially, through acting too much on his own initiative,
ran foul of the national committee, and the movement fell down
on actual organization—profitable areas were overworked, until
local contacts took offence, canvassing was neglected, and meetings poorly publicized.[4] By 1869, in consequence, several cherished
projects remained unrealized: the Union had, for instance, in spite
of the valiant efforts of the Birmingham secretary, been unable to
win for the freedmen the very considerable balance of the Lancashire Distress Fund. (Since Americans had contributed generously to this fund, it was felt that a return, via the Negro, would be
most appropriate.)[5]

However, similar charges of bickering and inefficiency can be
brought against United States abolitionists, and while these faults
hampered progress on occasion in both movements, they were
essentially the product of excessive zeal, and cannot ultimately
destroy the grandeur of the anti-slavery impulse or its achievement.
Richard Webb of Dublin made perhaps the best case for the defence when he wrote to his kinsman William:[6]

[1] See letters in A.P. C117/5, 9, 19, 21, 22, 25, C118/66, 68, 71, C119/107, C120/56, 68;
C121/168, 172; and T. Phillips to A. Hampson, 28 January 1866, A.P. C119/103.
[2] J. Hodgkin to A. Hampson, 1 March 1866, A.P. C118/101; and A. Albright to J. C.
Galloway, A.P. C121/148.
[3] See letters in A.P. C118/14, 112.
[4] See letters in A.P. C38/54, 58, 62, 76, 87, 104—Albright and Phillips particularly
had differences; also (on Albright's feuds) C38/19–21, 24, 61, C39/10, 12, 19, 22; and
(on poor organization) C117/49, C121/118, C38/71, C38/40a, C39/166, C119/112.
[5] See letters in A.P. C39/32, C118/106, C121/33, 88.
[6] Dublin, 24 January 1857, Estlin Papers, 24. 125 (54).

I heard your Anna saying (owing to the quarrels it gave rise to,) that there was nothing she so much disliked as Slavery except *Anti*-Slavery. There is no help for it. Any thing which calls forth strong feelings causes dissensions—and no people get so quietly through the world, as those who have no strong opinion about any thing.

In the end, it seems, there was as much danger in the enormous idealism of workers on both sides of the Atlantic as in their quarrels. H. L. Swint has suggested that 'An awakening was inevitable. No group, whatever its merits, powers, or potentialities, could have realized the expectations of the radical abolitionists.'[1] Thus an American Quaker who in 1867 was informing British Friends that the freedmen should enjoy the suffrage as of right, by 1871 wrote 'the condition of the Freedmen is by no means encouraging or satisfactory. . . . The greatest difficulty arises from their extreme ignorance under the rights and responsibilities of full citizenship— their legislation has been a great failure with a few exceptions.'[2]

On the English side, expectations were similarly high, hence Arthur Albright felt obliged to write to American abolitionist J. M. McKim in 1866 protesting at the tales of Negro ignorance and degradation which were being circulated, and which discouraged prospective donors in Britain.[3] There was still, perhaps, something of the spirit detected in an earlier generation of abolitionists, who in 'England's Romantic Age . . . represented the Savage who had only to be released from his chains to become a free and noble man'.[4]

Finally, we may consider the complaint made by some contemporaries, that freedmen's aid and the anti-slavery movement generally made unreasonable demands on public generosity, when so much distress and injustice prevailed at home. Since national felicity is seldom perfect, most missionary work is open to this kind of attack. And if we look at the activities of those involved in freedmen's aid we shall find that the most substantial contributors were nearly always involved in a number of charities.

As the Edinburgh Ladies' Emancipation Society pointed out in its own defence, 'it is generally those who are most liberal to the poor at home who make an extra effort to help the poor abroad, and, in like manner we think it may be found that those who

[1] Op. cit., pp. 56–8, 68.
[2] Francis King of Baltimore to A. Albright, 10 December 1867, A.P. C121/18; and to J. Taylor, 16 May 1871, A.P. C121/90.
[3] A. Albright to J. M. McKim, 16 February 1866, Anti-Slavery Papers, Cornell University.
[4] F. Thistlethwaite, op. cit., p. 116.

would shut up their sympathies from the distant sufferers, are not likely to let them flow very freely even towards those around them, for the principle of love and charity is, like Him from whom it emanates, world embracing'.[1] The Birmingham association was anxious to point out that it did not 'ask persons for contributions who had nothing to spare', while the Duke of Argyll made the telling observation that, though no one should ignore

the misery and poverty in our own country . . . yet I will never admit—for I think it would be confounding great moral distinctions—that the miseries which arise by way of natural consequence out of the poverty and vices of mankind, are to be compared with those miseries which are the direct result of positive law and of a positive institution, giving to man property in man.[2]

When all the criticisms have been made, however, the British freedmen's aid societies may be said to have aroused a final burst of public interest in the anti-slavery movement, and to have encouraged, by their moral support, the American workers in the field. In financial terms the $800,000 raised (the official estimate of W. L. Garrison, but almost certainly too small, in view of the difficulty of estimating donations accurately and the continuing efforts of individuals after official bodies had disbanded) was a fraction of the sum required to maintain operations in the South. During 1865–6 the American Freedmen's Union Commission alone spent approximately $318,670 in cash and $90,755 in supplies.[3] But a clearer idea of the resurgence of anti-slavery feeling which the freedmen's aid movement represented can be gained by comparing its income—around £25,000 annually for the five years 1863–8—with that of the Anti-Slavery Society itself, which during the 1850s and 1860s averaged only £1,000 a year.[4] In view of the pecuniary problems of the latter, the money collected by the freedmen's societies was a credit to the energy and dedication of those who raised it, and a not unworthy contribution towards the relief and education of the American Negro.

[1] *Annual Report . . . 1867*, op. cit., p. 18.
[2] *Birmingham Daily Gazette*, correspondence, 6 and 13 February 1865; *Proceedings at the Public Breakfast Held in Honour of William Lloyd Garrison*, London, 1868, p. 25.
[3] See McPherson, op. cit., p. 403.
[4] See Temperley, op. cit., p. 74, for figures relating to the Anti-Slavery Society's income.

CHAPTER V

Freedmen's Aid in Britain: The Campaign

'By our own past conduct to the negro race, we have placed ourselves under special obligation to come forward and help them freely in their present exigency. Whether the first cargo of slaves was conveyed to North America by the English or the Dutch, it is undeniable that we at a very early stage participated in this nefarious traffic, and ... have largely shared in the profits of this cruel and unrighteous toil.'

Freed-Man, 1865[1]

The broad and underlying purpose of the British freedmen's aid movement was to continue the fight against slavery and its tragic legacy, which had occupied many of the participants or their families—the Gurneys, Allens, and Peases, the Sturges and Alexanders—from the early part of the century. The situation in America was closely parallel to that which had prevailed in Jamaica after the emancipation by Britain of its slave population, except that the West Indian planters had been handsomely compensated for their loss of property. In spite of the anxious care of abolitionists, as we have seen, neither the island nor its Negro population had prospered, and they had finally been rewarded in 1865 with a violent freedmen's revolt, violently put down. Many sceptical eyes would now be turned on America, and although the anti-slavery movement had accomplished much since the 1830s, there was work still to do.

The freedmen's societies in Britain were fully aware how vital would be the 'influence of success in the American problem on the great work yet to be effected in Cuba, Brazil, etc., and the consequent extinction of *slavery* and the *slave Trade* the world-over', and it was pointed out that 'if Slavery, whether in name or in substance, resume her desperate grip on the negroes of the United States, the hopes of freedom for the slaves of Cuba, of Brazil, and of all the South American States, are dashed it may be for half a century.'[2] The work of abolitionists in America had not ended, but

[1] 1 August, p. 12.
[2] J. Hodgkin to A. Hampson, 24 July 1865, A.P. C118/95, and *Reporter*, October 1866, p. 57.

was simply entering a new phase, and the freedmen's associations accordingly launched a duel campaign to re-kindle British pride and British consciences.

Queen Victoria, in her speech at the opening of Parliament in 1866, observed that England 'has always been foremost in showing abhorence of an institution repugnant to every feeling of justice and humanity'.[1] 'May not all *English men . . . unite* on the broad ground of sympathy and help for the slave?' asked the London society in 1863, confident that 'There are thousands of Englishmen who are eager to prove that they have not lost their interest in the slave, and who will *thankfully welcome* their opportunity of doing so.'[2] References to Britain's splendid anti-slavery record came from the platform at most freedmen's meetings, and frequently appeared in press comment.[3]

A more reproachful tone was also common, and a sense of almost personal guilt strong among the religious elements in the movement. An article in the *Friend* in 1864 suggested that 'the sins of the whites against the blacks, in which the people of Great Britain have been so flagrantly guilty, can be partially atoned only by deep repentance and such restitution as can be made'. Writing a year later in the *Friend's Review*, Edmund Sturge predicted

that as the slavery and degradation of the negro in the Western World have been so largely due to the crime and cupidity of the Anglo-Saxon family, their religious, moral and social elevation will . . . be for a long time dependent on the residence among them of those of the superior race who can elevate and not degrade by their example. This is a debt which professing Christendom has contracted through the misdeeds of ages, and we need the Christian labors, and faith and patience of more generations than one, to cancel the debt and roll away its reproach.[4]

It was felt by Radicals like Bright and Argyll that concern and magnanimity would not be easy after the Civil War for Southerners, 'brought up from childhood under the influence of slavery'; unless the Negroes received help from the North and outside

---

[1] *Beehive*, 10 February 1866.

[2] *Prospectus*, The Freed-Man's Aid Society, London, 1863.

[3] See *Sheffield and Rotherham Independent*, 19 May and 18 October 1865; *Birmingham Daily Gazette*, 13 February and 12 June 1865; *British Workman*, 1 May 1865, p. 18.

[4] *Friend*, 1 September 1864, p. 202; *Friends' Review*, (Philadelphia), 3 March 1866, p. 488 (and 7 October 1865, pp. 93–4); see also *Birmingham Daily Gazette*, 31 March 1864, p. 7; A. J. Naish in *Friend*, 1 October 1864, pp. 241–2; *Minutes and Proceedings . . . 1865*, pp. 25–6.

sources they might grow up 'in much of the absolute ignorance and immorality which were the crowing wrong and . . . deepest crime of Slavery'. 'Those who have denounced Slavery', warned the *Freed-Man*, 'must watch over the Freed-men during the transition period, and not allow the want of liberal aid to result in anything which may endanger the stability of freedom.'[1]

Although the British freedman's aid societies maintained close links with the abolitionists in the United States, their priorities— shaped by distance and domestic considerations—were inevitably somewhat different. Americans themselves were divided in their approach to post-war racial problems, with the moderates such as Garrison, S. J. May, and J. M. McKim, though anxious that the freedmen should acquire full civil and political rights, also emphasizing other needs, for instance education, and favouring co-operation with organizations and individuals outside the anti-slavery movement, in conflict with men like Parker Pillsbury and Wendell Phillips, to whom the question of 'suffrage for the negroes is now what immediate emancipation was thirty years ago. If we emancipate from slavery and leave the European doctrine of serfdom extant, even in the mildest form, then the coloured race, or we, or perhaps both, have another war in store.'[2]

While abolitionists of the latter group especially took an anxious interest in the political fabric of Reconstruction, the main purpose of the American freedmen's aid societies was to bring the rudiments of education to illiterate Negroes, subsidiary aims being to alleviate distress, to provide Christian instruction, and, if possible, the opportunity to acquire land.[3] Phillips and his followers attacked these societies as paternalistic—the freedmen, they felt, wanted justice and not charity. Such charges were naturally repudiated, McKim defending freedmen's aid as 'a reconstructive movement. It is to remodel public opinion in regard to the black man by fitting him for [the responsible exercise of equal rights] . . . It is a movement established and conducted in the interest of civilization.'[4]

The British societies, which operated almost exclusively in conjunction with voluntary American groups, both secular and religious, inclined as a result to their rather conservative viewpoint,

---

[1] *Speech of . . . the Duke of Argyll . . . May 17, 1865*, pp. 16, 24; John Bright in *Reporter*, May 1866, p. 7; circular of A. Albright, 3 July 1866, A.P. C121/195; *Freed-Man*, 1 March, 1866.
[2] McPherson, op. cit., p. 306, quoting Pillsbury.
[3] Ibid., p. 393.   [4] Ibid., pp. 397–8.

but were also influenced by very different circumstances. Clearly powerless to influence either property or suffrage reform in the South, and anxious, as we know, to steer clear of domestic and foreign politics alike, the freedmen's movement in Britain, as represented by the national Union, confined its energies to the realization of a few practical goals, with which contributors could identify themselves; namely, the relief of physical suffering through gifts of money and clothing, the provision of simple agricultural equipment, and of schools and teachers for the Negroes.

During and immediately after the Civil War, the most urgent need was to ease physical distress among the four million freedmen, often homeless, invariably without possessions. Freedom was a great gift in itself, but 'the circumstances under which that boon had been bestowed have often mingled the bitterness of destitution and disease with the cup of blessing, and have in many instances been followed by death'.[1] Without constant work and watchfulness, the evils of freedom might even appear to outweigh those of slavery; and it was a matter of common sense that the freedmen had to 'have *food and raiment* before they can take in the elements of intellectual culture'.[2]

Appeals for help based on harrowing accounts of the sufferings of ex-slaves were published regularly in the *Freed-Man*, the *Reporter*, and the Quaker journals; pamphlets were put out by the Society of Friends, approximately 32,000 copies of which circulated, all underlining an aspect of freedmen's aid which led Wendell Phillips to describe it sourly as a work of charity, an 'old clothes movement', but to which British workers attached importance, if only as a preliminary to the great task of education.[3]

It seems, too, that the emphasis on Christian charity and suffering humanity was designed to move those who might feel little fondness for Negroes as such, and was certainly intended to touch female hearts, as the anti-slavery movement had always done. As the Ladies' London Emancipation Society put it, 'There are various considerations connected with the institution of slavery, which make it, far more than is the case in ordinary politics, a

---

[1] *Minutes and Proceedings . . . 1864*, p. 51.   [2] *Friend*, 1 January 1866, pp. 8–9.

[3] *Freed-Man*, 1 September 1865, pp. 20–2; 1 January 1866, pp. 140–1; 1 April 1866, pp. 221–2; 1 March 1868, pp. 38–9; *Reporter*, September 1866, p. 49; December 1866, pp. 86–7; March 1867, pp. 1, 111, 113–4; *Friend*, 1 May 1865, pp. 94–6; 1 October 1865, pp. 207–8; 1 December 1865, pp. 258–9; *British Friend*, 1 July 1864, pp. 169–71; 2 October 1865, pp. 250–1; see also *Report of the Central Committee*, pp. 2–3; McPherson op. cit., p. 397.

question especially and deeply interesting for women, and demanding the fullest exercise of their influence and activity.'[1] After as before 1863, women of sufficient leisure and philanthropic bent were entreated to form sewing circles and make clothes for the Negroes; once they had raised a small sum to finance these activities, the British freedmen's Union was prepared to augment their funds.[2]

A series of circulars issued by the Birmingham society during 1864 and 1865 placed great emphasis on physical distress; in the latter year, a typical appeal entitled *A Plea for the Perishing*, referring especially to conditions in Georgia and Alabama, pointed out that normal hardships were[3]

being made more terrible by the intensely severe American winter, . . . many thousands [of Negroes] will actually die from want and exposure to the cold, notwithstanding public efforts put forth on their behalf; and these not only the aged, the weakly, and the young (very many of those being fatherless, motherless, or parentless), but also the able-bodied—both men and women.

Freedmen's aid activities received a fair amount of coverage in the press, especially in areas—such as Birmingham—where strong societies existed, and newspapers generally chose to highlight physical suffering, either because it made good copy or as the least controversial aspect of the work.

'Our aid in this good service is greatly needed', wrote the *Manchester Examiner and Times* in 1865; 'We require no special evidence to convince us that numbers of the freed negroes must be in a state of deplorable destitution.'[4] The *Daily News*, while acknowledging the achievement of American workers and the self-reliance of the able-bodied freedmen, reminded its readers of 'the large army of women and children, the sick and aged, many of whom have no natural protectors, and all of whom must, in some way, be provided for until they are able to provide for themselves'.[5]

A leader in the *Birmingham Daily Gazette* at the end of 1864 drew attention to the 'thousands of our fellow creatures dying from

---

[1] *The First Annual Report of the Ladies' London Emancipation Society*, London, 1864, p. 4.

[2] See *Reporter*, December 1867, p. 21 and November 1866, pp. 66–7; also *Darlington Telegraph*, 24 June 1865; *Birmingham Daily Gazette*, 3 November 1864, 30 March and 3 April 1865; letter in A.P. C120/13; *Annual Report of the Birmingham and Midland Freedmen's-Aid Association, to May 19, 1865*, p. 8.

[3] Circular letter written by B. H. Cadbury, Birmingham, 27 December 1865, A.P. C39/50.

[4] 20 May 1865.   [5] 14 June 1865.

famine, cold, and disease'; 'poor black pilgrims who have broken down on their journey to the promised land of freedom, [who] must die by the wayside unless timely aid is given to comfort their hearts and heal their bodies'; its appeal, as a later editorial explained, was expressly directed 'to those who are ready to aid the suffering and succour the distressed, without too minutely considering the causes [namely Civil War] which brought them to grief'.[1]

Similar appeals to the emotions were made at public meetings on behalf of the freedmen. Presiding over a gathering in the city in 1865, the Mayor of Sheffield remarked 'that all people must be aware of the deep distress that existed amongst the free coloured people on the other side of the Atlantic. The reports in the papers had shown . . . a very harrowing state of things', and he hoped his audience would not fail to respond to such a cause.[2] At a meeting in Preston the same year, one of the principal speakers spoke of the Negroes as:[3]

deeply in want of all the aid which Christian benevolence can bestow upon them. Hunger and nakedness are pleading for your assistance; . . . the perishing are praying, hoping to be delivered. They who have hurried into freedom from the lash and the fetters of the slave-holder have suddenly found themselves held fast by the bonds of poverty, which it is hoped your Christianity will help them in removing. The infirm, the aged, and the orphan, of whom there are great numbers, require particular consideration. . . .

American deputations to Britain for the most part sensibly adopted a comparable approach. Thus the Negro preacher Sella Martin suggested to an assembly at Sheffield that in the face of starvation, disease, and death, there was no place for the political feuds of wartime; 'Practical men will not stop to deal with the dead things of the past, and the question which presses for immediate solution by America and England is—What must be done to rescue these perishing ones ?'[4] An earlier meeting in the city had listened to a report from the Western Freedmen's Aid Commission

---

[1] 29 December 1864, and 2 January 1965; see also, for typical appeals, *Christian World*, 15 and 22 September 1865; *Dublin Evening Mail*, 11 and 27 January 1866; *Preston Guardian*, 4 March 1865; *British Workman*, 1 May 1865, p. 18; *Birmingham Daily Post*, 5 January 1865; *Birmingham Daily Gazette*, 12, 18, 30 January 1865, 3 April, 4 May, 18 July 1865; *Darlington Telegraph*, 8 April 1865.

[2] *Sheffield and Rotherham Independent*, 19 May 1865.

[3] *Preston Guardian*, 11 March 1865; also *Blackburn Patriot*, 17 June and 1 July 1865.

[4] *Sheffield and Rotherham Independent*, 24 October 1865.

of America, describing the freedmen as 'in a condition of wretched-
ness and want—men, women, and children—clothed in rags, toil-
worn by marches, depressed and afflicted by privations and exposure', a state of affairs confirmed by the Commission's representative, Levi Coffin.[1]

The freedmen's societies were careful to stress, however, that the
Negro was neither responsible for nor anxious to prolong his degradation, and that Americans were themselves striving to alleviate
distress. Some British observers were inclined to blame conditions
on the Federal government, which had failed to make ample provision for emancipation.[2] To such individuals the Birmingham
society suggested that:

> Whether our sympathies be with the North or with the South . . .
> whatever our estimate of slavery, . . . whatever our view of the negro's
> place in nature . . . matters little. Those who think him merely a
> brute will yet acknowledge that he is a brute who needs food, shelter,
> . . . clothing. Those who think slavery his proper condition ought to be
> ready to mitigate, so far as they can, the hardships of the unnatural
> lot of freedom, which, in their view, though not in his own, has been
> forced upon him by a cruel military tyranny.[3]

The activities of freedmen's groups in the States were publicized
in the journals of the British movement, and by visiting lecturers.
An 'Appeal to the People of England', issued by the National Committee (forerunner of the Union) reminded critics that 'the American Government, by the supply of abundant rations, and the
people, by the formation of several very efficient Freedmen's Aid
Associations, and by individual sacrifices of the highest order, all
freely and efficiently rendered amidst the pressure of a gigantic
war, and the anxieties of its sudden collapse, have clearly acknowledged their full . . . obligation in this work of humanity.'[4]

But perhaps, most of all, it was necessary to vindicate the character of the Negroes themselves. If Victorians tended to regard lazi-

---

[1] *Sheffield and Rotherham Independent*, 18 October 1864.
[2] See for instance *Birmingham Daily Gazette*, 5 May 1864, p. 6, col. 6; 1 July 1864, p. 7,
col. 2; 7 July 1864, p. 7, col. 2; 29 December 1864, Leader; letter from Birmingham
M.P., Mr. Scholefield, 12 June 1865, p. 5., col. 2; 23 February 1865, p. 3, col. 6.
[3] *The Freedmen's Aid Commission*. See also, for stress on work being done by the American
government, pamphlet issued by Birmingham society in 1864; *The Case of the Freed
Refugees from Slavery in America*.
[4] *Four Millions of Emancipated Slaves in the United States, etc.*, op. cit., p. 2; also *Plea for the
Perishing*, pp. 4, 6; *The Freedmen's Aid Commission*; *Daily News*, 14 June 1865; letter by
Albright in *Birmingham Daily Gazette*, 2 January 1865.

ness as the chief vice and downfall of West Indian freedmen, they had no wish by excessive charity to encourage a similar trait among the coloured population of the South. The Birmingham society therefore argued:[1]

> Whether we regard the welfare of the Negroes, the interests of the owners of estates in the South, or those of the English people as the largest consumers of cotton, it is most important to sustain a movement which furnishes the freed man at once with continuous employment, and, as far as possible, in the cultivation of the soil, without that interregnum of idleness which would prove . . . disastrous to his future career.

Appeals emphasized that the freedmen 'are not only capable of sustained labour, but most desirous to obtain employment'.[2] The Ladies' Negro's Friend Society for Birmingham testified to the Negroes' 'ability and willingness to work under the stimulus of the same motives that influence other races to labour', and Edinburgh Ladies suggested that even if not all the coloured people were self-sufficient, 'shall we not . . . find cause for admiration that, notwithstanding all . . . difficulties, so many have become independent; . . . It is abundantly proved that the negroes, when favoured with ordinary advantages, are not indolent'.[3]

Meetings of the Birmingham and Leeds freedmen's associations, and the Ladies' London Emancipation Society during 1865 stressed that the Negroes 'may not only be helped, but educated and habituated to self-help'.[4] 'The voluntary missionaries of humanity', it was reported, 'who labour among them exercise judgment and discrimination in their work, particularly in the distribution of gratuitous relief. To raise the people by instruction and to help them to help themselves are steadily kept in view.'[5] Tribute was paid to the freedman's 'eagerness for work, and aptitude . . . in learning different trades', and a pamphlet put out by the Birmingham group commented approvingly, that 'no feature presents itself more encouraging and auspicious for the future of these now destitute people than the steady organization of

---

[1] *Considerations on the Transition State of the Freed Coloured People in America*, Birmingham, 1864.

[2] *Freed-Man*, 1 November 1865, p. 73.

[3] Report for 1864 (39th), p. 7, in Birmingham Reference Library, and *Annual Report of the Edinburgh Ladies' Emancipation Society . . . 1867*, pp. 7, 13, 11; see also *Report [II] of the Central Committee*, pp. 11, 12, 19; *Friend*, 1 October 1864, p. 227; *Minutes and Proceedings . . . 1864*, pp. 51–2.

[4] *Annual Report of the Birmingham and Midland Freedmen's-Aid Association to May 19, 1865*, pp. 10–11.

[5] *A Plea for the Perishing*, p. 7.

employment producing the necessaries of life, by the cultivation of the soil, and of education combined with industry. It is thus that the true emancipation of the Negro will be best secured.'[1]

American reports were similarly encouraging. The Quaker superintendent of Negro schools in Tennessee and Alabama maintained that his charges were diligent and would not require permanent support; 'I know nothing', he wrote, 'of the *idle lazy negro* basking in the sun', tales of which had so infuriated opponents of British policy in Jamaica.[2] The Rev. W. H. Channing vouched for the 'enterprise, industry and skill of the freedmen', and the Negro leader Frederick Douglass, while he initially opposed aid 'on the ground that [it] would foster in the public mind the popular idea, that the negro in a state of freedom cannot take care of himself', came to regard the work of freedmen's societies as essential, 'a real charity—one which the merciful Father will own and bless'.[3]

The Negro, we should notice, is presented throughout the appeals of the British movement as fulfilling essentially his pre-war economic role in American society: he was to be an agricultural labourer, working probably on a cotton plantation, different only in his possession of freedom (which might itself prove precarious without the backing of civil and political rights).

It is unlikely that philanthropists in Britain could have influenced in the slightest degree the position of land or labour in the South, even if they had shown any disposition to quarrel with contemporary assumptions about the sanctity of property and the place of the Negro in society, which basically they did not. Recent historians have deplored the defeat of American Radicals and abolitionists by the race prejudice and economic attitudes of the nation at large, which saw the freed slaves in terms of a pliant labour force, poor, and thus, by implication, inferior, and which expressed a characteristic nineteenth-century opposition to any form of initiative sapping paternalism.[4]

An interesting questionnaire prepared by the Boston Emancipation League in 1863 and sent to all the camps at which Negro

---

[1] *The Second Annual Report of the Ladies' London Emancipation Society*, p. 24; (see also *Birmingham Daily Post*, 5 January 1865); and *Birmingham and Midland Association for the Help of the Refugees from Slavery in America, by a Vessel to be Freighted with Stores*, Circular no. 2 of the Birmingham Society, Birmingham, 1864, p. 4.

[2] *The Freedman in Tennessee and Alabama*, Circular no. 13 of the Birmingham Society, Birmingham, 1865.

[3] *The Rev. W. H. Channing on the Freedmen of America*, op. cit.

[4] Stampp, op. cit., pp. 120–35, and McPherson, op. cit., pp. 407–16.

refugees had gathered, inquired of those in charge whether the freedmen were 'fit to take their places in society, as a laboring class, with a fair prospect of self support and progress? Or do they need any preparatory training and guardianship?'[1] The fact that friends of the Negroes could doubt their need for special help, and ignore the government's duty to provide it, illustrates well the prevailing climate of opinion from which the freedmen's aid movements in both countries could not escape.

A New York Friend advised British Quakers who wanted to help the Negroes to buy land for them, as much as possible, and in as many states as possible, and the Birmingham association was anxious to assist them obtain homesteads under the provisions of the 1862 Act, but apparently nothing was achieved in this sphere.[2] The only practical help Britons could offer was in the form of agricultural equipment, the lack of which, combined with their far more serious lack of capital, prevented the freedmen from becoming independent small farmers.

Self-interest is in evidence here, as in the appeals for working-class support. At its annual meeting in 1865, the Birmingham and Midland society reported that many local tradesmen members had contributed simple implements (one man had given £100 for the purchase of hoes) as well as household goods and clothing for the Negroes, and these would, it was felt,[3]

prove, in their degree, invaluable instruments in procuring the livelihood of the free people ... in the supply of the finest cotton to the mills of Lancashire; and will also prove the means of reviving commerce, and promoting the material and social well-being of the dwellers on both sides of the Atlantic.

A special appeal for hoes circulated by the principal officers of this association stated: 'We believe that, at a computation *very far indeed* within the truth, every hoe now sent out may be looked upon as a seed that will bear a whole bale of cotton before the year is out.'[4]

From a long term point of view, however, the supplying of

---

[1] *Facts Concerning the Freedmen. Their Capacities and Their Destiny. Collected and Published by the Emancipation League*, Boston, 1863, p. 3.

[2] *Friend*, 1 January 1866, pp. 8–9, and *Reporter*, August 1866, p. 27.

[3] *Annual Report of the Birmingham and Midland Freedmen's-Aid Association to May 19, 1865*, pp. 7–8.

[4] *Birmingham and Midland Freedmen's-Aid Association*, n.d., John Rylands Library pamphlet; see article in *National Freedman*, Vol. II, 1866, pp. 44–5, in which Americans praise this venture.

material needs came second to 'the endeavour to impart education in its full and Christian sense to the forlorn outcasts'.[1] The need was obvious, since slaves by Southern state laws had been explicitly barred from receiving even rudimentary instruction. Equal civil and political rights were now promised, but while they remained illiterate the Negroes could neither exercise such rights fully, nor even be sure of keeping them. As McKim told Arthur Albright:[2]

> If the blacks are kept in ignorance they can be subjected to a system of serfdom . . . If we enlighten them they are secure against the machinations of their old enemies—to which they will always be subject until educated.

There were, however, domestic reasons for attaching great importance to this aspect of freedmen's aid. The 1860s in Britain were marked by a growing preoccupation with educational reform—with the need to provide simple instruction for those who needed it. W. E. Forster told the Commons in 1870 that 'On the speedy provision of elementary education, depends our industrial prosperity, the safe working of our constitutional system and our national power. . . . if we are to hold our position among the nations of the world, we must make up for the smallness of our numbers by increasing the intellectual force of the individual.'[3]

If education was essential to the future of Britain, small wonder that the freedmen's societies hoped it might prove a panacea for the problems of American Negroes. Thus their declared aim 'was not only to supply the present pecuniary wants and to relieve . . . [the freedmen] in their present need, but also to impart to them religious and moral education, so as to fit them for the exercise of their rights and duties as freedmen'.[4]

A Leicester contributor wrote in 1869, 'I do not know of any better object for promoting the best interests of this class than in furnishing the means for the extension of education.'[5] Joseph Simpson of Manchester felt after a four-month trip to the United States that 'What is now wanted is, that . . . [the freedmen] shall be educated, so as to fit them for the duties of citizenship; and, though it may even be years before they obtain their full and equal rights, I feel sure that we cannot aid them better in this matter than by furnishing them with those educational advantages which have

[1] *Friend*, 1 March 1864, p. 60.   [2] Quoted in McPherson, op. cit., p. 393.
[3] See Young, op. cit., p. 115.   [4] *Birmingham Daily Gazette*, 28 July 1864.
[5] T. Burgess to T. Phillips, 1 October 1869, A.P. C39/4.

hitherto been so studiously denied them.'[1] In 1865, a Hitchin Quaker, Frederick Seebohm, described the new schools as 'the one hopeful element in the present condition of things'.[2] The Ladies' Negro's Friend Society of Birmingham and district, which maintained a keen interest in freedmen's aid throughout and beyond the sixties, emphasized the importance of education, and took pleasure that (in 1869) 'the cost of 1,000 teachers [for the Negroes] is mainly provided for' by the British movement.[3]

American workers confirmed the British diagnosis. Thus J. M. McKim reported: 'We find that instruction and physical aid—to make either *fully* effective—must go hand in hand. Instruction adds one hundred per cent to the value of material relief.'[4] The British public was clearly receptive to this type of appeal, for the papers of the National Union contain many such, from American organizations promoting educational work among the Negroes, those chiefly concerned being the Garnet League (a Negro group); the Friends' Freedmen's Associations of Philadelphia and New York; the American Missionary Association; the Baltimore Association for the Moral and Educational Improvement of the Coloured Race; the American Freedmen's Union Commission; the Western Freedmen's Aid Commission; and the Pennsylvania Freedmen's Relief Association; all of which received financial support from Britain.[5]

Both movements were similarly impressed by the eagerness of the freedmen to acquire education, and their ability to learn. A Bristol society circular on the subject quoted an ex-Confederate General as saying:[6]

The negro is very teachable. . . . Education will not be lost upon him. It is our duty to do all in our power to place the lamp of learning in his hands. The Freedmen only require to be educated to make excellent citizens. I did not think so ten years ago, but do now.

[1] *Freed-Man*, 1 November 1865, p. 73.
[2] F. Seebohm to A. Hampson, 2 November 1865, A.P. C120/7a.
[3] See Reports for 1864, 1865, 1866, 1868–9, 1871, in Local History Collection of Birmingham Reference Library; especially Report for 1865, Appendix, pp. 56–8, and for 1868–9, p. 20.
[4] Circular no. 15 of the Birmingham society, Birmingham, 1865, John Rylands Library.
[5] See letters in A.P. C39/78, 80a, 100, 120, C117/144, 146, C118/28, 77, 117, 120, C119/4, 37, 133, C120/23, 27, 48, C121/36, 43, 79, 80, 87, 88, 90, 100, 103, 104.
[6] Bristol circular, 1 January 1868, A.P. C120/84; for other American assurances about Negro capabilities see *A Plea for the Perishing*, op. cit., p. 5; Circulars no. 11 and 13 of the Birmingham society.

Writing home from America in 1868, Bristol abolitionist Mary Estlin was able to confirm these claims, and commented enthusiastically on a meeting of teachers returned from the South for their summer vacations, to which she had been taken by William Lloyd Garrison, Maria Weston Chapman, and other friends of the Negro. 'I must not attempt to repeat their narratives', she confided, as 'some were thrilling, all touching as showing the devotedness of these laborers and their trials, and every report was encouraging; proving the rapidity and eagerness with which the negroes learn, and their progress towards independence.'[1]

The *British Workman* told its readers, 'the eagerness of the freedmen in learning to read and write is most extraordinary, as the various reports of the Freedmen's Aid Societies pleasingly testify. A few years will doubtless see many of those emancipated slaves taking a high stand in the schools of learning'.[2] Edinburgh ladies noted that the Negroes 'beg harder for a school than for food or clothing', and cited their 'eagerness for learning . . . [as] another proof of energy and perseverance'. Coloured children, it was felt, were as bright as white, and 'Of the capacity of the negro to receive and use the education he is seeking, there can be no doubt'. The London society echoed these beliefs.[3]

Attention was frequently drawn in the British freedmen's aid journals to the eagerness of Negroes of all ages to learn, even after the novelty had worn off; to their capacity to benefit from it; to the growing skill of coloured teachers; to the need to educate and elevate an innocently illiterate people, thus equipping them for their new life; and to the danger of relying on the initiative of an obviously poor and embittered South.[4]

As far as the importance of education was concerned, philanthropists found themselves for once in agreement with public opinion as a whole. Neither the British press nor travellers of the period really questioned the ignorance of the majority of Negroes, and would have been foolish to do so. Slavery indeed, as J. M.

---

[1] Mary Estlin to Rebecca Moore, 18 July 1868, Estlin Papers, 24.121(6).

[2] 1 June 1866, p. 166.

[3] *Annual Report of the Edinburgh Ladies' Emancipation Society, and Sketch of Anti-Slavery Events and the Condition of the Freedmen During the Year Ending 1867*, pp. 13, 15, 16–17; and *The Second Report of the Ladies' London Emancipation Society*, p. 24.

[4] See for instance, *Reporter*, December 1867, p. 21; May 1866, pp. 4, 10, 13; November 1866, p. 74; July 1866, p. 35; March 1867, p. 116; *Freed-Man*, 1 September 1866, pp. 22–4; 1 December 1866, p. 63; 1 December 1865, p. 122; 1 June 1867, pp. 166–9; 1 July 1867, p. 180.

McKim testified, 'darkens the mind—dulls the intellect—perverts the affections'; while Henry Rowntree, an English Quaker who had gone out to help in the new schools wrote bluntly that 'The work is immense. The Negro has little conception of his duty to God or man . . . and it requires labour, steady untiring labour to convince [him].'[1]

The only question which remained was whether the freedmen were susceptible to education, and if so, up to what level. It was on this point that freedmen's aid workers often parted company with other British observers, the latter inclining to the view of popular journalist W. H. Dixon that the Negroes' desire to learn was 'a spark—a flash—and it is gone'.[2]

There were some, however, who shared the philanthropists' optimistic attitude. Thus Sir George Campbell, Liberal M.P. and colonial administrator for many years, writing in the late seventies, noted that 'The negroes show a laudable zeal for education', had made enormous progress since emancipation, and that some displayed 'an educational capacity quite equal to that of good whites'. (He did add, though, the familiar criticism, that 'while the younger children are as quick and bright as white children, they do on the average fall off in some degree as they get older'.)[3]

In the same way Scottish writer and missionary David Macrae, a not uncritical commentator, was delighted by the 'extraordinary spectacle . . . of an ignorant and enslaved race springing to its feet after a bondage of two hundred years, and with its first free breath crying for the means of education'. The Negro children, he wrote, 'were wonderfully eager over their lessons', but then so too were the older freedmen, and 'it would be interesting to know how many uneducated adults in England, Scotland, and Ireland—white people though they be—are striving, as the negroes in these night-schools are doing, to make up for the educational deficiencies of early years!' Macrae dismissed stories that the freedmen could not be raised beyond a certain stage, and concluded that such men would 'cease to be exceptional when the negro has come

[1] J. M. McKim to A. Albright, 6 March 1866, Anti-Slavery Papers, Cornell University; and *Friend*, 6 June 1863, pp. 144–5.

[2] *The White Conquest*, London, 1876, 2 Vols., Vol. II, p. 169; see also J. Bryce, *The American Commonwealth*, London, 1888, 3 Vols., Vol. 3, pp. 92–3; G. A. Sala, *America Revisited*, London, 1882, 2 Vols., Vol. 1, p. 295.

[3] See Swint, op. cit., pp. 71–4 and H. Donald, *The Negro Freedman*, New York, Schunan, 1952, pp. 100–1. Also Campbell, *White and Black*, London, 1879, pp. 130–6.

to enjoy, as he is now beginning to do, the same opportunities as the white man for developing what power he has'.[1]

At the Washington Embassy one of the most conservative members of the British delegation, Clare Ford, admitted privately to Lord Stanley that attempts to teach the freedmen 'have been readily responded to by negroes of both sexes and of every age', who showed 'an ardent desire to avail themselves of every means of gaining instruction', with the result that many Southern planters 'find advantage in the employment of negroes whose educational attainments, however scanty, are a guarantee for good conduct'.[2]

The freedmen's associations in both countries originally concentrated almost exclusively on imparting the most rudimentary education to the masses. But when, by 1866, the enormous expense and difficulty of such a programme had been realized, there was a movement towards the establishing of normal schools and colleges to train Negro teachers—perhaps also in recognition of the hopelessness of desegregating existing establishments.[3] This change of emphasis is reflected in the appeals of the British movement, and the hope was that qualified freedmen might continue the work of educating their race once outside help was withdrawn.[4] A fund-raising circular drawn up in 1867 declared:[5]

Bishop McIlvaine [of Ohio] at [a] ... Meeting of the National Freedmens Aid Union at Birmingham ... speaking as one of the Trustees of the Peabody Fund[6] stated that their great want would be that of suitable Teachers and he therefore would much estimate the proposal to train colored Teachers.

The Yankee school marm who went South on what W. E. B. DuBois called the 'Ninth Crusade'—'a mission that seemed to our

---

[1] Op. cit., Vol. II, pp. 57–69; see also Marquis of Lorne, *A Trip to the Tropics, etc.,* London, 1867, pp. 309, 335; W. Saunders, *Through the Light Continent,* London, 1879, pp. 85–7; Dilke, op. cit., Vol. I, p. 24; F. B. Zincke, *Last Winter in the United States,* London, 1868, p. 61.

[2] Ford to Stanley, 28 September 1867, F.O.5 1108, no. 9, Public Record Office, London.

[3] See McPherson, op. cit., pp. 405–6.

[4] For letters on the change, see above p. 125, n. 5; and see B. H. Cadbury to T. Phillips, 27 July 1868, A.P. C39/70; also on the importance of normal schools in British eyes, A.P. C38/43, C40/52, C118/144, C119/125, C120/21.

[5] Draft appeal for educational funds, 29 October 1867, A.P. C118/114.

[6] Fund of c. $3,500,000 (in existence until 1914; set up by American philanthropist George Peabody for the promotion of education in the South). See J. L. M. Curry, *A Brief Sketch of George Peabody, and a History of the Peabody Education Fund Throughout Thirty Years,* Cambridge, Mass, 1891.

age far more quixotic than the quest of St. Louis seemed to his'—
and in fact all who taught in the freedmen's schools or settled in
that region during Reconstruction experienced considerable local
hostility.[1] An obvious solution to the educational problem, it
seemed, and one which would foster self reliance among the
Negroes, at the same time relieving them of the unpleasant feeling
of dependence on white charity, was to train coloured teachers.
(Though it should be noted that some of the voluntary religious
agencies opposed the establishment of normal schools, perhaps
because it would weaken their hold on the Negro.[2] However, W.
F. Mitchell and Francis T. King, two American workers on whose
advice the British movement heavily relied, were in favour of the
programme.)

Unfortunately this practice while removing one difficulty raised
another, of lasting significance. The freedmen's aid movement,
for all its idealism, failed to prevent practical segregation from
developing in its schools; in June 1867 of its 111,442 pupils, only
1,348 were white.[3] Very often this state of affairs was the fault of
the whites, who refused to allow their children to attend mixed
classes—sometimes teachers simply abandoned the unequal
struggle, adopting the compromise principle of separate but equal.

An interesting example of this (as it now appears) short-sighted
policy, and the situation which produced it, is the school founded
at Mandarin, Florida, by Harriet Beecher Stowe, which was
partly supported by anti-slavery stalwarts in Bristol, including the
Estlin family. Mandarin was a fairly typical venture—the school
built by the Freedmen's Bureau, tuition undertaken by 'a missionary and a female teacher', land provided and salaries paid by
Mrs. Stowe. In 1869, six months after the school had been established, she wrote to Mary Estlin:

you have no idea what it is to start such a school amid the prejudices
of such a community. In the first place, tho' they are pleasant and kind
enough,—the old white settlers regard us Yankees with some suspicion.
They also despise the negroes and hate them. The negroes naturally
are wary and do not give their confidence at once. They are *very*
ignorant and untaught.

Although Mandarin was to cater for black and white children,

---

[1] *The Souls of Black Folk*, London, 1905, p. 25.
[2] See W. F. Mitchell to J. M. McKim, Nashville, Tennessee, 12 April 1866, Anti-
Slavery Papers, Cornell University; also A.P. C121/88.
[3] See McPherson, op. cit., p. 400.

for 'Teaching the whites is the only way of protecting the blacks', they were to be separated, 'To try to put them in ... [the same] room would raise a rebellion at once.'[1] Obviously her British correspondents felt some concern about this feature of the new school, for two months later Mrs. Stowe was writing, 'In relation to the subject that you mentioned—it has been found expedient as yet, at the South, to teach the white and black in separate schools. The white children will *not* come to the same school with the black ones ... no inducement would ever persuade parents to let their children come to them—they would greatly prefer that they should grow up, without any education at all.' The only way was to establish schools for the whites and 'get them under our influence. You would yourself see the necessity of pursuing such a course, if you were on the ground.'[2]

Such arguments were, of course, very difficult for the English societies to refute. Mrs. Stowe's Bristol friends may have had qualms, but they continued to support the Mandarin scheme. The President of the London Freedmen's Aid Society, Frederick Tomkins, when in America saw the tendency towards segregation clearly indicated in the work of the Peabody Fund, and protested vigorously against such a 'deplorable and cruel mistake'; but there was little else either he or anyone in Britain could do, when the American associations spoke out for equal rights and integration, and could achieve neither.[3]

Perhaps not entirely free from a sense of white superiority, and because of its special wish to avoid political controversy, the British movement placed particular emphasis on the need for industrial or vocational education for the Negroes.

The veteran Levi Coffin noted in 1869 that 'Some Friends think there is a danger of the coloured people neglecting agriculture for science and pedagogueism', and urged the Negroes to concentrate on practical instruction (though he himself welcomed education as a social asset, and contended that knowledge would 'make its professor a more valuable working machine than if he were a hopeless, spiritless slave').[4] Rather in the vein of Booker T. Washington, the London President advised the freedmen to 'advance in

---

[1] Harriet Beecher Stowe to Mary Estlin, 7 April 1869, Estlin Papers, 24.123(4). Copy.

[2] H. B. Stowe to Miss Wigham, copy by M. Estlin, 4 June 1869 in ibid., 24.123(6). See also 24.123(2) and (3) and note by A. L. Murray in *American Quarterly*, Vol. XII, no. 4, Winter 1960, pp. 518–9.

[3] *Freed-Man*, 1 January 1868, p. 2.   [4] *Friend*, 1 October 1869, p. 227.

knowledge, virtue and religion, and . . . in due time God would bring all things to pass'.[1] In a cause dominated by clergymen and Quakers, such advice was not very singular, its apparent callousness reflecting only the normal nineteenth century acceptance of social inequalities.

The Mandarin school, supported by Bristol donations, taught 'not only the ordinary branches of intellectual education, but also some industrial calling, by which . . . [the pupils] may get a living, beginning with sewing, cutting, fitting, and laundry work for the girls, together with bread making and plain cooking. For boys . . . some elementary instruction in agriculture.'[2] In 1865, George Dixon, superintendent of the Quaker industrial school at Ayton in Yorkshire, resigned his post to go to America, where for nearly five years he worked in and founded similar schools for coloured people.[3] Benjamin Tatham of New York, perhaps influenced by the land grant scheme, commented as Dixon was beginning his work, 'your plan of agricultural schools is just the thing most wanted, and . . . if it be carefully introduced, *with the sympathy and approbation* of the whites of any locality, it will work its way admirably'.[4] In this way the freedmen's aid movement sought to meet the criticisms of white Southerners that to educate the Negro was simply 'to ruin him as a laborer'.[5]

Although one or two Englishmen went out to teach in the South, aid was generally in the form of money to found or sustain existing schools. In response to W. F. Mitchell's enthusiastic endorsement of the programme to train coloured teachers, a committee of seven Friends was set up to supervise the raising of £5,000 annually among English members of the Society for normal schools, and Quakers in Ireland agreed to give £1,000 a year for five years.[6] Letters in the *Friend* during 1867 record the setting up of a coloured orphanage with British financial aid; the correspondence between Levi Coffin and J. M. McKim, stressing the continued need for Negro education, makes frequent reference to British contributions in this connexion; while the files of the

[1] *Freed-Man*, 1 January 1868, pp. 2–3.
[2] H. B. Stowe to M. Estlin, Hartford, 21 December 1868, Estlin Papers, 24.123(2).
[3] See letters of G. Dixon to A. Hampson, 28 September–15 December 1865, A.P. C118/29–35. Also *Reporter*, November 1866, p. 74, and December 1867, pp. 31–2.
[4] *Friend*, 1 January 1866, pp. 8–9.
[5] *Paducah Herald*, quoted in McPherson, op. cit., p. 395.
[6] A.P. C118/114, and *Friend*, 7 June 1867, p. 137.

national Union are full of letters from grateful American recipients
—one such from New York acknowledging a gift of £10,000 from
England.[1]

As time passed, however, some of the early optimism was lost by
British workers, for the onslaught against Negro illiteracy was perhaps the most daunting aspect of freedmen's aid. An editorial in
the *Friend* emphasized that, while American agencies and the
government had done much, 'school provision . . . for . . . 400,000
children and 10,000 adults is a gigantic work beyond even their
. . . power to supply', and a Quaker secretary to the English freedmen's Union urged the need for patience; 'it seemed strange', he
wrote in 1869, 'that there were persons who knew that it had taken
hundreds of years to educate the Anglo-Saxon, even up to his
present state; but seemed to think that four millions of coloured
people—who while in slavery were debarred from every advantage
—could be sufficiently educated in four years; an error of great
magnitude'.[2]

The whole question was still claiming the attention and financial
support of Friends in Britain long after the formal freedmen's
societies had been disbanded, in December 1868. Appeals were
successfully published in the *Friend*, and in the course of 1869
nearly £500 was raised, part of which went, at Albright's suggestion, to found a scholarship at Howard University, Washington.[3]
It was reported that, in the areas worked by Western Friends, at
least thirty-nine Normal schools owed their existence to English
money.[4] Another general appeal for educational funds was issued,
as we have seen, by the London Yearly Meeting in 1877, and by
the following year over £1,500 had been received.[5]

But the difficulties still remained immense. The secretary of the
national Union once observed that, in spite of the magnitude of
Reconstruction, and the vast numbers of freedmen involved, 'how
comparatively few there are with the heart to feel the obligation
and the grace to afford them relief! To a sad extent is this the case

---

[1] *Friend*, 1 March and 1 October 1867; Coffin to McKim, Cincinatti, 14 December
1866, 27 December 1867, 8 January and 22 May 1868, Anti-Slavery Papers, Cornell
University; letters from Philadelphia Friends, A.P. C39/120, and C121/43; also A.P.
C39/100 from New York acknowledging the £10,000.

[2] *Friend* 1 April 1869, p. 69, and 1 January 1869, p. 13.

[3] See for instance *Friend*, 1 April 1869, pp. 81–2; 1 May 1869, p. 108; 1 July 1869, pp.
159–62, 170; 1 October 1869, p. 227; 2 December 1878, pp. 320–1.

[4] Ibid., 1 October 1869, pp. 241–2.

[5] *At a Yearly Meeting Held in London . . . 1877*, pp. 631, 655–7, and ibid., for 1878, pp.
48, 50–4.

on both sides of the Atlantic.'[1] Friends confirmed that 'The adversaries [of the work] are many. The Freedmen are surrounded, to a large extent, by a hostile white population; then there is the adversary of poverty, even if the whites were friendly, and there is again the adversary of indifference to their fate in the Northern States of America and in this country.'[2] During the succeeding decade in Britain, only the Quakers steadfastly concerned themselves with the increasing social disabilities of the Negro, and felt that 'Nothing is truly settled that is not settled right.'[3]

One Friend, chancing to visit the South in 1878, when Reconstruction was theoretically at an end, was shocked by what she saw. Her verdict was that

> There are a few—a very few—in America who are continuing to fight the battle of freedom under this new aspect; and, as in the old days, it is to the unprejudiced Christianised common sense of the British people that they mainly look for moral support in accomplishing the work. Should we not, then, disregard the cry of 'British interference', and endeavour, both by act and word, as opportunity may offer, to obtain the recognition of the dark-skinned man as truly a *man* and a *brother*?[4]

William Forster Mitchell had predicted with truth, in the early stages of freedmen's aid, that 'One thing you may depend upon—However many friends the colored man now has, in a few years, he will be left where he was before the war, in the hands of the Quakers and old line Abolitionists.'[5] Unhappily the valiant exertions of these few proved insufficient to the task.

It would be wrong to leave the British freedmen's aid movement, however, without some consideration of the last of its basic aims, namely the improving of Anglo-American relations. At a large meeting of the London Freedmen's Aid Society, held in Exeter Hall on 15 February 1865, at which Levi Coffin and other American visitors were present, the audience was invited to 'embrace this opportunity of showing their good-will and friendship to their kinsmen in America. . . . There were, unhappily, people in both countries who were willing to excite feelings of hostility between the two countries, and they ought therefore to take every means in their power to frustrate these efforts. . . . If they wished for the . . . prosperity of the whole British Empire, and of the whole

---

[1] *Friend*, 1 November 1866, pp. 240–1.   [2] Ibid., 1 October 1869, pp. 241–2.
[3] Ibid., 2 September 1878, pp. 240–2.   [4] Ibid.
[5] W. F. Mitchell to J. M. McKim, Nashville, Tennessee, 22 December 1866, Anti-Slavery Papers, Cornell University.

English speaking community, they should take every means of cementing all branches of the Saxon race together.' These feelings were shared by the Americans present, who believed that such charities as freedmen's aid could 'promote international harmony and good-will'.[1]

Similar sentiments were echoed at provincial meetings of the movement. At Weymouth, in May 1866, the Rector expressed a hope that 'we may not only, in fact, perform the duties of Christian philanthropy, but we may also be the means of drawing more closely those bonds of sympathy and real love which ought to unite together the branches of the great Anglo-Saxon family, upon the unity, sympathy, concord, and affection of which the happiness, civilization, and Christianity of the whole world so much depend.'[2]

W. E. Forster, M.P., President of the Bradford Society, remarked at a meeting in the city in November of the same year that he 'thought no excuse was necessary for asking Englishmen to assist the Americans in any good work, and for this reason, that we could not help sympathising with them, they were so bound . . . [to us] by ties of common interest, of feeling, of blood, of language, and institutions', and these ties were not to be loosened by any amount of political hostility.[3] At an anniversary breakfast in Birmingham in June, Goldwin Smith and the Rev. W. Dale welcomed the freedmen's movement 'as an illustration of the sympathy really existing between the American people and ourselves'.[5]

Experienced observers, including John Bright, agreed that 'every manifestation of good feeling shown in that great cause, to that unhappy race, the negro, would not only tend to balance, but even to obliterate, all traces of the . . . evils . . . [resulting from the American Civil War] nay, would tend to produce a better feeling between the two countries than existed before the war began.'[5] In 1868, when Charles Francis Adams was about to return home after seven years in Britain, the freedmen's societies showered the Ambassador with good wishes and presented him with an address expressing the hope that his 'great influence' would 'continue to be given to the promotion of two objects which you, as well as ourselves, have . . . sincerely at heart, namely the advancement of the

[1] Coffin, op. cit., pp. 693, 695, 700, and *Freed-Man*, 1 March 1866, p. 168; see also *Reporter*, April 1866, pp. 12–13.

[2] *Freed-Man*, 1 June 1866, p. 263.   [3] *Reporter*, December 1866, p. 84.

[4] Ibid., July 1866, pp. 30–1.

[5] John Bright reported in *Friend*, 1 July 1865, p. 142; see also Albright, in ibid., 1 September 1864, p. 203.

welfare ... of the Emancipated Negroes throughout your land, and the maintenance of harmony and co-operation between the government and people of the United States and of Great Britain.'[1]

There was a strong feeling in Britain that the Americans were entitled to assistance, not only because of the plight of the freedmen, but also because of the American aid, amounting to some £100,000, made to the distressed English cotton operatives during the Civil War. This gesture seems to have made a tremendous impact on the freedmen's societies—certainly it would be hard to find many appeals during their five years of existence which did not mention the donation (and that made by America during the Irish potato famine of 1846).[2]

The freedmen's aid *Reporter* summed up these kindly sentiments in its leader pages in 1866. 'By wise and generous co-operation with transatlantic Christians and philanthropists, in the elevation of the Freed people', the British movement would, it was felt, 'be useful in helping to achieve results for America, for Britain, and the world, the magnitude, value, and duration of which are incalculable', and should 'feel encouraged to persevere, alike because the work is essentially good in itself, from the fact that the coloured people are progressing admirably; and because we shall draw into closer friendship the spiritual and moral conservatism of the two great branches of the Anglo-Saxon race.'[3]

It is impossible to hazard how far, if at all, this aim was successful at a national level, since the only assessments come from partial sources. (Thus Joseph Simpson reported after a tour of America in 1865, 'the sympathy and aid of the English people in this great work are most gratefully appreciated, and have already done much to soften the hostile feeling which was engendered towards England during the war.' '[F]ew things pleased me more in my travels than the oft-repeated expressions of gratitude to the "mother country" for her timely aid. I know that these thanks were sincere, and am equally satisfied that few things will tend more to bring the two great countries into that true concord which

---

[1] See letters in A.P. C38/78, 118, C39/76, C121/71, 96.
[2] See for instance *Minutes and Proceedings . . . 1864*, p. 52; *Friend*, 1 January 1863, pp. 12–13, and in the John Rylands library, *Leeds Auxiliary to the Freed-Men's Aid Society*. *A Plea for the Perishing*, Leeds, 1865, p. 16; *The Freedmen's Aid Commission*; *Why Should Birmingham Workmen Help the Freed Refugees from Slavery in America, etc.*; also *Preston Guardian*, 4 March 1865, *Daily News*, 14 June 1865; *British Workman*, 1 May 1865, *Birmingham Daily Gazette*, 29 September and 29 December 1864; *Birmingham Daily Post*, 5 January 1865.
[3] June 1866, p. 17.

K

should ever exist between them, than such an evidence of brotherly sympathy as our English subscriptions would afford.')[1] It is possible, however, to estimate the impact of aid from Britain upon the American societies which received it.

By the 1850s at least, abolitionists in the United States appear to have been divided between gratitude for past British help, and a feeling that the anti-slavery struggle was becoming an increasingly American affair, inseparable from their own domestic policies. Maria Weston Chapman, while writing in 1863 to thank English friends for their efforts over the years, was forced to acknowledge that their financial aid was no longer welcome in America.[2] A similar ambivalence characterizes post-war relations.

In the first place, although a great many agents on behalf of the freedmen came over from the United States, they were anxious not to appear importunate.[3] Levi Coffin, for instance, replied to an accusing letter from J. M. McKim, 'I fully appreciate thy feelings or sensitiveness on that subject. I *too* have some American pride; but it so happens that the most of the begging and call for help has gone from New York [where McKim worked] and not from Cincinatti, [Coffin's headquarters] ... When I was in Europe, I felt quite humiliated.' 'I pursued a very different course. I told them I did not come to beg.'[4] But then, of course, such tours would hardly have been undertaken without hope of financial gain, and visitors were generally concerned to take home what they could, and for their own particular association.[5]

For their part, the British societies objected to overt American requests for money and wished to take full credit for the contributions made by members.[6] It was also feared that funds from

---

[1] J. Simpson to J. H. Tuke, the *Freed-Man*, 1 November 1865, p. 73.

[2] See Thistlethwaite, op. cit., pp. 115–19; letters in Estlin Papers, 24.122 (37), 24. 122 (41), and 24.122 (140).

[3] For instance Rev. R. J. Parvin (A.F.U.C.); Levi Coffin (Western Freedmen's Aid Commission); Joel Cadbury Jnr. (Philadelphia Friends association); Sella Martin (A.M.A.); Rev. J. A. Thorne (A.M.A.); Rev. W. W. Patton (A.M.A.); Dr. A. M. Storrs (W.F.A.C.); Dr. J. C. Holbrook (A.M.A.); W. F. Mitchell (A.F.U.C.); Crammond Kennedy (A.F.U.C.); C. C. Leigh (National Freedmen's Relief Association of New York); George Cabot Ward (A.F.U.C.); William Lindsay, ex-slave, student of Oberlin.

[4] L. Coffin to J. M. McKim, 5 January 1866, Cincinatti, Anti-Slavery Papers, Cornell University; also in ibid., Coffin to McKim, 14 January 1867. (See similar testimony from Rev. R. J. Parvin, A.P. C119/133; from Philadelphia Friends, A.P. C120/27; from J. M. McKim, A.P. C121/101.)

[5] See W. F. Mitchell to J. M. McKim, Nashville, 12 April 1866 and 6 February 1867, and also A.P. C120/46, C121/79, 80, C118/120.

[6] See letters in A.P. C120/121, 84, and C39/14, 19.

Britain might not be distributed according to the wishes of the donors and might even be dissipated on salaries and other administrative expenses—charges that the American Freedmen's Union Commission strongly repudiated.[1]

Thus the American Missionary Association, for instance, received English funds because Joseph Simpson could give good account of its work and assurances that gifts would be properly used; and the correspondence of Levi Coffin contains angry complaints to the American Freedmen's Union Commission that he was not receiving British donations sent out via that body but intended specifically for his own society's use.[2]

However, the papers of the British movement do contain many sincere tributes to the valuable part played by American agents in stirring up interest as well as moving letters of thanks—often for quite trifling amounts—from those actually working among the freedmen.[3] A Baltimore Friend promised Albright 'that if you will aid us with some of your funds either directly or through N[ew] Y[ork] Union—we will have a handsome tablet erected upon the building [a normal school] commemorative of your aid and sympathy—we shall do that, whether you aid us or not, for we wish every child we teach, who has been rescued from the degradation of slavery, to know the history of British sympathy and aid first in their freedom and then in their elevation'.[4]

Those in Britain were clearly anxious to know that their gifts were useful, and at the inaugural meeting of the Union in 1866, the Duke of Argyll informed possible cynics that, according to a recent report of the Western Freedmen's Aid Commission, 'the collection in Great Britain was not very far short of one half of the whole funds which have been contributed to this particular Society, and Great Britain has also contributed liberally to nearly every other existing American Freedmen's Association'.[5] Arthur Albright recorded a crisis for the friends in New York so serious 'that they were on the point of suspending schools and withdrawing Teachers

---

[1] See letters in A.P. C121/101, 103, 104, and C119/37 in which McKim denied charges of misappropriation and showed how British funds were being spent.

[2] See A.P. C120/122, C40/64, C39/24, 56, 109a; and letters from Coffin to McKim in Anti-Slavery Papers, Cornell, 11 September 1866, 1, 22, 24 November 1866, 14 and 27 December 1866, 14 January 1867, 28 July 1868.

[3] See letters in A.P. C38/26, 63, C117/11, C118/21, C119/115, for tributes to American agents; also letters of thanks in A.P. C39/78, 80a, 100, 120, C118/28, 77, C120/27, 50, C121/87, 137.

[4] F. T. King to A. A. Albright, 10 December 1867, A.P. C121/88b.

[5] See letter in A.P. C118/144, and Argyll quoted in *Reporter*, May 1886, p. 5.

[.] Ge[orge] C[.] Ward [the treasurer] smiled at the hope that money would come from England. [A] days respite was granted and the next day came my Letter advising £2,550 as voted.'[1]

If bias be suspected in these two instances, further tributes can be taken from American sources. In 1868 M. C. Cooper of Philadelphia wrote, 'We have rejoiced in the active sympathy and very liberal pecuniary aid furnished by our brethren in England and Ireland. It has cheered and sustained us in the work so far as we have been able to carry it on.'[2] All differences forgotten, the A.F.U.C. in 1869 had nothing but praise for the British Union:

> Extraordinary service and the most valuable aid has been rendered to the cause by this body. Its leading members entered into the work with the liveliest sympathy and the most ardent zeal. Had their own country been directly responsible for the condition of the freedmen, they could hardly have been more energetic. They raised large sums for relief and education. . . . The money which we have been spending during the past year . . . in building up normal schools in the South, is money which was raised in chief part by the National Freedmen's Aid Union of Great Britain and Ireland.[3]

Writing in the same year on the financial contribution of the British freedmen's societies to those in America, the New England abolitionist William Lloyd Garrison declared in similar vein 'that, on this side of the Atlantic, we have nothing but wonder to express, thanks to give, and congratulations to proffer, at such a splendid contribution in so short a period, in aid of a hapless race three thousands miles away, on the part of our British friends, . . . They have far exceeded our highest expectations, and set a brilliant example of international benevolence.'[4]

The closeness of the ties between the two national associations is illustrated by the fact that they wound up their affairs simultaneously, the British movement following the advice of the American, and both making a virtue of necessity. Therefore, although some sensible observers in the States recognized that freedmen's aid was 'not the labor of a year, nor of years, but that of an age, and may as much occupy the attention of our children as it does our own', and that the real reasons for disbanding were lack of funds and 'the growing apathy of the public mind', it was also

---

[1] A. Albright to T. Phillips, 29 January 1868, A.P. C38/63; for other similar reports see C121/87, 161.

[2] M. C. Cooper to A. Albright, 2 January 1868 A.P. C121/43.

[3] *National Freedman*, Vol. III, 1869, p. 2.   [4] Ibid., p. 3.

suggested that Negroes could and should now take care of themselves.[1]

The cause of the freedman, wrote McKim, would not be furthered '*by keeping him before the public as an object of benevolence.* . . . We have reached a point when self-respect as well as regard for the cause admonishes us to be careful in our appeals.'[2] Adopting a similar line, the Union justified closing operations on evidence of 'the daily increasing development of self-reliance on the part of the freedmen', and B. H. Cadbury felt satisfied that it had 'been able to render a helping hand in laying the foundation towards the education of the Freed People of the U[nited] States a work that will take years to accomplish and will . . . be better done by their own efforts and if the White Population will not help . . . they will do it of themselves'.[3] (The British and Foreign Freedmen's Aid Society, however, though forced to abandon its efforts late in 1868 because of financial difficulties, in an article published in the last issue of the *Freed-Man*, entitled 'Is This the Time to Stop?', ridiculed arguments that the advance of education among the Negroes had rendered further aid unnecessary.)[4]

Adversely affected by events in Jamaica, the ferment for political and social reform at home, by difficult economic conditions, especially during 1866, and growing apathy on both sides of the Atlantic, as well as difficulties within its own ranks, the British freedmen's aid movement was also, and not surprisingly, unable to escape the influences of environment.[5] The public which made *Uncle Tom's Cabin* a bestseller responded with equal enthusiasm to the gospel of Samuel Smiles, as preached in his four main works, *Self Help* (1859), *Character* (1871), *Thrift* (1875), and *Duty* (1887).

According to Smiles, the gulf between different social classes could be crossed not by charity handed down from the prosperous, but by effort and application among the less privileged. 'Whatever is done *for* men and classes', he wrote, 'to a certain extent takes away the stimulus and necessity of doing for themselves.' Men could not be 'raised in masses' but 'must be dealt with as units';

---

[1] See report from Philadelphia Friends in A.P. C118/109a; (also A.P. C121/43); and J. M. McKim to A. Albright, 21 August 1868, A.P. C121/103; and P. C. Garratt to T. Phillips, 7 February 1868, A.P. C39/120.

[2] J. M. McKim to A. Albright, 21 August 1868, A.P. C121/103, (also A.P. C121/36).

[3] *National Freedman*, pp. 2–3, and B. H. Cadbury to T. Phillips, 27 July 1868, A.P. C39/60.

[4] *Freed-Man*, 1 September 1868, p. 138.

[5] See letters in A.P. referring to distress in Manchester, Leeds, Plymouth, and Nottingham, C40/51, C118/126, C39/109.

and 'As steady application to work is the healthiest training for every individual, so is it the best discipline of a state. Honourable industry travels the same road with duty; and Providence has closely linked both with happiness. The gods, say the poet, have placed labour and toil on the way leading to the Elysian fields.'[1]

In the face of such popular pronouncements, it is perhaps understandable that many freedmen's aid workers felt they had done all that *should* be done for the Negroes (although the more thoughtful among the Quakers, recognizing that here was a special case requiring a new approach and infinite patience, did of course continue their efforts on an unofficial basis throughout the 1870s). As Emerson had put it, more than twenty years earlier, unless coloured men could prove their own powers and native ability (and he believed they could), there was no help for them: 'a compassion for that which is not, and cannot be useful or lovely, is degrading and futile . . . I say to you, you must save yourself, black or white, man or woman; other help in none.'[2]

[1] A Briggs, 'Samuel Smiles and the Gospel of Work', in *Victorian People*, London, Pelican, 1965, pp. 124, 131, 133, 141.
[2] *The Emancipation of the Negroes in the West Indies. An Address Delivered at Concord, Massachusetts, on 1st August, 1844*, London, 1844, p. 51.

CHAPTER VI

The Growth of Racial Consciousness

'What have the English people done that the irrepressible negro should make an irruption into their daily papers, disport himself at their dessert, chill their turtle, spoil their wine, and sour their pineapples and their temper? ... Is it not enough that he has divided and distracted one population of thirty million Caucasians [in America], but he must needs also come to divide another population of equal numbers and similar combative qualities? Are we henceforth to be separated, as a nation, into negrophilites and anti-negroites? Is every dinner-party and every tea-party, every society of geographers and every society of social twaddlers, to be worried and wearied by prosy conversationalists on the brutal inferiority or the angelic superiority of the sons of Ham?'

Saturday Review, 1866[1]

During the 1860s and 1870s it is clear that both Britain and America were becoming increasingly fascinated by questions of race, and that in Britain racial awareness, which often degenerated into colour prejudice, fostered ideas of Anglo-Saxon solidarity, if not yet of a 'special relationship' in the modern sense.

Although the freedmen's aid societies differed radically from the majority of Britons over the political and racial aspects of Reconstruction, on the desirability of encouraging cordial relations with the United States, all were at one. There were at the same time, in the press especially, plenty of the familiar criticisms of the American political and protective systems, but even critics now recognized the need for caution. Thus the *Manchester Courier*, self-interest overcoming its normal hostility, argued that 'In proportion as America developes her wealth will she develop her trade with England. The moral therefore is that we ought to rejoice in the prosperity of the nation which originally sprang from us, and whose friendship may do so much to augment our material prosperity and the happiness of the world.'[2]

The major London journals all draw attention to the significance for Britain of America's growing prosperity, an anonymous

---

[1] 13 October, p. 446.
[2] 3 May 1866; See also 21 January 1867.

contributor to the *Edinburgh Review* looking forward to more vigorous commercial relations between the two countries in the belief that 'The bonds thus woven across the sea will be stronger than those of either race or sympathy; they will be bonds of mutual interest and of a common prosperity, and will be an effectual assurance that between us two there shall be always peace.'[1] And in spite of certain fears about the fact 'that the Union is now', as the *Spectator* put it, 'a power of the first class, a nation which it is very dangerous to offend and almost impossible to attack', the consciousness of Anglo-Saxon unity and destiny, implicit in the freedmen's aid movement, continued to gain strength.[2]

Among British travellers of the period, F. B. Zincke commented after a trip to America in 1867 that 'there is no part of the world which Englishmen ought to find so instructive and interesting', since that continent formed 'part of the great Anglo-Saxon race, with all its rich inheritance of law, literature and traditions'. (Zincke was Vicar of Wherstead in Suffolk, and one of Queen Victoria's chaplains; active in local politics as a Radical he won high praise for his work from C. E. Norton, who described it as 'the book of a good observer, a gentleman, and a man accustomed to reflection'.)[3] Similarly David Macrae admonished his readers to familiarize themselves with American affairs, since 'The two nations are knit together as parts of one body. What affects the one affects the other. Disaster to America means disaster to us, though it may temporarily benefit a few; progress in America means progress here, though it may involve changes hostile to class interests.'[4]

In his perceptive survey of the post-war South, John Kennaway hoped that improved acquaintance would 'strengthen the bonds of union between the two great families of the Anglo-Saxon race', believing that 'On the future relations of England with the United States will depend possibly, results, the importance of which can scarcely be adequately estimated—results which may affect in no slight degree our national prosperity, perhaps even our national

---

[1] *Economist*, 18 November 1865, p. 1399; *Spectator*, 22 August 1868, p. 982; *Saturday Review*, 18 November 1865, pp. 526–7 and 15 June 1867, p. 743; *The Times*, 13 February 1866; *Daily News*, 8 June 1872; and *Edinburgh Review*, 1872, Vol. CXXXVI, p. 179.

[2] *Spectator*, 17 February 1866, pp. 177–8.

[3] Op. cit., p. 100; See *Letters of Charles Eliot Norton* With Biographical Comment by his Daughter Sara Norton and M. A. De Wolfe Howe, Boston, 1913, 2 Vols., Vol. I, p. 350.

[4] Op. cit., Vol. I, p. xvi.

existence. ... Sharing in the same hopes and fears, the same objects and interests, the world is large enough for us both, and our rivalry should not degenerate into jealousy.'[1]

A more elaborate exposition of this view was put forward by Charles Dilke, who, on the threshold of his political career, published in 1868 his first and best book, *Greater Britain*. It was enthusiastically reviewed by the press, and by politicians and scholars; it quickly ran through four editions in England and in pirated editions sold even more copies in America.[2]

In the preface, Dilke explained his 'Greater Britain' as 'a conception, however imperfect, of the grandeur of our race, already girdling the earth'. He believed that 'In America, the peoples of the world are being fused together, but they are run into an English mould. ... Through America, England is speaking to the world.' After considering the strain placed upon Anglo-American relations by the Civil War, Dilke concluded that 'The chief reason why America finds much to offend her in our conduct is, that she cares for the opinion of no other people than the English.' From this gratifying premiss was evolved the theory that 'America offers the English race the moral dictatorship of the globe, by ruling mankind through Saxon institutions and the English tongue'.[3]

Dilke later regarded this vision of a 'Greater Britain' as 'the best piece of work of my life', and the phrase passed into common usage among Victorians.[4] Writing in 1882 Goldwin Smith declared himself to be 'a loyal and even ardent citizen of The Greater Britain, and [I] most sincerely wish to see all children of England, including the people of the United States, linked to their parent by the bond of the heart'.[5] The following year J. Seeley, a Cambridge don, published his *The Expansion of England* (which helped to bring about the Imperial Federation League of 1884); in this influential work he observed that '. . . Greater Britain is not in the ordinary sense an Empire at all. Looking at the colonial part of it alone, we see a natural growth, a mere normal extension of the English race into other lands. ... It creates not properly an Empire, but only a very large state.'[6]

[1] Op. cit., Vol. I, pp. viii, 276–7.
[2] See R. Jenkins, *Sir Charles Dilke, A Victorian Tragedy*, London, Collins, 1958, p. 42.
[3] Op. cit., Vol. I, Preface, pp. 304–5, 318.
[4] Memoir, the Dilke Papers, British Museum, Add, Ms. 43930.
[5] *A Selection from Goldwin Smith's Correspondence, 1846–1910*, A. Haultain (ed.), London, 1913, p. 137.
[6] London, 1883, p. 296.

One of the most publicized of British peace offerings to America during these early post-war years was the series of public breakfasts given in 1867 to honour William Lloyd Garrison. At the principal gathering in London, among the distinguished panel of speakers—and invited at his particular wish—was Lord John Russell who took advantage of the occasion to repent of his wartime policy towards the North; he hoped, too, that 'that the friendship of the United States and the United Kingdom . . . may endure unbroken, and that . . . our meeting here to-day has tended to the better union of two races who ought never to be separated'. Speaking at the same meeting the Duke of Argyll urged that it was 'time to forget ancient differences'; England desired peace with America and the 'friendship and affection' of her people, and in travelling to that great republic Englishmen were 'going only to a second home'.

Garrison's visits to Manchester, Newcastle, South Shields, Edinburgh, Birmingham, Leeds, and Liverpool provoked a similarly cordial reponse, and the working men of North Shields, acknowledging gratefully their debt to American democracy, looked forward 'with hope to the time when the British people . . . in firm and friendly union with the American people, may jointly lead the nations towards a nobler civilization, true liberty, and lasting peace'.[1]

Nor were such kindly sentiments and sense of mission confined to British Radicals, who saw in American institutions much to envy and inspire. The Liberal leader Gladstone, whose wartime utterances had not endeared him to the North, was writing in lavish praise of the United States a decade later in the *North American Review*, and at a reform demonstration in Liverpool in 1866 he pledged concern for 'the welfare of that nation in every part and portion of it, whether it be white or black, whether it be North or South'.[2]

Disraeli, who had pursued a more decorous course during the Civil War, but was no devotee of the American political system, referred to it during the reform debates of 1867 as 'framed by the children of our loins, and certainly under the inspiration of as pure a patriotism as ever existed', and to the American nation as 'in-

[1] *Proceedings at the Public Breakfast Held in Honour of William Lloyd Garrison*, op. cit., pp. 28–9, 31–3; and W. P. and F. J. Garrison, op. cit., Vol. IV, pp. 224–5.

[2] 'Kin Beyond Sea', *North American Review*, September–October 1878, p. 186; *The Times*, 7 April, 1866; See also Gladstone's condemnation of his wartime stand in 'Some of My Errors', 1894, Gladstone Papers, British Museum, Add. Ms. 44790, f. 131.

ferior to us in no point; it is of the same blood, the same brains, the same intelligence, of equal energy, perhaps of more enterprise'.[1] As one might expect from their pre-war activities, both John Bright and Christopher Newman Hall continued to act as vigorous and influential exponents of Anglo-American unity.[2]

British newspapers of every class and political affiliation, whatever their views on the conflicting policies for Reconstruction in America, also expressed a friendly interest in the affairs of that country.

The *North British Daily Mail*, a Glasgow paper of advanced Liberal opinions, laid it down in 1867 that 'The foreign politics that concern us the most relate to the North American, and not to the European Continent. . . . Accordingly, the public events transpiring in the United States absorb the attention of our countrymen to a degree that surpasses very much the regard they are accustomed to pay to the internal affairs of any other people.'[3]

Most of the important Irish journals took a sanguine view of the future of Anglo-American relations. 'The people of this country', wrote the *Dublin Evening Mail* (which yet poured bitter scorn upon the Radical Republicans' Reconstruction policies), 'are animated by the best feelings towards the American people', and even 'those who think it would have been better for the Northern population and Northern interests and morals that the South had succeeded, must wish that the American Government may now surmount the difficulties of its success, and no other feelings but such as are honourable to the English people have found expression with respect to those difficulties.'[4]

The influential *Irish Times*, commenting on the friendly tone of President Johnson's Message of December 1867, noted that 'A great alteration has taken place, also, in England feeling towards America; and, when two most powerful nations, connected so closely by race, language, and civilisation are animated by a spirit of confidence in each other's rectitude of principle, there is little danger of hostility, no matter what embarrassing questions may arise.'[5]

Quoted in H. C. Allen, *The Impact of the Civil War and Reconstruction on Life and Liberalism in Great Britain* New York, A. Knopf (forthcoming).

[2] See John Bright reported in *Times*, 27 February 1868; Christopher Newman Hall, *The Assassination of Abraham Lincoln*, London, 1865, pp. 7–8, letter to Gladstone, 7 February 1868, The Gladstone Papers, Add. Ms. 44188, Vol. CIII, and *From Liverpool to St. Louis*, New York, 1868.

[3] 11 April 1867. [4] 16 May 1865; see also 30 June 1865.

[5] 5 December 1867; see also *Freeman's Journal*, 10 June 1865 and 7 November 1872; *Northern Whig*, 11 December 1876.

In the summer of 1866, the laying of the Atlantic telegraph cable prompted the leader writer of the *Daily Telegraph* to comment, as regards the United States, that 'the time for petty rivalry and jealousy' was 'well nigh over; that of a cordial human fellowship at hand. . . . Our messages are now of peace and of goodwill.' The *Economist* observed, in addition to the misunderstandings which sometimes arose between the two nations, the peculiar closeness of their relationship, as did the *British Workman*, while the *Manchester Examiner and Times* and the *Courier*, so unlike in many ways, both stressed the importance of uniting 'in unbroken friendship the two great branches of the Anglo-Saxon stem'.[1] Sustained by these powerful feelings of kinship and affection, by a growing awareness of the racial concept of Anglo-Saxon or Anglo-American strength, even supremacy, British interest in the United States during Reconstruction not unnaturally revolved around the crucial figure of the Negro. Nor should we be surprised at the popular prejudice which prevailed not only towards the American freedmen but against coloured races everywhere.

The freedmen's aid movement in Britain clearly did not decline because of any lack of awareness of racial problems among educated observers, although not all of them might be personally acquainted with the races about whom they wrote. Certainly, as the *Saturday Review* pointed out, Englishmen who stayed at home would encounter few Negroes (exact figures are not available until the present century). This perhaps explains Charles Dilke's description of them as 'a monster class of which nothing is yet known'; while in 1899 the Aborigines Protection Society commented: 'One of the difficulties with which the Society has always been confronted . . . in its efforts to arouse the public interest necessary to the advancement of its objects, arises from the fact that in many cases so few have accurate knowledge about the people with embarrassing names on whose behalf it appeals, or about the places, with names as embarrassing, in which they live.'[2]

Yet in spite of such ignorance—or perhaps because of it—many Britons appear from this study to be not only eloquent but vio-

[1] *Daily Telegraph*, 2 August 1866; see also 16 April 1866; *Economist*, 10 December 1870, p. 1, 482; *British Workman*, 1 July 1868, p. 172; *Manchester Examiner and Times*, 5 May 1868; *Manchester Courier*, 7 May 1868, 19 April 1866; see also *The Times*, 30 July 1866 and 5 May 1868; *Spectator*, 11 August and 8 September 1866, pp. 880 and 993–5.

[2] Op. cit., Vol. I, p. 20; and *The Aborigines Protection Society: Chapters in its History*, London, 1899, p. 1.

lently prejudiced on the subject of race; in the rather surprising words of *The Times* during Reconstruction,

The advocate of the negro can cite general principles and special instances. He can appeal to the common origin of our race and the common brotherhood of man, and can ask, with a voice the electric tones of which shall vibrate on the religious heart of America, 'Why do ye this thing to your brother?' . . . He can appeal to the gratitude and honour of the people, and demand the guerdon earned by the negro's sacrifice. On the other side stands arrayed that strong, dull, dumb, and unreasoning prejudice . . . which the Anglo-Saxon feels against all coloured races the longer he knows them, and feels most strongly against the negro.[1]

Although attention so far has been confined almost exclusively to the American and Jamaican Negroes (and attitudes towards the former, among the general British public, will presently be considered), it is clear that British comments are related to the broader question of the treatment of coloured races throughout the colonies. (The freedmen of the South are frequently referred to as Africans, though colonization proposals are rare, and the vices of the Negro —again an all embracing term—felt to be much the same the world over. Thus the *Daily Telegraph*, specifically discussing the prospects of free labour in America after the Civil War, observed: 'Wherever the white and . . . black are placed on an equal footing, the Anglo-Saxon will drive the African out of the field in the battle of life'.)[2] And in fact it seems to have been the sense of fear and frustration produced by the problems of administering an empire which shaped British attitudes to the racial aspect of Reconstruction.

The *Saturday Review*, in two articles about 'the Government of Coloured Races in Colonies', described this task as 'one of the greatest problems which can puzzle the ingenuity of statesmen'. Most Englishmen, it was felt, were indifferent to the difficulties involved, and those Negroes whom they encountered failed 'to excite sympathy or liking beyond the unctuous pale of Exeter Hall'. In the opinion of the writer the only suitable government for freedmen was strong government: 'We do not say that mere brute force or mere brute courage is sufficient to keep an alien race in subjection, but we say that both are indispensable conditions.' Furthermore, an outstanding feature of colonial life was the extent

[1] 4 November 1865.
[2] 23 June 1865.

to which 'the prejudice against people of colour had grown in proportion to the mitigation of their civil disabilities', and this was explained as 'the natural recoil of a policy [of equality] violently and prematurely urged'.[1]

Charles Dickens well expressed the nervousness of many Britons when he wrote in 1865, 'That platform-sympathy with the black —or the native, or the devil—afar off, and that platform indifference to our own countrymen at enormous odds in the midst of bloodshed and savagery, makes me stark wild. Only the other day, here was a meeting of jawbones of asses at Manchester, to censure the Jamaica Governor for his manner of putting down the insurrection! So we are badgered about New Zealanders and Hottentots, as if they were identical with men in clean shirts at Camberwell, and were to be bound by pen and ink accordingly.'[2]

Radicals acknowledged the existence of such feelings with alarm, Frederic Harrison complaining,

For fifty years our armies, ever in the field, have never but once met with an equal foe. Fighting often with savages, generally with rebels and citizens, always with rude enemies, never with Europeans or really organized armies, their task has been chiefly one from which soldiers of honour recoil. It is plain to me . . . that there are growing up under the constant excitement of these miserable conflicts, indications of a temper which is degrading to the army. Horrible stories come out quietly of deeds in India, in China, in New Zealand. . . . The terrible Indian rebellion has sown evil seeds enough in the military as well as in the civil system. It called out all the tiger in our race. That wild beast must caged again.[3]

A similarly unflattering picture of British opinion on racial questions was drawn by the *Spectator*, which described the average Englishmen, both before and after the Civil War, as 'Blinded by a prejudice against colour which in its strength and permanence is to cool reasoners scarcely intelligible.'[4]

In his *Greater Britain* Charles Dilke noted that 'if it is still impossible openly to advocate slavery in England, it has, at least, become a habit persistently to write down freedom. We are no longer told that God made the blacks to be slaves, but we are bade

---

[1] 20 January 1866, pp. 73–4, and 3 February 1866, pp. 134–5.
[2] Dickens to M. de Cerjat, Higham by Rochester, Kent, 13 November 1865; *The Letters of Charles Dickens*, C. Hogarth and M. Dickens (eds.), 1880–2, 2 Vols., Vol. II, p. 241.
[3] *Martial Law. Six Letters to 'The Daily News'*, London, 1867, Jamaica Papers, no. 5, London, 1867, p. 41.
[4] 25 August 1866, pp. 932–3.

to remember that they cannot prosper under emancipation.'¹ Speaking at the last meeting of Manchester Union and Emancipation Society, Goldwin Smith reminded his audience, with the example of Jamaica before them, of 'the perils of a community composed of the ex-slave owner and the ex-slave. What will cleanse away the taint which seems not to quit the blood of the man who has owned slaves—or of his children—or of his children's children? How, with the ineradicable difference of colour, to which fatal memeories will . . . cling, and with the physical antipathy the existence of which it is vain to deny, can we hope for social fusion? Without social fusion, how can we hope for political equality? And without political equality, what security can there be for justice?'²

In a moment of candour the *Pall Mall Gazette* conceded that the British 'mode of governing alien and discrepant races' left much to be desired (an admission strongly endorsed by the Dublin *Freeman's Journal*.)³ 'We fail', it wrote, 'By the combined operation of our pet national virtue and our pet national vice—our passion for doing justice and giving freedom to all the Queen's subjects, on the one hand; and our ignorant conceit, on the other hand, in fancying that all the Queen's subjects, of whatever origin, habits nature, and complexion, can be dealt with in the same fashion . . . without any knowledge of their peculiarities or any study of their wants. We have bungled Ireland; we have bungled India; we have bungled Jamaica; we have mismanaged Celts, Kaffirs, Hindoos, Maories, and Negroes, and all from the same case—because we refused to see that they were not Englishmen, or have fancied that we would make them Englishmen.'⁴

Apportioning blame for existing difficulties very differently, the *Daily Telegraph* commented that 'Africa is a bore. The most enthusiastic student of voyages and travels loses heart and hope when he hears the forlorn old names of Timbuctou and Khartoum. No one can be really much interested in a black wilderness, inhabited by foul, fetid, fetish-worshipping, loathsome, and lustful barbarians.'⁵

The Times repeatedly drew attention to the troublesome nature of the colonies, concluding that: 'The most barbarous races are recognized as "men and brothers", but Governors, Generals, and

---

¹ Op. cit., Vol. I, p. 25.   ² *The Civil War in America*, p. 69.
³ 20 February 1866.   ⁴ 13 February 1866.
⁵ 17 August, 1866.

all men placed in authority are treated as of a different race. "The quality of mercy is not strained" for them, and the excessive tenderheartedness of Philanthropy towards aboriginal races is brought down, after all, to a not very startling average by its extreme harshness to persons of our own.'[1] It was felt to be essential 'to keep ever displayed before the eyes of barbarians the signs and symbols of civilized authority', for though individual Negroes might rise and prosper, 'yet the mass remains very low, both intellectually and morally. Two or three generations hence instruction and increased civilization may have made a change, but every age legislates for its own wants, and according to its own circumstances; and it seems to us that the best policy for any people who have to deal with the black race is to keep a strong hand over them.'[2]

Apart from specific shocks like the Indian Mutiny and the Jamaica Revolt, a number of other factors are likely to have influenced the growth of racist feelings in mid-Victorian Britain, though no explanations can ever be entirely satisfactory. The economic motive for empire, which brought conflict between both expansionists and philanthropists at home and Britons and natives abroad, though held in check during this the ascendancy of free trade ideas, was clearly a potential source of friction. White colonists in Africa and elsewhere strove to rationalize their actions, it has been suggested, on the grounds of the inferiority of the races they encountered.[3]

The myth of an innately (and therefore permanently) superior race was fostered during this period by Darwinian ideas (the *Origin of the Species* was published in 1858, the *Descent of Man* in 1871), or rather the Spencerian gloss of the survival of the fittest as applied to human history, though more obviously racist works were neither unknown nor confined to Britain. Thus in 1854 Count Arthur de Gobineau published his *The Inequality of Human Races*, in which he divided men into three types, black, yellow, and white, and stated bluntly 'The negroid variety is the lowest, and stands at the foot of the ladder. The animal character, that appears in the shape of the pelvis, is stamped on the negro from birth, and foreshadows his destiny. His intellect will always move within a very narrow circle.' Gobineau was equally convinced of 'the immense superiority of the white peoples in the whole field of the intellect'

---

[1] 11, 12, and 13 December 1865; See also *Daily Telegraph*, 7 December 1865.
[2] *The Times*, 4 November 1865; and 13 November 1865, and see 27 January 1866.
[3] M. Perham, *The Colonial Reckoning*, London, Collins 1963, pp. 82, 60.

and 'the undisputed superiority of those groups of the white races which have remained the purest', thus retaining their original 'monopoly of beauty, intelligence, and strength'.[1]

The prevalence of opinions such as these was recognized and deplored by Charles Saville Roundell, secretary of the Royal Commission on Jamaica in the 1860s. In his opinion the current doctrine that 'the history of colonization is the history of the annihilation of the native races; that, in the order of Providence, savage man is destined to disappear before civilized man: that in the "struggle for existence," the inferior races must give way to the superior' was merely 'a short and simple way of salving over our consciences'. Roundell urged instead 'the rejection of all *a priori* assumptions, and the patient investigation of facts, including the causes of our miscarriages in the past'.[2]

For those actually involved in the work of colonization, the problem was doubtless aggravated by the very apparent technological and material superiority of the West, and by the fact that they were frequently drawn from a class in Britain which would consider it had little in common with working men, let alone with foreign tribes which, by Victorian standards, lacked both possessions and culture. Pride of birth and pride of race, as Roundell put it, 'together induce a sort of caste-like spirit' and build up 'a hard, impassable barrier against the better and more generous feelings of human nature'.[3] Though Britain possessed a proud anti-slavery record, there may well be some truth in the adage that those long held up as an object for pity will in time become subject to contempt. Then, as the century and empire building progressed, and women joined the original settlers, fears of miscegenation no doubt increased. Nor is it hard to see how the sense of mission towards coloured races felt by philanthropists in Britain—in the words of the Aborigines Protection Society, the realization 'of the ability which we possess to confer upon them the most important benefits'—could be transformed into a sanction for imperialism, on the grounds that 'the British Empire was, under Providence, the greatest instrument for good that the world has seen'.[4]

What emerges undeniably, however, from a study of Victorian opinion—in so far as it can be estimated through travellers' books,

---

[1] Translated by A. Collins, Vol. I, London, 1915, pp. 205, 207–9.
[2] *England and Her Subject-Races, With Special Reference to Jamaica*, London, 1866, pp. 4–5, 9.
[3] Op. cit., p. 19.   [4] Op. cit., p. 4, and Perham, op. cit., p. 83.

L

reviews and newspapers, and the testimony of eminent individuals —is the existence during the 1860s and 1870s of an impatient hostility towards the Negro. A complex phenomenon, with its roots apparently in memories of an unhappy colonial experience, and nurtured by the ideas of race consciousness and white superiority which were to flower a decade later in a second great period of imperialist expansion, this hostility forms a background to activities of the British freedmen's aid movement, and make its success the more remarkable. There were, clearly, still men in Britain proud of her record in anti-slavery endeavour, but their influence had a waning force.

When we examine the comments on the Negro during Reconstruction made by Britons unconnected with freedmen's aid, race prejudice is starkly revealed, for popular attitudes to the problem were determined to a high degree by a belief in both the innate and apparent inferiority of the Negro.

William Rathbone Greg, writing in the *Pall Mall Gazette*, noted that some races, including the African, were not fitted to stand alone, though 'most valuable when guided and ruled by superior intelligence', so that to turn the American Negroes free without education or training, was pure madness. The abolitionists would 'cease to interest themselves about a race from whom personally they always shrank', and the freedmen would become 'a nuisance, an offence, and an eyesore'.[1] An angry letter in reply attacked this attitude, but owned that 'such opinions, put forward indeed with less ability and impartiality, have become very common of late'.[2]

The *Spectator* also felt impelled to take Sir Samuel Baker to task for a letter to *The Times* in which he maintained that the African Negro had 'little in common with the white man beyond the simple instincts of human nature'; in the course of its lecture, however, the Liberal journal, referring to coloured races, commented 'The more inferior they are to us, the more mercy we should have supposed that we owe them.'[3] It is interesting to note in this, the most enlightened of British papers on the subject of race, a complete absence of the modern distinction between man and his immediate condition, his environment; the African by European criteria was neither prosperous nor cultivated—he was, therefore,

---

[1] Greg was a well-known essayist; wrote for a number of periodicals, mostly on political and economic affairs; see *Pall Mall Gazette*, 21 April 1865, pp. 3–4.
[2] Ibid., 25 April 1865, pp. 3–4.   [3] 22 September 1866, p. 1,042.

simply inferior. (Although it was paradoxically admitted that Negroes might be elevated by altering environmental factors—for instance by providing education, or the opportunity to acquire property.) Similar standards of judgement were applied to the American freedmen.

Indicative of this attitude of superiority was the use of insulting slave labels like 'Cuffee' or 'Quashee' and even 'Sambo'. Thus we find the leader writer of the *Daily Telegraph* declaring that the best thing the government of the United States could do for itself and 'Cuffee' (elsewhere referred to as 'the poor childlike African') was to take him into some form of apprenticeship, since 'Under the regime of a professed but impossible political and social equality, no superior race ever comes into contact with a race inferior in character and numbers without constant degradation and injury to the lower. The slave system alone seems to induce the superior tribe to protect the inferior for the sake of its own interest.'[1] In the same vein the *Saturday Review* poured scorn upon proposals to give political power to the freedmen at the expense of their late masters, since 'A privileged aristocracy has never yet been constituted from an inferior race.'[2]

Observers on the spot tended to confirm these opinions. If we look briefly at the diplomatic dispatches on this period, we find British consular representatives saying in private what British journalists did not hesitate to write publicly. Consul Tasker Smith in Savannah, who, having served for many years in South Africa, claimed to be an experienced judge of the Negro—being of the opinion that 'no climate nor situation changes ... [his] essential temperament'—described the freedman as a 'perpetual minor'; 'Docile and tractable when he knows that the orders given to him must be executed; but when left to his own discretion in the matter, careless and fitful as a child; without the least thought for to-morrow; ... relying upon the superior intelligence and activity of the white man to direct his efforts.'[3]

From South Carolina H. P. Walker wrote that emancipation would have been a boon 'if the moral and physical improvement of the emancipated class were thereby secured', but in fact a 're-lapse towards barbarism is apparent to every observer', and in particular a situation was deplored in which the Negro, 'who is unfitted for such duties either by natural instinct, education,

[1] 21 April 1865.   [2] 2 February 1867, p. 127.
[3] Consul Tasker Smith to Earl Russell, 5 July 1865, F.O.5 1031, no. 14.

principle, or self-restraint, is involuntarily placed in positions of high responsibility.'[1]

Travellers in the United States often betrayed an involuntary feeling of revulsion on coming into contact with the freedmen, even where this was not associated with contempt for their abilities. Thus Goldwin Smith alluded to the 'Physical repulsiveness of the negroes', and Sir George Campbell felt sorry for mulatto children forced to attend school 'among the blacks, many of whom are very black and hideous. I hardly knew before what an ugly race some of the blacks are.'[2] Charles Dilke, in his judicious survey of the Southern racial question commented that 'our common English notions of the negro'—of his vacant amiability, love of show and the like—'are nearer the truth than common notions often are', adding, however, unlike most British observers, that such characteristics were the product of environment and not nature—'That the negro slaves were lazy, thriftless, unchaste, thieves, is true; but it is as slaves, and not as negroes, that they were all these things.'[3]

A stereotype portrait of the Negro 'child of nature' was presented by author and popular entertainer George Rose, who saw the freedman as an amusing, good tempered, 'thoughtless creature, incapable of even seeing his own interests; he is insensible to the charms of domestic life, being, when left to himself, neither a good husband nor a good father. His sole delight is to bask in the sun, and indulge in every low gratification of sense.'[4] In his study *Black and White*, published in 1867, Henry Latham stated quite bluntly that 'At the present time there can be no doubt that the black race is inferior to the white', both in 'mental vigour' and 'bodily stamina', which view was confirmed by the Scot, David Macrae.[5]

Although he recognized the adverse influence of slavery, deplored that institution, and acknowledged 'the affection and docility of the negro' (qualities which, it was felt, made him 'a polite and admirable servant'), Macrae also described the freedmen as

---

[1] Consul H. P. Walker to Lord Russell, 19 May 1865, F.O.5 1030, no. 40; R. G. Watson, deputy to the Ambassador, to Lord Derby, 4 September 1874, F.O.5 1484, no. 91.

[2] A. Hautain, *Goldwin Smith, His Life and Opinions*, London, 1913, p. 291, and Campbell, op. cit., p. 294.

[3] Op. cit., pp. 19–25.

[4] Op. cit., p. 152; also pp. 151, 153, 155–7, 177; Rose was prone to refer to the 'darkey' and 'Sambo'; W. H. Dixon favoured 'Sam': *New America*, London, 1869, p. 426.

[5] London, 1867, pp. 275–6; also pp. 263, 277.

'an ignorant, degraded, and often brutalized people', and dismissed all possibility of their supremacy in the South, since the 'power of filling other heads with his thoughts—of making other hands the willing instruments of his purpose—belongs to the Caucasian far more than the negro, and belongs pre-eminently to the Anglo-Saxon. . . . And if, under any circumstances, two millions of negroes in the Gulf States prove themselves able to control the destinies of even one million of whites, either the white people must greatly deteriorate, or the black people must greatly improve.'[1]

Other British visitors bore witness to the Negroes' need for constant supervision, deficiency in matters regarding intellect, to their lack of application, proneness to crime, and to the likelihood of their dying out altogether, when placed in competition with the whites.[2]

Some of this antagonism towards the American Negro appears to have been founded on fear. Englishmen had their own experience—though, not, of course, in most cases first-hand—of race riots and native wars, and could sympathize with those who feared that Radical policies might provoke racial conflict in the United States. Many predicted the realization of De Tocqueville's prophecy that the Negroes 'may long remain slaves without complaining; but if they are once raised to the level of free men, they will soon revolt at being deprived of all their civil rights; and as they cannot become the equals of the whites, they will speedily declare themselves as enemies'.[3]

The British consuls in the South, not surprisingly in view of their situation, issued the most strident warnings about an impending war of races.[4] A report from Alabama in 1867 was typical of many in its belief that 'the ill feeling between the races has increased ten

[1] Op. cit., Vol. II, pp. 12–14, 17–18, 46–61; Vol. I, pp. 262–3, 268–9, 361–2.
[2] Sala, op. cit., Preface, p. viii, Vol. I, pp. 250, 295; Marquis of Lorne, *A Trip to the Tropics, and Home Through America*, London, 1867, p. 272; F. B. Leigh, *Ten Years on a Georgia Plantation Since the War*, London, 1883, pp. 15, 24; Zincke, op. cit., pp. 61, 92–93, 95, 105–7, 291; A. Granville Bradley, 'A Peep at the Southern Negro', *Macmillan's Magazine*, Vol., XXXIX, November 1878, pp. 61–6; G. Campbell, op. cit., pp. 138, 145–6, 170, 285.
[3] *Democracy in America* New York, 1899, 2 vols., Vol. I, p. 383.
[4] See H. P. Walker to Lord Stanley, 22 March 1867, F.O.5 1114, no. 17; to Lord Derby, F.O.5 1546, Political no. 3, 24 November 1876; William Barnes to Lord Stanley, 27 May 1867, F.O.5 1113, no. 10; Consul Fonblanque to Lord Derby, 13 November 1876, F.O.5 1545, Political no. 1, and 28 April 1877, F.O.5 1588, Political no. 2.

fold and openly the Blacks declare they will have revenge on the whites, though the whites suffered most. From all I can hear and from personal observation I can see but one end to such a state of things. The minds of the Blacks are poisoned by Northern fanatics in their midst . . . [and] already the white population of Mobile is disposed to take the law into its own hands and rid themselves of the blacks by violence, be the result what it may.'[1]

Comparable views were also expressed publicly in Britain, notably in all sections of the press. In Georgia, according to *The Times*, 'both the black and white inhabitants are continually engaged in murder and pillage. . . . The whites and blacks engage in open battle in some of the towns, and martial law has been declared at several places. A more unfortunate condition of affairs can scarcely be possible. The slightest spark will cause a negro insurrection to burst out in all parts of the State.' Later in 1866 the paper's Philadelphia correspondent commented: 'The line that separates the blacks and the whites in the South has been gradually widening since the end of the war. Where once there was nothing but friendly feeling they now regard each other with the bitterest hatred.'[2] Noting the 'intense hostility' which prevailed between Negroes and whites 'all over the Southern States', the *Scotsman* predicted that the Reconstruction policies of 'Northern fanatics' could well precipitate a war of races.[3]

It is clear that (contrary to the now widely accepted view that racial discrimination and hatred, as well as segregation in the South, were more marked after than during Reconstruction) many British commentators were convinced of a rapid deterioration in race relations throughout the late sixties and early seventies, a belief which was not simply based on racism or fear.[4]

The *Freeman's Journal*, for instance, which felt some sympathy for Radical Reconstruction, commented in 1876, 'We have been conversant for some months past with the unhappy state of things which prevails in the Southern States owing to the enmity of the black and white races—the one rejoicing with the joy of the semi-savage in the freedom for which they were unprepared, and it is to be feared not yet fitted; and the other smarting under the sense of

[1] F. J. Cridland, Alabama, to Lord Stanley, 16 May 1867, F.O.5 1111, no. 19.
[2] 4 January 1866, and 13 January 1866; see also 15 January 1866.
[3] 12 March 1866, 9 November 1876; see also *Daily Telegraph*, 30 November 1876; *Dublin Evening Mail*, 11 November 1876.
[4] See C. V. Woodward, *The Strange Career of Jim Crow*, New York, Galaxy, 1957.

defeat and the mortification of beholding those who, a few years ago, were their bond-slaves, now their political equals and in many localities even . . . their political superiors.'[1]

A journal of similar outlook, the *Northern Whig*, reported in 1874 a situation verging on anarchy—'That the defeated slave-owners and their Democratic supporters may yet join in a life and death struggle against the negroes is not at all impossible'; the sympathetic *Spectator* was almost alienated from the Republican party by the racial unrest which developed in the South, while the steadfast *Daily News* admitted in 1877 that 'The position of the South is one in which nothing that makes for moderation can safely be dispensed with. The elements of confusion are rife there, the danger of a war of races has from time to time been, and may again be, imminent.'[2] It should be noted, too, that disturbances were not simply blamed on the excitability of the Negro, but rather on Northern impolicy, and the activities of the Ku Klux Klan found no supporters.[3]

Sir George Campbell, writing in 1878, underlined the fact that 'Since the North has insisted that the blacks should be admitted to political equality neither North nor South has made any movement whatever towards admitting them to social equality; in fact, the movement has been rather the other way.' (He also felt, however, that there was 'generally no bad feeling or incivility attending the caste separation', and that this had broken down as regards public transport, where the mixing of races was such that 'even an English Radical is a little taken aback at first'.)[4] The extremist Dixon described the situation in Texas, where there were not only Negroes but also Indians, as one of perpetual conflict, 'each race against the other two races'.[5] Reference was often made to 'the bitterness with which some of the Southerners regard the negro race as a chief cause of their misfortunes', a bitterness which was 'of recent date in the South, where, in former times, the black man

---

[1] 9 November 1876.
[2] *Northern Whig*, 19 September 1874; *Spectator*, 16 November 1867, p. 1280; *Daily News*, 3 March 1877; see also *Economist*, 22 August 1874, pp. 1020–1, 31 October 1874, p. 1308; *Banner of Ulster*, 2 October 1866.
[3] See *Economist*, 3 October 1868, pp. 1131–2; *Freeman's Journal*, 7 November 1876; *North British Daily Mail*, 26 April 1871; *Edinburgh Courant*, 8, 17 April 1871; *Manchester Examiner and Times*, 13 November 1876; *Irish Times*, 15 April 1871; *Beehive*, 9 May 1868; R. Somers, *The Southern States Since the War*, London, 1871, pp. 152–5; E. Dicey, *Fortnightly Review*, July–December 1874, Vol. XVI, pp. 832–3; G. Campbell, op. cit., pp. 172–3.
[4] Op. cit., pp. 194, 195, 196–9.   [5] *The White Conquest*, Vol. I, p. 330.

experienced far kinder treatment than he did from his Northern champion.'[1]

The separation of races in the South was also pointed out by British journalist and politician, William Saunders; 'there is', he wrote, 'no social intercourse between the two. I never saw white and coloured men in friendly conversation, and so great is the separation that not in a single instance did I find white and coloured children playing together. As fellow workmen, and as master and servant, the two races get on well, but socially there seems to be an impassable barrier between them.'[2]

What made this state of affairs particularly distressing to Englishmen was, very often, a belief that the two races in the South were mutually dependent; if Radical rule were not to last for ever, they ultimately would have to get on together, and left to their own devices were, in fact united by curiously durable bonds of understanding and affection. The North, on the other hand, did not love the Negro though it courted his vote, a fact the freedmen ultimately recognized by voting the Democratic party back into power. In the words of George Rose, 'It is almost laughable to hear the Northerner put forth a claim to be the negro's friend, for he hates him intensely, and would expel him from every place frequented by the white man. You . . . are induced to think that all the professions of love for him, all the desire for his emancipation, arose from nothing but a desire to annoy and humiliate the South.'[3] Such views were not held to be inconsistent with the 'war of races' theory of Reconstruction, and a belief in the development of colour prejudice in the South.

The two attitudes were often combined in the press. Thus the *Daily Telegraph* argued in 1867 that 'Where a vast territory has been for generations occupied with a population of which the elements have become blended, and when the interests of the labourer and the employer are mutually dependent, the wit of man can devise no scheme by which the country may be so governed as to punish the master and impair his prosperity, without an injurious reaction upon the servant.'[4]

A similar outlook was reflected in *The Times*. 'The great and overwhelming argument for the admission of the Southern States into Congress without delay', wrote its New York correspondent, 'is this—that to keep them out ruins the negro as well as the white

---

[1] Latham, op. cit., pp. 151–2, and Rose, op. cit., p. 151.
[2] Op. cit., pp. 78–9.   [3] Op. cit., p. 151.   [4] 22 February 1867.

man. . . . Already the labour system of the South has been struck away at a blow. . . . Undoubtedly the future welfare of the negro ought to be very carefully considered and guarded in the work of reconstruction which has to be done; but observation in the South will satisfy any one that his interests are being sacrificed by the measures which tie up his master's hands.'[1] Punitive measures against the Southern planters were deplored by the Dublin press— 'The black man', wrote the *Mail*, 'will have new masters, of a new race, and a worse race. He will be free, but in all likelihood not really happier . . . Men who have obtained large tracts by their swords will hold them by harsh measures.'[2]

Nor were these simply the opinions of conservative supporters of the South. In 1865 the *Daily News* issued a clear warning that 'Any fierce conflict, political or social, entered into by the negroes' friends with the Southern whites will injure nobody so much as the freed people, and nothing is so necessary to the security and prosperity of the Southern whites as full justice to the negroes.'[3] The *North British Daily Mail*, while criticizing some aspects of President Johnson's policy, admitted that he 'has to a great extent been right in saying that the Southern planters were the only men who knew how to deal . . . with the negro. . . . The great error of the Northern Radicals has been to endeavour to maintain in opposition to each other the planters and the negroes, and to attach the latter to themselves rather than to those among whom their lot was cast.'[4] Furthermore the North itself did not scruple to deal vigorously with the freedmen, where necessary forcing them to work.[5]

Concern was also expressed by the *Spectator*, for 'Whatever the fitting position of the two races, it is not fitting that the blacks should have more than equality. . . . Justice must be done against blacks as well as whites, and we suspect the Republicans in places of not doing it.'[6] The only true solution for the South was one which involved the two races living together in harmony.[7]

These feelings of concern and disappointment were well

[1] 2 January 1866; see also 2 March 1864; and *Saturday Review*, 17 November 1866' pp. 191–2.

[2] *Dublin Evening Mail*, 2 June 1865; see also *Irish Times*, 4 July 1865.

[3] 18 November 1865; see also 15 February 1866.   [4] 11 April 1867.

[5] *North British Daily Mail*, 27 May 1865.

[6] 16 November 1867, p. 1281; see also 14 November 1868, p. 1330.

[7] See also *Daily Telegraph*, 8 August 1865; *Manchester Courier*, 3 January 1866; *Freeman's Journal*, 10 June 1865; *The Times*, 29 February, 2 March 1864, 2 January 1866, 27 September 1867; Zincke, op. cit., pp. 57, 102, 104; Dixon, *New America*, p. 426; Marquis of Lorne, op. cit., pp. 234–7, 242, 293; Sala, op . cit., Vol. I, pp. 231, 234.

summarized by A. V. Dicey, Vinerian Professor of Law at Oxford, who visited the States with Bryce in 1870. His biographer relates that for Dicey, the abolition of slavery in America 'had brought with it unlooked-for disappointment. The relationship between white and black, in the conditions of slavery had been, if often . . . immoral, still a human, relationship, and it has been succeeded by an inhuman relationship.'[1]

There remained, however, to do justice to the long tradition of British humanitarianism, a small but loyal group of Liberal papers in London, Manchester, Belfast, and Glasgow, and Radicals such as Bright, Mill, and the Argylls, which though stressing the importance of amicable race relations in the South, demanded for the Negro all the civil and legal rights necessary to ensure his freedom.[2]

Basic assumptions about the inferiority of the Negro, the mutual dependence of the two races in the South, feelings of sympathy towards the whites, and concern at the apparent deterioration of race relations in that region, all combined to affect British comments on the economic and political prospects of the freedmen, and it is clear that these aspects of the Negro problem, rather than, for instance, the debates over the civil rights legislation, most interested observers in Britain.

After the Civil War many American abolitionists believed that the freedmen required economic independence just as much as political and educational opportunities, if they were not to remain at the mercy of their former masters. The confiscation and redistribution of rebel property was urged throughout the war, and carried out on the South Carolina Sea Islands, and the coastal regions of South Carolina, Georgia and Florida.

Although the expectations of both abolitionists and Negroes were ultimately disappointed—under the terms of President Johnson's amnesty proclamations most Confederates were restored to their former political and property rights; many of the freedmen were ejected from their newly acquired lands; the achievements of the Bureau, private enterprise, and the Southern Homestead Act were slight; and Northern support for confiscation

---

[1] Memorials of *Albert Venn Dicey*, R. S. Rait (ed.), London, 1925, pp. 49–50.
[2] *Spectator*, 27 June 1868, pp. 760–1 and 22 August 1868, p. 982; *Daily News*, 18 November 1865, 10 and 11 April 1866; *Manchester Examiner and Times*, 17 April 1866; *Banner of Ulster*, 2 and 23 October 1866; *Northern Whig*, 12 June 1866; *North British Daily Mail*, 11 April 1866; J. S. Mill in the *Friend*, 1 November 1865, pp. 231–2; Bright in *Proceedings*, p. 147; Elizabeth Argyll in ibid., Vol. XLVII, p. 106.

schemes could not be mustered—conservatives in America and Britain were outraged. Not only did the Radicals appear to threaten one of the most sacred of social rights, they also in the process kept the Negroes in a state of restless anticipation, which alienated them from steady labour.[1]

The Freedman's Bureau was regarded cynically by *The Times* as a ruthless agency destined to supervise confiscations rather than to protect the Negroes, and Radical proposals for the redistribution of land were given a chilly reception.[2] Since it had violently denounced President Johnson's early plans for confiscating the property of wealthy Southern planters, the *Saturday Review* not surprisingly opposed the more extreme Radical plans; 'the creation of a gigantic Ireland, or of a black Poland, in the United States' it wrote, 'would be an enterprise rather difficult than glorious. The final result might perhaps be the extermination of the negro race, and in the meantime a chronic civil war would perpetuate the misery of the South.'[3]

Walter Bagehot, in the *Economist*, made no objection to the breaking up of the great Southern plantations, but stopped short of suggesting the redistribution or sale of such land to the Negroes, who were, however, criticized as unfit for the franchise not simply because of ignorance, but because of their lack of property.[4] Even John Bright advised caution on this issue, the best policy in his opinion being for '*Lands* already seized and sold to remain with their present possessors. In other cases a *large generosity and mercy* will be most wise.'[5]

But discounting fears about property redistribution, and assuming (as they generally did, in spite of such fears) that the bulk of the freedmen would remain agricultural labourers, many British observers felt that the Negroes were, and would remain for years to come, restless, lazy, and improvident.

The share cropping system was regarded with particular disapproval, as liable to encourage such vices. 'If the negro does not work well now,' wrote Robert Somers, a British journalist and

[1] See McPherson, op. cit., pp. 246–59, 407–16; Rose, op. cit.; Lawanda Cox, 'The Promise of Land for the Freedmen', *Mississippi Valley Historical Review*, Vol. XLV, December 1958, pp. 413–40.
[2] 28 July 1865, correspondent, and 2 January 1866, correspondent.
[3] 5 August 1865, p. 163, and 23 March 1867, p. 356.
[4] 17 June 1865, pp. 719–20; see also *Irish Times*, 24 June, 4 July, 3 August 1865, 9 March 1866; *Freeman's Journal*, 27 July 1865; *Manchester Courier*, 3 January 1866; *Banner of Ulster*, 18 September 1866.
[5] Bright to Sumner, 17 February 1865, London; *Proceedings*, p. 135.

economist who visited the South in 1870, 'one must be sorry for him. The planter gives the land, his stock and implements, working capital and credit, his skill, and plodding care and watchfulness from day to day for the chance of half the cotton which his hands may be induced to plant and till, or may think it worth their while to gather when . . . ripe.' In spite of these advantages, however, the freedmen were invariably in debt—'The soul is often crushed out of labour by penury and oppression. Here a soul cannot begin to be infused into it through the sheer excess of privilege and license with which it is surrounded.'[1]

Little, if any, allowance was made by British writers for the fact that before the war Negroes had been unable to move about freely, and could scarcely be blamed for wishing to do so now; nor was there much sympathy for the natural feelings of revulsion aroused by plantation work which hitherto had been the hallmark of slavery. Although the *Telegraph* ridiculed the 'popular cant about the dignity of labour', worthy exhortations along these lines were commonplace, and Britons saw no reason for encouraging indolence among the coloured population by such instruments as the Freedmen's Bureau. Thus a Dublin journal complained in 1866 that the current budget of that body was more than three times the total expenditure for the relief of the poor in Ireland, and asked why such privileges should be 'established for the exclusive benefit of blacks'.[2]

It would be wrong to expect most Victorians—even in the case of ex-slaves—to abandon their faith in the virtues of self-reliance and improvement, but there were a few capable of a wider and more charitable attitude. David Macrae reported that some of the planters wanted emancipation to be a failure, 'and in many cases, by withholding their land and refusing to employ negro labour, did something to make it a failure'. As a class, the freedmen were no more idle than the whites, and when they refused to work it was usually because they had no guarantee of receiving wages; while there were signs of 'provident habits rapidly forming' among the 'better class of emancipated slaves in the South'.[3]

Writing at the end of the 1870s, William Saunders confirmed that the freedman 'as a labourer, succeeds as well in manufactures as in agriculture', and was, in some areas, becoming a land-

---

[1] Op. cit., pp. 121, 129, 60; also Latham, op. cit., pp. 127–8.
[2] *Daily Telegraph*, 23 June 1865; *Freeman's Journal*, 7 March 1866.
[3] Op. cit., Vol. II, pp. 49–53, 55.

owner 'to a very respectable extent', and in his much earlier work, Sir Samuel Morton Peto, well-known contractor and Liberal M.P., wrote '. . . I do most heartily concur with those who believe that, as the result of the emancipation of the slaves, such new life, energy, and vigour will be introduced into the cultivation of those States, as will render them far more productive than they ever have been heretofore.'[1] Even a racial extremist like W. H. Dixon conceded after his trip to America in 1866 that while for some years the freedmen might be 'sorely tried', and compelled to be 'servants in the families, toilers on the plantations, in which they have recently been slaves', many would ultimately rise and prosper.[2]

The *Spectator* painted an encouraging picture of the diligence and prosperity of the Southern Negroes, and the *Daily News* came vigorously to their defence, attacking 'the worn out nonsense about negro . . . squatting . . . there is enough of co-operation and social action to dispose of the charge of a disposition to squat'; in fact abolition had brought about a change which would be 'in every way a happy one. Almost everywhere the negroes have worked well, whether for wages, or for a share of profits, or on land owned or occupied by themselves'.[3]

The *Economist* and the *North British Daily Mail*, though more critical, felt some sympathy for the Negro. The former envisaged as an ideal solution a system of apprenticeship or supervised labour (something, no doubt, on the lines of what was tried— without much success—in the West Indies after emancipation), but recognized that 'honest agents for such a task may not be readily found, or found at all'.[4] For its part, the *Mail* congratulated the Radicals on having at least prevented in the South, under cover of the Black Codes, 'the substitution of serfdom for slavery, or the acquisition of submissive free labourers who might be compelled to accept any wages that might be given to them'.[5]

Of all Radical proposals, however, that concerning Negro suffrage aroused the most indignation and concern, both when it was first made, and after the coloured race began to play a part in Southern politics. At a time when proposals to extend the suffrage

---

[1] Saunders, op. cit., pp. 75, 76; and Peto, *Resources and Prospects of America*, London, 1866, p. 407.
[2] *New America*, pp. 433–5.
[3] *Spectator*, 22 August 1868, pp. 982–3, 27 July 1872, pp. 957–8; *Daily News*, 18 November 1865 and 20 June 1865.
[4] 17 June 1865, p. 719.   [5] 11 April 1867.

in Britain were being fiercely resisted, and comparisons between British and American democracy were commonplace, such hostility was to be expected. (It is interesting to notice in this context the *Saturday Review's* complaint that English 'advocates of negro enfranchisement'—and there were very few of these—were 'also, for the most part, zealous supporters of an extended suffrage at home'. As it happens, the *Spectator*, the most active 'advocate' among the press, was not whole-heartedly in favour of extending the vote to British working men.[1]

In his autobiography the American abolitionist, M. D. Conway, recalled that 'When the odious epoch of reconstruction arrived . . . Froude and Carlyle urged on me the absurdity of enfranchising the negroes. . . . Carlyle did not suggest any alternative to negro enfranchisement. But Froude argued that the rebellion . . . was in defence of what certain States believed their constitutional rights . . . and the Northerners would find in the end that their Union had a South on its hands like the Ireland that England had.'[2]

Both men appear to have opposed the suffrage on account of its unacceptability to the Southern states, and Carlyle's famous racist views seem to have mellowed with age, if Conway's testimony can be trusted.[3] But he did still warn his American friend, 'All the worth you have put into your cause will be returned to you personally; but the America for which you are hoping you will never see; and never see the whites and blacks in the South dwelling together as equals in peace.'[4] For his part, Froude was at least prepared to admit that though the Radical demand 'that every one who held office [in the Confederacy] during the war should be disabled for the future, seems . . . most irrational', the Southern states 'ought to agree to have the number of their representatives diminished—if the negroes are not to vote, they ought not to count.'[5]

Far more vigorous than Carlyle, however, in his denunciation of Negro suffrage was Charles Dickens, who reported from Baltimore in 1868—'The ghost of slavery haunts the houses; and the old, untidy, incapable, lounging, shambling black serves you as a free man. Free of course he ought to be; but the stupendous absurdity

---

[1] *Saturday Review*, 30 September 1865, p. 410.
[2] *Autobiography, Memories and Experiences of Moncure D. Conway*, London, 1904, 2 Vols., Vol. II, pp 186–7.
[3] M. D. Conway, *Thomas Carlyle*, London 1881, pp. 93–102.
[4] *Autobiography . . . Conway*, Vol. I, p. 358.
[5] Dunn, op. cit., p. 345.

of making him a voter glares out of every roll of his eye, stretch of his mouth, and bump of his head.'[1]

There is ample evidence of a similar attitude in the conservative sections of the British press, where it was undoubtedly strengthened by the almost unanimous hostility to admitting any ignorant or property-less individual to the franchise. As the *Economist* put it, 'There never was in the history of democracy so dangerous an experiment as that of entrusting full electoral power to nearly four millions of black persons, but just emancipated from actual slavery, totally uneducated, and hungry for material advantages.'[2]

Many Britons maintained, in fact, that the franchise was being bestowed, in the words of the Ambassador to Washington, 'with reference to party interests among the whites'—in order to manufacture Republican voters, rather than because the Negro was fitted for it by 'moral and intellectual aptitude', and much capital was made from the 'notorious and undeniable' 'repugnance which all classes North feel to admitting the negro to the franchise'.[3] Furthermore, it was argued, the Negroes were harassed and manipulated when voting; the experiment endangered good government and racial harmony, and ultimately, the *Irish Times* concluded, not without satisfaction, in 1876, the freedmen became as tired of Reconstruction as the whites, since 'it was actually the black vote that has won Democratic victories in more centres than one'.[4]

There were occasional instances where such conservative observers entertained the possibility of a graduated suffrage: *The Times* favoured 'educational conditions', the *Saturday Review* preferred a property qualification for Negroes, a measure which would have excluded the bulk of them from polls.[5] Only very occasionally does there seem to be an awareness that without the vote, without a political stake in the South, the freedmen's chances of

---

[1] *The Letters of Charles Dickens*, Vol. II, p. 349.

[2] *Economist*, 9 November 1872, p. 1367.

[3] Lord Frederick Bruce to Lord Stanley, 10 September 1866, Washington, F.O.5 1067, and *The Times*, correspondent, 11 July 1867, on base motives behind granting Negro suffrage; *The Times*, 31 January, 1866, on Northern opposition to it; and *Saturday Review*, 30 September 1865, p. 411, *Daily Telegraph*, 8 August 1865, on unfitness of Negroes to vote.

[4] *Irish Times*, 6 November 1876; and see *Scotsman*, 28 February and 12 March 1866, 23 March 1867; *North British Daily Mail*, 27 April and 5 December 1867; *Edinburgh Evening Courant*, 2 June 1866; *Manchester Guardian*, 16 December 1865; *Freeman's Journal*, 18 April 1866; *Banner of Ulster*, 18 September and 23 October 1866.

[5] *The Times*, 22 February 1877; *Saturday Review*, 28 October 1865, p. 636.

obtaining land and education were slender—as the *Telegraph* felt obliged to admit in 1867, 'No amount of statutes could have secured the freedman fair play had not the leaders of the North placed the ballot-paper in his hand.'[1]

Even philanthropic Britons tended to regard the Negro vote as a desperate last resort, in the event of no other means being found to protect the freedmen in their rights, and there was a real appreciation both of Northern deficiencies and the problems involved in forcing political changes on an unwilling South.

'The negro suffrage question', wrote Goldwin Smith to an American friend, 'is the one which to a distant observer seems most difficult and almost desperate. . . . I cannot help thinking that negro emigration on a large scale will prove the best way out of the wood. And happily our West India dependencies . . . lie close at hand.'[2] It is interesting to find such conservative, authoritarian views—which would have done credit to *The Times*—expressed by a staunch friend of the United States, and indicative not only of the anxiety which racial questions aroused during the sixties, but of the gulf separating English and American Radicals on these issues.[3]

The attitude of John Stuart Mill to Negro suffrage, though highly creditable to a British Liberal, was equally out of touch with reality. Recognizing that unconditional amnesty for the South might jeopardize the rights of the freedmen, but opposed to any form of 'despotic' Federal rule in that region, Mill suggested granting self-government 'only to a mixed community, in which the population who have been corrupted by vicious institutions will be neutralized by black citizens and white emigrants from the North. . . . I have no objection to requiring, as a condition to the suffrage, education up to the point of reading and writing, but upon condition that this shall be required equally from the whites. The poor whites of the South are understood to need education quite as much as the negroes, and are certainly quite as unfit for the exercise of the suffrage without it.'[4]

The difficulties encountered in disfranchising the Confederate

---

[1] 4 November 1876.

[2] Goldwin Smith to C. E. Norton, Oxford, 18 October 1865, Goldwin Smith Papers, Cornell University.

[3] Bright, however, wrote Sumner in 1862 (*Proceedings*, p.110, Llandudno, 10 October 1862), 'Surely that childish project of removing the black people from America will cease to be talked about. It damages the character of your President and Government.'

[4] *Friend*, 1 November 1865, p. 231.

leaders should have warned Mill of the opposition which his proposal about the poor whites would have aroused, and he failed to realize—something in which, as we have seen, he was not alone—the futility of demanding qualifications, such as education, from the Negroes, when they had no means of securing these things.

The Duke and Duchess of Argyll, throughout the war staunch supporters of the North, and abolitionists by conviction, were also unable to see the need for granting full political rights to the freedmen. Writing to Charles Sumner in 1865, the Duke commented: 'I have great confidence that the United States will get through their political-social difficulties—at last—as they have done through the war. But I don't like the present aspect of things. Of course *here* where the suffrage is considered a right, I don't feel sure of the negro suffrage being good policy. But if there is any risk of re-enslavement it may be the only protection.'[1]

His wife, who exchanged letters regularly with the American Radical, was similarly cautious. 'Do not think too little of the great gains already won,' she wrote, 'even if the political rights are delayed.'[2] On another occasion the Duchess confessed 'Though, so much interested, I do not feel able to judge of the state of things at Washington at all. I do not understand the *degree* of Importance you attach to Negro Franchise, when it seems to us from old experience that it may be worth very little to such an entirely dependent class as they must be, and the political awkwardness of forcing it on the South *before* the North gives it, seems very great. Why not urge the abolition of the black codes, the equal rights in the courts of law, as the great necessity?'[3] Here again one sees the British willingness to take things gradually, the failure to appreciate the temper of Southerners on the question of race, and the belief that the North itself was anything but enthusiastic about Negro suffrage.

Something of the same apprehension about the suffrage was expressed by John Bright, who also corresponded with the Radical Sumner during this period. The Englishman confided in 1865, 'I can see some difficulty in the way of the President if he attempts to give the suffrage to the negro. . . . even in a majority of the free States, the suffrage law does not appear to be the same for the two

---

[1] Argyll to Sumner, Privy Seal Office, 7 July 1865, *Proceedings*, pp. 89–90.
[2] Elizabeth Argyll to Sumner, Inveraray, 27 October 1865, in ibid., p. 106.
[3] Elizabeth Argyll to Charles Sumner, 20 March 1866, Argyll Lodge, in ibid., p. 106; see also letter from Inveraray, 23 July 1866, p. 106.

M

races. How then could he insist on doing that in the South which
he cannot enforce in the North?'

These doubts were not only strengthened by the comments of
the British press, but by Americans themselves. Bright reported
that the U.S. Ambassador was strongly opposed to Negro suffrage,
and had suggested that most Northerners felt the same—as witness the rejection of a proposal to give coloured men the vote in
Connecticut. A note in Adams' diary confirmed this—'Then came
Mr. Bright, who spent a couple of hours talking over our internal
process of reconstruction. The policy of Mr. Johnson excites much
uneasiness in the extreme class in America, which reacts upon our
friends here. I did what I could to reassure him. As to making
negro suffrage an issue, it is simply suicide, in the state of popular
feeling in America.'[1]

A handful of British commentators were, however, prepared to
urge the adoption of Negro suffrage, in spite of the risks involved.
The *Northern Whig, Daily News,* and *Spectator* lent their support to
this Radical proposal, and some of the more thoughtful travellers
of the period could see its advantages.[2] Charles Dilke thus declared firmly, with an insight which was rare, that 'A reading and
writing basis for the suffrage in the Southern States is an absurdity.
. . . Though pretended to be impartial, [it] would perpetuate the
antipathy of colour to which the war is supposed to have put an
end. . . . If the negroes were to vote as soon as they could read, it is
certain that the planters would take . . . care that they never
should read at all.' Dilke was even willing to concede that to 'be
able to examine into the details of politics is not entirely necessary
to the working of representative government. It is sufficient that
. . . [individuals] should be competent to select men to do it for
them.'[3]

As a colonial administrator of some eminence, Sir George Campbell was interested to see how the freedmen reacted to political
privileges, being of the opinion that British practice in withholding
such rights in the Empire had not always proved just. After his
visit to the South, Campbell felt able to vindicate the Radical
governments except on the charge of corruption; criticized the local
whites and Democrats for their ruthless determination to get rid

[1] *Proceedings*, pp. 145–7.
[2] *Northern Whig*, 3 and 29 September 1866; *Daily News*, 26 June 1865, correspondent,
and 30 June 1865; *Spectator*, 23 February 1867, p. 206, 9 March 1867, p. 264.
[3] Op. cit., Vol. I, pp. 29–30.

of these governments; and felt it to be 'absolutely necessary that the South should honestly accept the 15th Amendment'. Elsewhere it was pointed out that 'Unrepresented blacks, and other unrepresented classes, are always liable to be treated unfairly under labour laws, vagrant laws, and revenue laws.'[1]

Dilke's cynicism about Southern intentions was shared by the Rev. David Macrae who, though recognizing the dangers inherent in Negro suffrage, inquired, 'in a government which derives its right from the consent of the governed, why should four millions of the governed be gagged? And, in a government which says that taxation without representation is tyranny, why should representation be refused to the coloured people, who are taxed as heavily as the whites are . . .?' 'It was unfair to ask for education qualifications when inadequate educational facilities for Negroes were the rule'; 'And perhaps, after all, the speediest way of preparing a Negro or any other man, to exercise the suffrage, is to give it to him.' Macrae concluded that the freedmen 'have, in general exercised their new power quietly, considerately, and well'.[2]

The freedmen's aid movement marked the last great effort of British abolitionists to mobilize public opinion at home and abroad against slavery and its aftermath. When it ended, race prejudice—aroused by events in India, New Zealand, South Africa, and Jamaica, and confirmed by the American experience during Reconstruction—triumphed in Britain.

Not even the philanthropists were free from the influence of this prejudice, as we have seen. Many became disheartened at the sheer size of the task they had undertaken in the South, began to feel that the early faith in the Negro had been misplaced, and to reason that charity, if too long continued, would sap will-power, initiative, and self-respect. Although the freedmen's aid societies were initially at pains to prove that the condition of Jamaica, by the 1860s, was the result of planter mismanagement and hostility towards the Negro, faith in the efficiency of free labour in the similarly placed Southern States had been shaken by the end of the Reconstruction. Declining public interest (and funds) as early as 1868 made British workers more susceptible to the propaganda which had always been directed against them: what right, after all, had outsiders—Northern or foreign—to interfere in the

---

[1] Op. cit., pp. x-xii, 126-7, 186, and 191.
[2] Op. cit., Vol. I, pp. 360-1; Vol. II, pp. 69-70.

internal affairs of the South, especially when such interference might defeat the avowed ambition of the freedmen's aid movement to improve Anglo-American relations. This seemed no idle fear. It had proved difficult enough to sustain an amicable understanding with the American abolitionists who solicited British aid. Nor were the British societies themselves free from internal strife, caused by personality conflicts and disagreements over policy.

Their decline was, of course, partly predictable: it was hard then, as it is hard now, to sustain public sympathy over long periods for whole peoples. Tragedies which bring personal involvement alone can do this. Many British abolitionists had no first-hand acquaintance with the Southern freedmen. Still more was this true of the Victorian public at large. And the former, having expected too much from a long enslaved race, surrounded by enemies, in spite of their acknowledgement of these difficulties, eventually compromised—accepted segregated schools as better than none, accepted a renewal of the old agricultural order in the South, since land for the Negroes was apparently unobtainable.

Those not actively involved in freedmen's aid in Britain—that is, the majority—went even further in their support for the Democratic approach to Reconstruction, contemptuous of the Negro, opposing major changes in his political and economic circumstances, approving civil rights and education indeed, but doubtful that the freedmen would ever benefit from the latter, or properly exercise the former.

We who criticize the failure of the Radical Republicans after the Civil War might well remember that no group in Britain was able, during these turbulent years, to see through the excesses and corruption to the intrinsic merits of the Northern programme for the Negro. On the whole, and not just because of an undeniable wish to avoid political controversy, British observers were luke-warm in their approval; those who threw caution to the winds, and committed themselves politically, sided with the Southern whites. The concept of Anglo-Saxon solidarity, which had once sustained humanitarian endeavour on both sides of the Atlantic, now served only to encourage the prejudice and sense of mission which, though unpleasant features of the 1860s and 1870s, were to become most marked during the next great period of British imperialism towards the end of the century.

SELECTED BIBLIOGRAPHY

A. *Primary or Documentary Sources*

I MANUSCRIPT SOURCES

Public Record Office
F.O.5. 905–1591—Dispatches of Sir Frederick Bruce and Sir Edward Thornton, British Ministers to Washington, and of British Consuls in America.
British Museum
Bright Papers; Cobden Papers; Dilke Papers; Gladstone Papers.
Dr. Williams's Library, London
Estlin Papers.
Friends' House, London
Manuscript records of the London Yearly Meetings of Friends, 1845–78; Manuscript records of the Devonshire House Monthly Meetings, 1863–7.
Rhodes House, Oxford
Anti-Slavery Papers (Manuscripts of the British Empire S18).
Birmingham Reference Library
Minutes of the Birmingham and Midland Freedmen's-Aid Association, 1864–5.
Glasgow Public Library
Smeal Collection.
John Rylands Library, Manchester
English Manuscripts 741.
Cornell University Library, Ithaca, New York
Anti-Slavery Papers; Goldwin Smith Papers.
Miscellaneous
Minutes of the Gloucester and Nailsworth Monthly Meeting of the Society of Friends; Minutes of the Banbury Monthly Meeting of the Society of Friends; Minutes of the Plymouth Monthly Meeting of the Society of Friends; Minutes of the Lewes and Chichester Monthly Meeting of the Society of Friends. (Quaker Ms. 52/8); John Farley Rutter Papers.

II PRINTED SOURCES

(a) *Official*

Hansard's Parliamentary, Debates, Third Series, Commencing With The Accession of William IV.
Extracts from the Minutes and Proceedings of the Yearly Meetings Held in London, 1847–1867.

Proceedings of the Yearly Meeting of Ireland, 1866–1888.

The Annual Monitor . . . or, Obituary of the Members of the Society of Friends in Great Britain and Ireland, London, 1843–1908.

Biographical Catalogue, Friends' House, London, 1888.

Minutes of the Methodist Conferences, London, Wesleyan Conference Office, 1868, Vol. XVI.

The Congregational Yearbook, London, 1866 and 1867.

The Baptist Handbook, 1865.

United Presbyterian Synod Proceedings, 1864–70, Glasgow, 1870.

Proceedings of the General Assembly of the Free Church of Scotland, 1864–8.

Fortieth and Forty-First Annual Reports of the British and Foreign Unitarian Association, London, 1865 and 1866.

Annual Reports of the Birmingham and Midland Freedmen's Aid Association, Birmingham, 1865 and 1866.

Annual Reports of the Ladies Negro's Friend Society for Birmingham, Birmingham, 1845–1889.

Annual Reports of the Edinburgh Ladies' Emancipation Society and Sketch of Anti-Slavery Events and the Condition of the Freedmen During the Years Ending 1866 and 1867, Edinburgh 1866 and 1867.

The Twenty-Fourth Annual Report of the British and Foreign Slavery Society, London, 1863.

First and Second Annual Reports of the Ladies' London Emancipation Society, London, 1864 and 1865.

(b) *Newspapers and Periodicals*

Friend
British Friend
Friend's Review
Freedmen's-Aid Reporter
Freed-Man

Wesleyan Methodist Magazine
Watchmen and Wesleyan Advertiser
National Freedman
American Freedman
Christian World

Daily Telegraph
Economist
Edinburgh Review
Fortnightly Review
Saturday Review
Spectator
The Times

Pall Mall Gazette
Beehive
British Workman
Daily News
Macmillan's Magazine
North American Review

Edinburgh Evening Courant
Scotsman

North British Daily Mail

Freeman's Journal
Irish Times
Dublin Evening Mail

Banner of Ulster
Northern Whig

Birmingham Daily Gazette   Birmingham Daily Post

Manchester Courier   Liverpool Daily Post
Manchester Examiner and Times   Preston Guardian
Manchester Guardian   Sheffield and Rotherham Independent
Blackburn Patriot   Darlington Telegraph
                                  Derby Reporter

(c) *Pamphlets*

(i) West Indies

The Outbreak in Jamaica, A Speech by the Rev. William Arthur, M.A., Delivered at the Anniversary of the Folkestone Auxiliary to the Wesleyan Missionary Society, November 21st, 1865, London 1865.

The West-India Labour Question; Being Replies to Inquiries Instituted by the Committee of the British and Foreign Anti-Slavery Society, Embracing Facts and Statistics on the Present Conditions of the Emancipated Classes, and on the Alleged Want of Labour in the West-India Colonies; but Especially in Jamaica, London, 1858.

The Emancipation of the Negroes in the West Indies. An Address Delivered at Concord Massachusetts, on 1st August, 1844 by R. W. Emerson, London, 1844.

Martial Law, Six Letters to 'The Daily News', London, 1867, Jamaica Papers, no. 5, London, 1867.

Jamaica Papers, no. 1, London, 1866.

Jamaica: Who is to Blame? by a Thirty Years' Resident, London, 1866.

Jamaica: Its State and Prospects, With an Exposure of the Proceedings of the Freed-Man's Aid Society, and the Baptist Missionary Society, London, 1867.

C. S. Roundell, *England and Her Subject Races, With Special Reference to Jamaica,* London, 1866.

Emancipation in the West Indies. Two Addresses by E. B. Underhill, Esq., and the Rev. J. T. Brown, the Deputation from the Baptist Missionary Society to the West Indies, Delivered at a Private Meeting, Held at Willis's Rooms, 20th February, 1861, London, 1861.

(ii) Freedmen's Aid

A Plea for the Perishing, Leeds Auxiliary to the Freed-Men's Aid Society, Leeds, 1865.

Four Millions of Emancipated Slaves in the United States, An Appeal to the People of England, from the National Committee of the British Freedmen's Aid Association.

'Help For the Freed Slaves, Large Public Meeting in Derby', from the *Derby Reporter* of 10 March 1865.

Reports I and II of the Central Committee of the Society of Friends for the Relief of the Emancipated Negroes of the United States . . . Also, List of Subscriptions and Letters from America, London, 1865.

Case and Claims of the Emancipated Slave of the United States, Society of Friends, London, 1865.

F. Seebohm, *The Crisis of Emancipation in America*, London, 1865.

Prospectus, Freed-Men's Aid Society, London, 1863.

Help for the Negro Refugees in America, Two Millions Free!

'The Freedmen's Aid Commission', Reprint of an article in the *Belfast Northern Whig*, December 1864.

Why Should Birmingham Workmen Help the Freed Refugees from Slavery in America? Who are in great distress.

Birmingham and Midland Freedmen's-Aid Association (An Appeal for hoes).

Birmingham and Midland Association for the Help of the Refugees from Slavery in America, By a Vessel to be Freighted With Stores, Birmingham, 1864.

Birmingham and Midland Association for the Help of the Refugees from Slavery in America, By a Vessel to be Freighted With Stores, Circular no. 2., Birmingham, 1864.

Birmingham and Midland Association for the Help of the Refugees from Slavery in America, By a Vessel to be Freighted With Stores, Circular no. 6.

Circulars no. 10 and 11.

General Howard, the Freedmen, and their Cause, Circular no. 12.

The Freedmen in Tennessee and Alabama, Circular no. 13.

The Rev. W. E. Channing on the Freedmen of America, Circular no. 14.

The Case of the Freed Coloured Refugees from Slavery in America, Birmingham, 1864.

Considerations on the Transition State of the Freed Coloured People in America, Birmingham, 1864.

Reception of the Special Delegation to Great Britain of the United States National Freedmen's Relief Association . . ., Birmingham, 1865.

Birmingham and Midland Freedmen's-Aid Association. The Speeches on behalf of the Four Millions of Coloured People freed from Slavery by the late Civil War in America, Delivered in the Town Hall, Birmingham, on Wednesday Evening, August 2nd, 1865, at a public meeting convened by the above Association, more especially in Connection With the assembling of the Wesleyan Conference . . ., Birmingham, 1865.

Facts Concerning the Freedmen. Their Capacity and their Destiny, Collected and Published by the Emancipation League, Boston, 1863.

The Freed Men of South Carolina. Address of J. M. McKim, at Samson

Hall, on Wednesday Evening, the 9th July, to an Audience invited by the Port Royal Committee, Stephen Colwell, in the Chair, London, 1862.

The Freedmen of South Carolina: Some Accounts of their Appearance, Condition, and Peculiar Customs, by Charles Nordhoff, Papers of the Day, Collected and Arranged by Frank Moore, no. 1., New York, 1863.

Speech of His Grace, the Duke of Argyll at a Meeting Held at the Westminster Palace Hotel, May 17, 1865, London, 1865.

(iii) Miscellaneous

Proceedings at the Public Breakfast Held in Honour of William Lloyd Garrison, London, 1868.

The Aborigines Protection Society: Chapters in its History, London, 1899.

Chronological Summary of the Work of the British and Foreign Anti-Slavery Society during the Nineteenth Century, London, 1901.

American and English Oppression, and British and American Abolitionists, a Letter Addressed to R. D. Webb, Esq., by an American in his Fatherland, London, 1853.

The Bible View of American Slavery, a Letter from the Bishop of Vermont (New England), to the Bishop of Pennsylvania, London, 1863.

An Epitome of Anti-Slavery Information, or a Condensed View of Slavery and the Slave Trade etc., London, 1842.

The National Anti-Slavery Societies in England and the United States, or Strictures on 'A Reply to Certain Charges Brought Against the American and Foreign Anti-Slavery Society, etc., by Lewis Tappan of New York, United States'; With an Introduction, by John Scoble, Dublin, 1852.

What the South is Fighting For, The British and Foreign Anti-Slavery Society, Tract no. 1, London, 1863.

The American War and American Slavery, a Speech Delivered by the Rev. Joseph Parker, D.D., . . ., Manchester, 1863.

Rev. W. Arthur, *The American Question. English Opinion on the American Rebellion*, London, 1861.

T. Hughes, *The Cause of Freedom: Which is its Champion in America, the North or the South*, London, 1863.

J. E. Ritchie, *Thoughts on Slavery and Cheap Sugar. A Letter to the Members and Friends of the British and Foreign Anti-Slavery Society*, London, 1844.

L. Stephen, *The 'Times' on the American War: A Historical Study*, London, 1865.

Rev. F. W. Tremlett, *Christian Brotherhood: Its Claims and Duties. With a Special Reference to the Fratricidal War in America*, London, 1863.

Report of a Meeting of the Unitarian Body Held at the Freemason's Tavern, June 13th, 1851, to Deliberate on the Duty of English Unitarians in Reference to Slavery in the United States, London, 1851.

The Duty of the United Kingdom Towards the Slave of the United States, A Letter by the Rev. Samuel J. May, of Syracuse, State of New York, Bristol, 1860.

(d) *Contemporary Works—Essays, Letters, Diaries, etc.*

H. Adams, *The Education of Henry Adams: an Autobiography*, Boston and New York, 1918.

George Douglas, Eighth Duke of Argyll ... 1823–1900, *Autobiography and Memoirs*, Dowager Duchess of Argyll (ed.), London, 1906, 2 Vols.

W. Armistead (ed.), *Five Hundred Thousand Strokes for Freedom. A Series of Anti-Slavery Tracts, etc.* London, 1853.

——, *A Tribute for the Negro: being a vindication of the moral, intellectual, and religious capabilities of the coloured portion of mankind, etc.*, Manchester, 1848.

——(ed.), *A 'Cloud of Witnesses' Against Slavery and Oppression, etc.*, London, 1853.

J. Bigelow, *Retrospections of an Active Life*, New York, 1909–13, 5 Vols.

John Bright, *Speeches of John Bright, M.P., on the American Question*, F. Moore (ed.), Boston, 1865.

——, *The Diaries of John Bright*, R. A. J. Walling (ed.), London, 1930.

——, *Speeches of John Bright, Esq., M.P., Delivered in Birmingham in October and November, 1868*, Reprinted from the *Daily Post* and revised by Mr. Bright, London and Birmingham, 1868.

J. Bryce, *The American Commonwealth*, New York, 1888, 2 Vols.

T. F. Buxton, *The African Slave Trade and its Remedy*, London, 1839.

G. Campbell, *White and Black, The Outcome of a Visit to the United States*, London, 1879.

T. Carlyle, *Occasional Discourse on the Nigger Question*, London, 1853.

——, *Shooting Niagara: and After?*, London, 1867.

L. Coffin, *Reminiscences*, Cincinatti, 1876.

M. D. Conway, *Thomas Carlyle*, London, 1881.

——, *Autobiography, Memories and Experiences of Moncure D. Conway*, London, 1904, 2 Vols.

J. Crosfield, *Letters Written During Joseph Crosfield's Second Journey in America from 19 August, 1865 to 26 January, 1866*, unpublished journal, Friends' House.

J. L. M. Curry, *A Brief Sketch of George Peabody, and a History of the Peabody Education Fund Throughout Thirty Years*, Cambridge, Mass., 1891.

R. W. Dale, *Impressions of America*, New York, 1878.

H. Deedes, *Sketches of the South and West, or Ten Months Residence in the United States*, Edinburgh and London, 1869.

G. Hogarth and M. Dickens (ed.), *Letters of Charles Dickens*, 1880–2, Vols. II and III.

C. W. Dilke, *Greater Britain*, London, 1868, 2 Vols.

W. H. Dixon, *New America*, London, 1869, 9th ed.

——, *The White Conquest*, London, 1876, 2 Vols.

R. Ferguson, *America During and After the War*, London, printed Carlisle, 1866.

S. Tuke (ed.), *Selections from the Epistles of George Fox*, London, 1848.

E. Fry, Sir, *James Hack Tuke, A Memoir*, London, 1899.

J. Gadsby, *A Visit to Canada and the United States of America. Also a Second Visit to Spain*, London, 1873.

W. P. and F. J. Garrison, *The Life and Times of William Lloyd Garrison, 1805–1879, as told by his children*, New York, 1889, 4 Vols.

A. de Gobineau, Count, *The Inequality of Human Races*, originally 1854, Vol. I, transl. A. Collins, London, 1915.

C. N. Hall, *The American War*, New York, 1862.

——, *The Assassination of Abraham Lincoln*, London, 1865.

——, *From Liverpool to St. Louis*, New York, 1868.

——, *Newman Hall in America*, New York, 1868.

O. O. Howard, *Autobiography of Oliver Otis Howard*, New York, 1907, 2 Vols.

T. Hughes (ed.), *Gone to Texas. Letters From Our Boys*, London, printed Oxford, 1884.

——, *Rugby, Tennessee: being some account of the settlement founded on the Cumberland Plateau by the Board of Aid to Land Ownership . . .*, London, printed Edinburgh, 1881.

L. J. Jennings, *Eighty Years of Republican Government in the United States*, London, 1868.

John Kennaway, Sir, *On Sherman's Track: or, the South After the War*, London, 1867.

H. Latham, *Black and White: A Journal of a Three Months' tour in the United States*, London, 1867.

Rev. G. G. Lawrence, *Three Months in America in the Summer of 1863 . . .*, Huddersfield, 1864, 2 parts.

——, *A Tour in the Southern States of America, in the Summer of 1866*, London and Huddersfield, 1867.

F. B. Leigh, *Ten Years on a Georgia Plantation Since the War*, London, 1883.

Lorne, Marquis of, *A Trip to the Tropics, and Home Through America*, London, 1867.

C. Mackay, *Life and Liberty in America: or, Sketches of a Tour in the United States and Canada in 1857–8*, London, 1859, 2 Vols.

———, *Forty Years Recollections of Life, Literature and Public Affairs*, London, 1877, 2 Vols.

D. Macrae, *The Americans at Home, Pan-and-late Sketches of American men, Manners and Institutions*, Edinburgh, 1870, 2 Vols.

———, *Amongst the Darkies, and other Papers*, Glasgow, 1876.

J. MacCarthy, *A History of Our Own Times*, London, 1882–97, 5 Vols.

J. G. Medley, *An Autumn Tour in the United States and Canada*, London, 1873.

H. Merivale, *Lectures on Colonization Delivered Before the University of Oxford in 1839, 1840 and 1841*, new ed., London, 1861.

J. S. Mill, *Autobiography*, London, 1908.

———, *The Letters of John Stuart Mill*, ed. and introduction by H. S. R. Elliot, London, 1910, 2 Vols.

Letters of Charles Eliot Norton, with Biographical Comment by his Daughter Sara Norton and M. A. de Wolfe Howe, Boston, 1913, 2 Vols.

L. Oliphant, *On the Present state of Political Parties in America*, Edinburgh and London, 1866.

T. D. Ozanne, *The South as It Is, or Twenty One Years Experience in the Southern States of America*, London, 1863.

S. Morton Peto, Sir, *Resources and Prospects of America, Ascertained During a Visit to the States in the Autumn of 1865*, London, 1866.

H. Richard, *The Memoirs of Joseph Sturge*, London, 1864.

A. Rooker, *Does it Answer? Slavery in America, a History*, London, 1864.

G. Rose, *The Great Country: or Impressions of America*, London, 1868.

Letters of John Ruskin to C. E. Norton, Boston, 1905, 2 Vols.

G. Sala, *My Diary in America in the Midst of War*, London, 1865, 2 Vols.

———, *America Revisited*, London, 1882, 2 Vols.

W. Saunders, *Through the Light Continent, or the United States in 1877–8*, London, 1879.

J. Seeley, *The Expansion of England*, London, 1883.

J. Shaw, *Twelve Years in America: Being Observations on the Country, the People, Institutions and Religion*, London, 1867.

G. Smith, *A Selection from Goldwin Smith's Correspondence, 1846–1910*, A. Haultain (ed.), London, 1913.

———, *England and America*, Manchester, 1865.

———, *The Civil War in America*, London, 1866.

———, *Reminiscences*, New York, 1910.

———, *The Moral Crusader, William Lloyd Garrison: A Biographical Essay*, Toronto, 1892.

———, *Goldwin Smith. His Life and Opinions*, A. Haultain (ed.), London, 1913.

R. Somers, *The Southern States Since the War, 1870–1*, London, 1871.

G. Stephen, *Anti-Slavery Recollections: in a Series of Letters Addressed to Mrs. Beecher Stowe etc.*, London, 1854.

H. B. Stowe, *Uncle Tom's Cabin. A Tale of Slave Life etc.*, London, 1853.

A. de Tocqueville, *Democracy in America*, New York, 1899, 2 Vols.

B. B. Underhill, *The Tragedy of Morant Bay*, London, 1895.

H. H. Vivian, Sir, *Notes of a Tour in America*, London, 1878.

The Complete Poetical Works of John Greenleaf Whittier, Boston, 1895.

E. Wigham, *The Anti-Slavery Cause in America and its Martyrs*, London, 1863.

H. Wigham, *A Christian Philanthropist of Dublin, A Memoir of Richard Allen*, London, 1886.

——, *A Sketch of the History of Friends in Ireland*, London, Friends Tract Association, 1896.

F. B. Zincke, *Last Winter in the United States. Being Table Talk Collected Through a Tour through the late Southern Confederation*, London, 1868.

B. *Secondary Works*

I BOOKS

E. D. Adams, *Great Britain and the American Civil War*, London, Longmans, 1925.

H. C. Allen, *Great Britain and the United States*, London, Odhams, 1954.

——, *The Impact of the Civil War and Reconstruction on Life and Liberalism in Great Britain*, read in manuscript.

G. H. Barnes, *The Anti-Slavery Impulse, 1830–44*, Gloucester, Mass., 1957.

A. A. Barter (afterward Cruse), *The Victorians and their Books*, London, Allen & Unwin, 1935.

A. F. Beard, *A Crusade of Brotherhood. A History of the American Missionary Association*, Boston, 1909.

G. R. Bentley, *A History of the Freedmen's Bureau*, Philadelphia, University of Pennsylvania Press, 1955.

M. L. Bonham, *The British Consuls in the Confederacy*, Studies in History, Economics and Public Law, Columbia University, Vol. XLIII, no. 1, New York, 1911.

J. B. Brebner, *North Atlantic Triangle. The Interplay of Canada, the United States, and Great Britain*, New Haven, Yale University Press, 1945.

A. Briggs, *Victorian People*, London, Penguin, 1965.

W. R. Brock, *An American Crisis: Congressional Reconstruction, 1865–7*, London & New York, Macmillan & Co., 1963.

F. M. Brodie, *Thaddeus Stevens. Scourge of the South*, New York, W. W. Norton & Co., 1959.

H. Carter, *The Angry Scar: the Story of Reconstruction*, Garden City, New York, Doubleday & Co., 1959.

W. J. Cash, *The Mind of the South*, New York, A. Knopf, 1960.

O. F. Christie, *The Transition From Aristocracy, 1832–1867*, London, Seeley & Co., 1927.

E. T. Cook, *The Life of John Ruskin*, London, Allen & Unwin, 1911.

E. M. Coulter, *The South During Reconstruction, 1865–77*, Baton Rouge, Louisiana State U.P., 1947.

R. Coupland, Sir, *The British Anti-Slavery Movement*, London, Oxford University Press, 1933.

R. McNair and Wilson Cowan, *The Newspaper in Scotland: a Study of its Expansion, 1815–60*, London, 1946.

Lawanda and J. H. Cox, *Politics, Principle, and Prejudice, 1865–6, Dilemma of Reconstruction America*, New York, Free Press of Glencoe, 1963.

D. P. Crook, *American Democracy in English Politics, 1815–50*, Oxford, Clarendon Press, 1965.

P. de Armand Curtin, *The Image of Africa. British Ideas and Action, 1780–1850*, London, Macmillan & Co., 1965.

H. Donald, *The Negro Freedman*, New York, Schunan, 1952.

T. E. Drake, *Quakers and Slavery in America*, New Haven, Yale U. P., 1950.

M. Duberman (ed.), *The Anti-Slavery Vanguard*, Princeton, Princeton U.P., 1965.

W. E. B. Dubois, *The Souls of Black Folk*, London, Constable, 1905.

——, *Black Reconstruction: An Essay Toward a History of the Part which Black Folk Played in the Attempt to Reconstruct Democracy in America, 1860–1880*, New York, Harcourt, Brace and Co., 1935.

D. L. Dumond, *Antislavery: The Crusade for Freedom in America*, Ann Arbor, University of Michigan Press, 1961.

W. H. Dunn, *James Anthony Froude. A Biography*, Oxford, Clarendon Press, 1961–3, 2 Vols.

P. H. Emden, *Quakers in Commerce: a Record of Business Achievement*, London, Sampson Low & Co., 1940.

T. H. S. Escott, *Masters of English Journalism. A Study of Personal Forces*, London, Unwin, 1911.

H. D. Fairchild, *The Noble Savage: a Study in Romantic Naturalism*, New York, 1961.

L. Filler, *The Crusade Against Slavery, 1830–60*, London, Hamish Hamilton, 1960.

J. H. Franklin, *Reconstruction: After the Civil War*, Chicago, University of Chicago Press, 1961.

——, *From Slavery to Freedom: A History of American Negroes*, New York, A. Knopf, 1948.

E. F. Frazier, *The Negro in the United States*, New York, Macmillan & Co., 1957.

H. R. F. Fox Bourne, *English Newspapers. Chapters in the History of Journalism*, London, 1887, 2 Vols.

F. E. Gillespie, *Labor and Politics in England, 1850–67*, Durham, N.C., 1927.

W. J. Graham, *English Literary Periodicals*, New York, Nelson, 1930.

J. Grant, *The History of the Newspaper Press*, London, 3 Vols., 1871–2.

J. Harris, *A Century of Emancipation*, London, 1933.

R. Harrison, *Before the Socialists: Studies in Labour and Politics, 1861–81*, London, Routledge & Kegan Paul, 1965.

W. B. Hesseltine, *The South in American History*, Englewood Cliffs, Prentice Hall, 1960.

E. Hildrith, *The 'Ruin' of Jamaica*, New York, 1955.

R. H. Jenkins, *Sir Charles Dilke. A Victorian Tragedy*, London, Collins, 1958.

R. M. Jones, *The Later Periods of Quakerism*, London, 1921, 2 Vols.

D. Jordan and E. J. Pratt, *Europe and the American Civil War*, London, 1931.

A. Jorns, *The Quakers as Pioneers in Social Work*, transl. T. K. Brown, New York, 1921.

F. J. Klingberg and A. H. Abel, *A Side-Light on Anglo-American Relations, 1839–58*, Association for the Study of Negro Life and History Inc., Lancaster, Penna., 1927.

H. Koht, *The American Spirit in Europe*, Philadelphia, University of Pennsylvania Press, 1949.

R. Korngold, *Thaddeus Stevens. A Being Darkly Wise and Rudely Great*, New York, Harcourt, Brace & Co., 1955.

P. Lewinson, *Race, Class and Party: a History of Negro Suffrage and White Politics in the South*, London, Oxford University Press, 1932.

G. D. Lillibridge, *Beacon of Freedom. The Impact of American Democracy Upon Great Britain, 1830–1870*, Philadelphia, University of Pennsylvania Press, 1954.

L. Litwack, *North of Slavery. The Negro in the Free States, 1790–1860*, Chicago, University of Chicago Press, 1965.

E. Lonn, *Foreigners in the Confederacy*, Chapel Hill, N.C., University of North Carolina Press, 1940.

W. L. Mathieson, *The Sugar Colonies and Governor Eyre, 1849–1866*, London, Longmans, 1936.

——, *British Slavery and Its Abolition, 1823–1838*, London, Longmans, 1926.

——, *British Slave Emancipation, 1838–49*, London, Longmans, 1932.

——, *Great Britain and the Slave Trade, 1839–1865*, London, Longmans, 1929.

E. L. McKitrick, *Andrew Johnson and Reconstruction*, Chicago, University of Chicago Press, 1960.

J. M. McPherson, *The Struggle for Equality: Abolitionists and the Negro in the Civil War and Reconstruction*, Princeton, University Press, 1964.

G. R. Mellor, *British Imperial Trusteeship, 1783–1850*, London, Faber & Faber, 1951.

J. T. Mills, *John Bright and the Quakers*, London, Methuen, 1935.

R. H. Mottram, *Buxton the Liberator*, London, Hutchinson, 1946.

G. Myrdal, *An American Dilemma, the Negro Problem and Democracy*, New York and London, Harper Bros., 1944.

Proceedings of the Massachusetts Historical Society, Boston, 1912–13, Vols. 46–7.

O. Patterson, *The Sociology of Slavery*, London, MacGibbon & Kee, 1967.

H. Pelling, *America and the British Left from Bright to Bevan*, London, A. & C. Black, 1956.

L. M. Penson, *The Colonial Agents of the British West Indies*, London, University Press, 1924.

M. Perham, *The Colonial Reckoning*, London, Collins, 1963.

J. G. Randall and D. Donald, *The Civil War and Reconstruction*, Boston, Little, Brown & Co., 1961.

W. L. Rose, *Rehearsal for Reconstruction. The Port Royal Experiment*, Indianapolis, Bobbs-Merill Co., 1964.

E. Russell, *The History of Quakerism*, New York, 1942.

B. Semmel, *The Governor Eyre Controversy*, London, McGibbon & Kee, 1962.

G. Shepperson, 'Reconstruction and the Colour Problem' in *British Essays in American History*, London, 1957.

D. C. Somervell, *English Thought in the Nineteenth Century*, London, Methuen, 1929.

K. M. Stampp, *The Peculiar Institution: Negro Slavery in the American South*, London, Eyre & Spottiswoode, 1964.

——, *The Era of Reconstruction. America After the Civil War, 1865–77*, London, Eyre & Spottiswoode, 1965.

H. L. Swint, *The Northern Teacher in the South, 1862–70*, Nashville, Tennessee, 1941.

F. Thistlethwaite, *The Anglo-American Connection in the Early Nineteenth Century*, Philadelphia, University of Pennsylvania Press, 1959.

The History of the Times, London, 1935–52, 4 Vols.

E. Wallace, *Goldwin Smith, Victorian Liberal*, Toronto, University of Toronto Press, 1957.

V. L. Wharton, *The Negro in Mississippi, 1865–1890*, Chapel Hill, University of North Carolina Press, 1947.

E. Williams, *Capitalism and Slavery*, Chapel Hill, University of North Carolina Press, 1947.

C. V. Woodward, *The Strange Career of Jim Crow*, New York, Galaxy, 1957.

II THESES

S. Van Auken, *English Sympathy for the Southern Confederacy*, B.Litt. thesis, Oxford, 1957.

M. Bullen, *British Policy Towards a Settlement with America, 1865–1872*, Ph.D. thesis, London, 1956.

H. Temperley, *The British and Foreign Anti-Slavery Society, 1839–1868*, Ph.D. thesis, Yale, 1960.

G.C. Taylor, *Some American Reformers and their Influence on Reform Movements in Great Britain, 1830–1860*, Ph.D. thesis, Edinburgh, 1960.

N

INDEX